D1570733

The Cheeses and Wines
of England and France,
with Notes on Irish Whiskey

The Cheeses and Wines of England and France

with Notes on Irish Whiskey

John Ehle

Drawings by James J. Spanfeller

HARPER & ROW, PUBLISHERS
New York, Evanston, San Francisco, London

FIRST EDITION

STANDARD BOOK NUMBER: 06-011167-4

LIBRARY OF CONGRESS CATALOG CARD NUMBER: 72-79659

Designed by Patricia Dunbar

Contents

About the Book

I have for many years written novels and have never written a book like this (nor has anybody else, I suspect), and my friends are wondering whether I am abandoning the main scheme of my life and following after strangers. No, not really. More simply, in eight years' time, purely as a hobby, I have acquired a stack of materials not available anywhere else which seemed to me to want to be a book, some sort of book, a book like this one, which describes how cheeses and wines have been made in homes for generations, and which shows, therefore, how you can make them in yours, with local modifications as you please. I have simply put the material together.

I gathered it in the first place because I am out of step with some of the noises and signs of this onrushing society we have in the United States. The French say the best is the enemy of the good, but we in our country have reversed all that, have managed to prove that the good is for us the mortal enemy of the best. Our best—the local and individual and traditional— is being battered down and strewn about by mass production and mass merchandising, and even most of our institutes and universities now teach the excellence of the new processes. Today our wines come from factories; our cheeses are made in factory presses. "What does it matter, if it tastes just as good?" some will ask.

And they *think* it tastes as good, which is the most discouraging aspect of all.

In France today each group of people—a family, a village, a town, a city, a department, no matter how small or large—has its excellent products which are its own, and which it makes for itself and will share with others. In America we come, lord knows, from all the countries of the world, yet we are willing to settle for products that are mass produced and mass distributed, so that the people of the families, the villages, the towns, the cities, the fifty states are now all opening the same infernal cans and boxes, the same frozen concoctions, the same plastic stoppers, and throwing out in all our many places tons of the same wrappers.

Isn't it a pity that out of our potentially rich diversity comes such protected sameness?

Perhaps no book will correct this malady. But I like to think that we will use this book, and others, and other means, to begin turning ourselves around, and that we will begin to make one or two essential things for ourselves. However, if you do nothing more than daydream about making them, I will accept that, for even daydreams will help; daydreams are attitudes, after all, and have influence. I admit myself that I spend as much time daydreaming about making wines and cheeses as I spend making wines and cheeses.

Five years ago when I first became interested in making cheeses, coming to this out of an interest in making wines, I was surprised to find that there were no instructions available. In a used-book store on Fourth Avenue in New York, finally I found two old, dusty, crumbly English booklets, which were most useful, and since then I have collected from every conceivable source—at least every source conceivable to me in Europe and the United States—the traditional procedures for making the best cheeses of England and France, and I have brought them together in this book.

Instructions for winemaking are readily available in other books. I have, however, gone back to original sources here, too, in order to find how the best home vintners of France and England make wines, and my discoveries now and again vary significantly from the ways recommended by those modern books on home winemaking which look to factory methods rather than home-vintner methods for guidance. As a rule, the best wines, as well as the best cheeses, are made in homes, not factories.

Not all the wines and cheeses are practical for home making today, though admittedly all of them in the places of their birth are made in homes by families. Some require a small press, some a large press, some a cellar, some a temperature- and humidity-controlled curing room, and so forth; not every home can provide what is needed, not for the more difficult varieties. I will enter these varieties regardless, because all about us are ingenious individuals who might figure out ways to use them; there are in this country many citizens waiting for a new opportunity to prove themselves: young people in communes or on their own, retired people, women who have more talent than opportunity to use it, and others—the fantastic assortment called the American people.

I will include a wide variety of cheeses and wines also because one reflects on another; each adds light to both these ancient crafts. They are related. They even share much the same equipment and require much the same temperament of their makers and serve each other well and comfortably in the making, the curing, the conversing, and finally, if all goes well, in the eating and drinking. I like the companionship each produces, too. Not for long will you be alone if you are making wines or cheeses, for these processes are festive occasions, and your home soon becomes a rallying point for family and neighborhood. People want to help. There seems to be in us all a romantic throbbing which attracts us to these ceremonies. In a time growing colder, and at a time when we grow older, I like such warm sensations and companionship, and the sense of accomplishment both the companionship and the manufacture bring.

I will at times give two methods for making a cheese, a contemporary and an old one, since changes in cheesemaking since 1940 have been drastic, particularly in England. The war brought about some of these alterations, and mechanization has brought about others. We can easily lose, if we don't take care, some of the great English cheeses, so I have recorded here old as well as, on occasion, new ways. A given round of cheese has a short life, a year or two at most, and memory is a poor repository for the taste of a Cheddar or a Cheshire or a Derby. We like to think a farmhouse Cheddar today is like the farmhouse Cheddar of our youth, or our father's. Well, it is not, as I will show, but I will show how both the old and the new can be made.

We are all served more and more by factory machines, maybe inevitably, and by schedules, even our own, and in time, as has often been pointed out, we come to serve them. Some of us are becoming chafed by it all. We seek to reaffirm ourselves, to do and make for ourselves, to find new ways to do so—many of them admittedly old ways, but new and revitalizing ones to us and our friends. We want to find out how the basic components of our lives are made and come to us to use. We seek to become part once more of the processes, and possessors once more of the details of our own

existence. This desire is natural and is as it should be, and
this book is meant to help along that way as it wanders
through two ancestral countries of my own and two ancient
food territories created over the years by hungry, thirsty men
and women, makers of genius and not much genius, many of
them flirtatious dairymaids and shiny-faced farm boys, who
have together left for us a wonderful lot of lore and goodness.

No, I have not made all these cheeses and have no idea that
I will. Nobody has made all of them. I would not care to enter
into such a lot of milk and curds and whey, except in my
fantasies. I have made six of them, all successfully except
one, the Colwick, which had disastrous, nose-tingling results
once I tried to cure it. It was in the slipcoat process that my
sense of world-rightness deserted me, or that its sense of
world-rightness deserted it. I suspect the room was too cool.
I prefer to think about the cheeses I made successfully, all of
which were miracles.

What I have done in this book, what I admit to trying to
do, is what, being a writer, I know best to do: I have done the
research necessary to find out how these fifty or sixty cheeses
were made by families—and most of them still are being so
made—and I have set down the methods exactly. Can you
now do these cheeses? Yes, you can, if you have access to
absolutely fresh milk and follow the same processes, the instructions. There is nothing uniquely intelligent about the
farm families of England and France, and there is nothing
exclusive about the cows of Cheshire or the fields of Normandy. Local conditions do contribute, but not decisively,
not with the controlling consequence of wine grapes, for instance, in winemaking. You cannot make in Indiana or Georgia or New Hampshire a wine as good as the French can

make—it is not ever done; but you can make as great a Cheddar as was made in Somerset in the golden ages of Cheddar, and a Stilton as good as any, and a Camembert to equal a Normandy product of the old farm makers, if you meet the needs, those here set down.

There is, of course, a body of opinion to the contrary, but that is exactly what it is—a body of opinion. Connoisseurs are valued for their opinions, which are largely based on their instincts and senses. I would not care to pit myself against them or compare myself with them—I would not like to be a connoisseur, anyway, because hosts don't dare serve you any cheese or wine at all—but I do feel obliged to tell you that when a connoisseur says in a book that a Stilton is made from milk taken from cows on certain fields, or that milk for Camembert is heavily enriched with cream, that he is arriving at these facts from his sense of taste. Indeed, Camembert is made from partially skimmed milk and Stilton's cows are today found in all sorts of places. It is all very well for the consumer of Stilton or Camembert or whatever cheese to think he is participating in a mystical or enriched experience, but you can't make cheeses that way, and you will do better to use the connoisseurs' books to decide how to appreciate cheeses and this one to decide how to make them.

I am interested in your successes, and in your devices and contrivances and innovations. What information you share with me, I will share with others, insofar as is practicable, in future editions of this book or in other books, if you will write me. Please do not, however, come to see me. I use this mountain place to write and expect to start a novel any day now.

I am particularly indebted to Professor J. J. Janzen of Clemson University and Jim Matthiason of the Milk Marketing Board's cheese center in Cheshire and Dr. Leroy Meek of Winston-Salem, food sciences chemist, for going through parts of this manuscript as it developed and helping to identify errors and suggest improvements, and to Mary McBride, who would come here to the house every morning, bringing her newborn baby with her, and would nurse the baby while she took this book down in dictation, using her right hand if the baby was nursing at her left breast and her left hand if the baby was nursing at her right, creating such a marvelous distraction that it is a dear wonder the book ever got done.

I want to dedicate the book to Mary, and to Bill and Jane Brown and the other craftsmen, makers of pottery and glass, weavers and the like, who have made Penland School the best craft school and one of the important craft centers of our country.

JOHN EHLE

Penland, North Carolina 28765
April 9, 1972

A Note on Weights and Measures Used in This Book

In this book quarts and gallons are the American size, not the imperial. Imperial gallons are 25 percent larger.
But a drop is a drop (we have that in common),
Sixteen drops are one cc.,
Fifty-six drops are one dram,
Eight drams make an ounce,
And an ounce is an ounce most everywhere.

Temperatures are in Fahrenheit.

The Cheeses

Yet this night you might have rested here with
me on this green leafage. We have ripe apples,
mealy chestnuts, and a wealth of pressed cheeses.

—Written some years ago now by a
disappointed Virgil

1

Small Holder Cheese

You can make this lightly pressed cheese easily enough, even on your first try, and it is quite a good one, a semisoft cheese with a fresh, mild taste which can be pressed into almost any shape, of any size. You will need a canning kettle—one of the lightweight black enamel pots that are purchasable inexpensively—or some other vat or cooking pot that will hold five or more gallons of milk. Any material will do.

You will need a thermometer that will register up to 90 degrees Fahrenheit. Take the one off the wall if you have no cooking thermometer at hand.

You will need fresh milk, taken from some dairyman's cooler, I suspect. Store-bought milk often is not fresh enough and always is two or three times as expensive. Get it as it arrives, if you buy it from a city dairy.

You will need rennet, which is a natural chemical found in our stomachs and those of other milk-consuming creatures. Usually it is commercially obtained from the fourth stomach of sacrificed calves and is available as a liquid extract at some drug and chemists' stores, and even from cheese factories if you ask politely, and through the mail (see Appendix 3 for markets for the various items I mention). It will keep in your refrigerator, losing about 10 percent of its power each year.

You will need coarse salt or table salt, non-iodized.

You will need a knife whose blade will reach to the bottom of the vat you plan to use.

And a press—a lard press or small wine press with a tin or plastic sleeve. If you don't have one, a well-washed paint can or coffee can with holes punched in it, to serve as a mold for the cheese, will have to do.

And a pot of coffee or tea, to keep you company as you work.

It will take four hours to make the cheese, so you will need that much time.

Rather than laying down procedural principles for cheese-making—I have put such notes in Appendix 1, and you can go back there and refer to them whenever you like—I suggest we start by visiting a cheesemaker while she works in her kitchen. The cheesemaker I have chosen to visit lives near my home. Her name is Lydia Kirby, and Mrs. Kirby is the only cheesemaker I know in the mountains of North Carolina who makes cheeses using an old English recipe.

The milk she uses is delivered to her home on cheesemaking mornings by a neighboring farmer. For two cheeses she uses 16 gallons of milk from his cooler. Essentially, since it has been chilled immediately and kept at low temperature, it is quite fresh. The farmer leaves it by the mailbox in two milk cans.

Mrs. Kirby lives alone now that her husband is dead. Occasionally her sister visits her from Baltimore or her son or daughter-in-law comes in from the next house down the rural road, but the white two-story house itself is all hers now, as is the work of making these cheeses, and even carrying the milk up from the road.

This past summer I drove up to sit in her kitchen and go through the process with her from start to finish. I arrived about 8:30 A.M., and by then she had put the milk on the electric range to warm.

"I take an hour to heat the milk," she told me. "I always wash up my dishes while my milk's awarming." She is gray-haired now, in her sixties. In stature she is average height for a woman, or maybe a bit shorter. Wearing a loose-fitting housedress and slippers, she seems thin and neat and small.

"I put the milk on at 8 A.M.," she said. "I stir it now and then to keep it from scorching or sticking but mostly I wash up."

I sat down at a table, one with a clean white cloth on it—everything was clean here—and began to write down what she told me so I could put it in this book. Mrs. Kirby's cheese is different from most other cheeses and is quite good—semisoft, loose textured, and with a mild tang to it. Also it has a good-tasting, edible rind.

"I put two 8-ounce cups of cultured buttermilk in the milk when I set it on the stove," she said. "That helps to get its ripening started. I buy cultured buttermilk at the store. You can buy starter from a company that makes it, or you can make your own starter from skimmed milk, which you let sour, which is what my mother did. If the evening's milk had been kept at 60 or 65 degrees overnight, I wouldn't need any starter, or not much. I've asked him to leave the milk out at least an hour or two, while he finishes milking. Milk has to ripen."

Out of the refrigerator she took a pint canning jar of rennet, a brown-colored liquid. Rennet and salt are the only two chemicals added by most home cheesemakers to their cheeses. "I mix half water with it when I buy it," she told me. "That makes measurements more accurate. It takes only 3 ½ teaspoons of full-strength rennet for this much milk. I use 7 teaspoons of my mixture." She measured out the rennet, mixed a cup of water with it, and poured equal quantities into the two 8-gallon enameled canners. A thermometer measured the milk's temperature as being 90 degrees.

She turned the two electric burners to "simmer." "I try to keep the temperature at 90 degrees," she said. "I used to rennet at 86 degrees, but the cheese factory in West Jefferson told me I could rennet at 90 degrees and it would do quicker. I stir it for five minutes and five minutes only, because it starts to coagulate soon after that." She began stirring. "The old people around here, in the old days, started making cheese when the cows came in fresh in spring, when they were first put on pastures again. Everybody made cheeses. Some of them skimmed their night's milk but left the cream in the morning's milk. I've been thinking of experimenting myself but haven't done any of it yet. My mother didn't have a thermometer. She tested the milk with her elbow; when it no longer felt chilly to her elbow, she put in the rennet."

Mrs. Kirby placed the two potlids under the hot-water tap and let them warm that way, then she put them on the pots. "You have to experiment a bit with your milk and rennet. The rennet will curdle the milk; I like to get a thick curd in thirty minutes. It will begin to coagulate in one-quarter to one-third that time. You can tell when it starts if you let a piece of a toothpick float on top of the milk; when the coagulation starts, the toothpick will stop moving. You can time how long that takes, then multiply that time by 2 ½ to judge how much longer you will need to wait. If it takes eight minutes to stop moving, then it will take eight times 2 ½ more minutes to be ready. That's twenty more, or twenty-eight from the time the rennet was put in. If it takes longer than eight or nine minutes to start, you will need to wait longer for the curd to set; if it takes less than eight minutes, you might want to cut the curd sooner."

She turned the heat off under the burners, or the eyes, as she called them. "I use enameled pots. You can use tinned pots. You might be able to use stainless steel. You can't use aluminum without eventually damaging the pots. Some of the old people used brass kettles, but in them you would have to keep the milk warm or it could 'brass.' The cold milk takes on a brass taste from the brass kettle, but warm milk doesn't seem to."

The milk was coagulating sooner than Mrs. Kirby's ideal eight minutes. This didn't seem to bother her very much. "The next time, I can use less rennet," she said.

By 9:30, one-half hour after renneting, the milk had become a firm, springy custard. "This is ready to cut," she said, "but I'm in no hurry to cut it."

I noticed in this matter, as in nearly all phases of Mrs. Kirby's cheesemaking, a contented, delaying tactic in her work, as if she intended to give the milk all the time it might need fully to mature, or herself something to do for the full morning.

"When the curd is ready to cut, it will break before your

finger when you run your finger through it. If you're going
to make cheese, you have to get your hands in it." She moved
her forefinger slowly through the custard-like mass, and a
tiny split opened just before her finger. She put her forefinger into the curd, and raised it, and the curd split neatly.

The next stage was to cut the coagulated mass into small
pieces. She set the pots on a table and got a kitchen knife.
She inserted it vertically into the mass and made a single cut,
from top to bottom, then parallel cuts until the curd in one
pot had been sliced into ½- to ¾-inch slabs. She then cut
crossways, again slicing the curd at ½- to ¾-inch intervals.
Finally she used a slotted spoon to cut horizontally. She
slowly moved the spoon through the mass in the pot, cutting,
while with her left hand she turned the pieces of curd, breaking up those that were oversize, until the curd was broken
into relatively even-sized cubes.

Then she did the other pot in the same manner. "If you
have a curd knife, you can save most of this work, but I
keep thinking I won't be making cheese long enough," she
said. "My mother just stirred it up with a wooden paddle
when it got ready. She never cut it. If you cut it too quick,
you won't get all the cheese out of your milk that you ought
to have. These are thick, firm curds—if it is much softer than
this, it takes longer to make. My grandson, when he visits,
loves to see me do this, make the milk come up in squares,
and he likes to taste the fresh cheese." She returned the pots
to the stove, with the burners set at the lowest point, on simmer, so they would heat the curds and whey slowly.

The time was 9:45. She made a cup of coffee for me and
a glass of tea for herself. Every now and then she would stir
the cubes of curd with her hand to keep them broken into
sections. I have known people making this cheese who would

increase the temperature of the curds and whey more rapidly, to get the work done, but Mrs. Kirby seemed to be content with her occupation. She ate none of the curds. I ate quite a few. They had a mild, rich, custardy taste, with a natural sweetness. They had a very soft texture at this point, almost like a cheese, but a type of cheese unobtainable at any store. The cubes exude whey, so by 10 A.M. each pot had several quarts of whey floating on the heavier cubes of curd. Two or three cups of whey Mrs. Kirby poured off into the sink. "I might stop making cheese, because it's difficult to carry the milk in. Sixteen gallons of milk, and I have a bad back, a disk wearing away," she said.

She kept turning and stirring the curds in the two pots with her hands. "I would make the cheeses in a single pot if I had a pot big enough, and an eye big enough to heat it with." She poured some whey into a dishpan, then into the sink. "If anybody wanted to keep hogs, this whey is awful fine hog food. When my husband was alive, we kept a few hogs."

The temperature was rising slowly in the pots. At 10:10 the thermometer registered 94 degrees. Mrs. Kirby said her thermometer was not really accurate; she estimated that the temperature was closer to 90 degrees. She preferred to work by feel, she told me, by touch and instinct. "It begins to stick together on you, so you keep stirring it, and keep it separated as best you can. I suppose you don't have to stir it so much, but I don't have anything else to do and would as soon be stirring."

I drank coffee and watched her. Hers was a bright, sunny kitchen, with nothing in it that Mrs. Kirby didn't use every day, or so I felt. Outside the open door flowers were blooming.

"My mother made this type of cheese and called it homemade. Everybody then made 'homemade cheese.' "

"Where do you get your milk?" I asked her.

"It's cheese milk, it's not Grade A milk. For cheese milk the cows have to be tested but you don't have to paint the inside of your barn and all that. I can buy cheese milk for thirty-five to forty cents a gallon, while Grade A milk would be higher, almost twice as much. I use the same milk they use in the cheese factory in West Jefferson."

Mrs. Kirby insisted the temperature of the curds and whey was 90 degrees; the thermometer indicated that it was 95 degrees, and by now it should have been much higher, but obviously to Mrs. Kirby time didn't make much difference. "The curds are getting tougher," she said. "If you turn the temperature up too fast, it makes a tough, dry cheese. Later I will turn the temperature up but not until the curds get tougher. If I had it all in one pot, it might be easier, but after all, it would take just as long to make it."

Now and then she dipped some whey off the pots, simply so she could begin consolidating the curds in one of the canning kettles. "This time of year the milk won't make as much cheese as it will in the fall of the year. The grass is tender now and succulent, you know. In rainy weather not as much cheese comes from milk, either. Another thing, if you don't feed cows on dairy feed as well as grass, you'll get a grassy taste. You ought to feed them some dairy feed even if they have all the grass they can eat."

I realized Mrs. Kirby couldn't read the thermometer; apparently her sight was such that she could hardly focus on the numbers.

She got a piece of cheese out of the refrigerator, an over-dyed Cheddar made at the cheese factory in West Jefferson, one aged six or more months, she said. I cut off a small piece and found it quite good.

"Cheese ought to be warm when you eat it; homemade cheese ought to be room temperature or warmer," she said. She took the slab of cheese away from me and set it in the kitchen window in the sunlight. "My homemade cheese will last three months after it is cut if it's kept in the refrigerator. I don't age my cheese. Old people sunned their cheeses a week, then kept them around the house a week or two, then ate them. You can age them for months if you want to, but you have to wipe mold off of them, or wax them. You shouldn't try to age them if they have cracks, but in spring and fall I rarely have trouble with cracks. If you wipe a cheese with a cloth wrung out in vinegar water, it won't mold so bad."

10:55. The thermometer said the curds and whey were 98 degrees. Mrs. Kirby didn't seem to think so. They were not that hot, she said. "The old people started making cheese in May when they put their cows on grass, and they would make it late enough so they would have cheese for Christmas. Then they would be out of cheese for a while. People born here in the mountains begin to crave cheese when the weather gets warm. A lady in West Jefferson—her mother used to make cheese—called me in March and said, 'I want you to save the first cheese you make for me.' "

Mrs. Kirby stirred the curds and whey. Sometimes she would dip some whey off into a pan, which once or twice she emptied into the sink. As she dipped whey out of one pot, she would move the curds from the other pot into that pot, so by 11 o'clock she had all the curds in the same one. It occurred to me that this variation might change the cheese and increase the time needed for the bits of curd to develop acidity—which it does, as I point out at the end of this chapter when I describe a faster way.

The thermometer registered 99 degrees, but Mrs. Kirby

didn't believe it. I judged it didn't matter to her, so long as the curds were gently, very gently, without haste, maturing, which meant losing some of their custardy quality and taking on a tinge of toughness.

At 11 o'clock when all the curds and some whey were in a single pot, Mrs. Kirby began to dip whey from that pot, a cup or two every few minutes. "I have cheese clients as far away as South Dakota. Their relatives live near here and mail the cheeses to them."

I asked her how much cheese she made a year ago. She said she had made as much as 1,000 pounds in a year.

11:25. The temperature in the pot was at 100 degrees. "As I take whey off, the temperature rises," she explained. "This 'Guernseyed' milk just won't make cheese at 100 degrees. I used to use pure Holstein milk, and it will make at 100 degrees, but this milk has some Guernsey in it and I have to heat it higher than that. The milk is 4 percent fat. I wouldn't mind to have milk with less than that. If it had more than 4 percent, the cheese would take even longer to make and would be too greasy. The 4 percent milk will make at about 104 degrees. A 3 ½ percent milk is what I prefer."

Mrs. Kirby now and then would stir the curds with her hand, and now and then she would dip off some whey. "As it gets done, curds float a little and won't mat so easily. You want to wait until it's spongy. When it's ready, if you squeeze a handful together, it will easily break apart when you open your hand."

At 11:32 the temperature was 100.5 degrees. "It's not hot enough yet. Holstein milk will finish at this. Guernsey milk won't finish at this, even if we wait. It's got all that butterfat. It's got to get hot enough to cook it. Holstein milk will make a whiter cheese, too. I used to use some coloring in my cheese; I prefer a cheese that is yellow—I don't know that I prefer as dark a yellow as the cheese factory's in West Jefferson. But I don't color my cheese now because I don't like to eat the coloring."

She dipped off some more whey.

"Sometimes the old people would color their cheese. I told you they didn't age it long. Most of the old people liked it fresh. There are six or eight or ten days when it has a sour or bitter taste; if you cut your cheese and it has a sour taste, wrap it up and put it in the refrigerator or spring house and it will cure itself. The old people didn't age it because, for one thing, they got hungry for it, and for another, they had no place to store many cheeses."

At 11:43 the temperature was 101 degrees. The burner was set to the next to lowest position. Mrs. Kirby took another cup of whey out of the pot. I found that the curds, when chewed, had begun to give a squeaky sensation on the teeth.

"My husband liked sweet curd better than cheese. He'd take a bowl of curds like this and eat them."

She took another cup of whey out of the pan.

"Old people took longer to make cheese, up to two hours longer. I used to take longer. Renneting at 86 degrees takes longer. It's just a longer process."

She left the cheese and got ham biscuits out of the cupboard.

"I don't fix much lunch. My husband could make a lunch of biscuits, preserves, honey, and fresh cheese."

She stirred the curds gently.

"I have some strawberries that have been thawing from being frozen, and some homemade lemon pie I made yesterday, that has kept. That was my husband's favorite pie."

I ate ham biscuits and pie and warm Cheddar cheese and fresh cheese curds and drank coffee. Mrs. Kirby ate little of anything.

At 12:20 the thermometer said 106 degrees. The curds

were tougher and left a more definite squeaky sensation on the teeth.

"It has a silky feel now as you run your hands through the curds and whey. My grandson says it tastes like silk, too, when it gets close to being done. It breaks apart easily when you press a handful of it. Can't you feel that it's silky when you run your hand through it? See how it squeaks even in your hand?"

The temperature rose to 108 degrees, according to the thermometer. Now the 8-gallon pot was about three-fifths full.

"I never get it higher than this temperature, whatever it is," she said. "I never watch the thermometer close, but I can tell by feeling when I'm not getting it hot enough." Gently she squeezed a handful of curds, then released them. She was able to break them apart easily.

The curds had a springy quality to them, and when chewed they actually did squeak.

"My sister tried to make cheese and couldn't make it. She came and watched and I said, 'You'll have to put your hands in here, go by the way it feels.' "

12:25. It was now time, Mrs. Kirby decided, to free the curds of the whey entirely. "If I had a big 3- or 4-gallon colander, it would be easier, but I told my daughter I doubt if I'll be making cheese that long. I've watched at country auction sales, but I've never seen one come up for sale."

12:30. 106 degrees. Mrs. Kirby still had not poured all the whey off the curds. I judged a quarter of the mixture was whey.

12:35. She removed the pot from the stove and set it on the table.

"You have to salt it while it's warm so the warmth can melt the salt," she said. "The salt stops the acid from developing further. You want very little salt, only enough barely to taste. I use rock salt, fairly fine ice-cream salt. I don't use regular table salt. You can use regular table salt, but it's best to use a coarser salt, which melts slower and gets more generally through the cheese. You don't use iodized salt, for that will taste in the cheese."

Mrs. Kirby didn't seem in a hurry to salt the cheese. She got out a half-pint of dandelion wine that somebody had given her years ago. She was more concerned about my lunch than her two cheeses.

"Do you know what dandelion wine's supposed to taste like?"

I admitted that I did, but wondered if I knew much about a three-year-old dandelion wine kept in a half-full pint jar.

"My son tasted it two years ago and said it was not ripe yet. Mr. Watts Hill tasted it last year and said it was just right. I don't know how it is this year."

The wine had a delicate, tantalizing aroma. It had a dry, almost puckering taste.

"How can I store it? In the refrigerator?"

"I would use it," I said. "It won't get any better."

She seemed to be inclined to want to store it.

"You might put it in a jar that it fills to the brim, to keep air off it," I said. "Air's likely to spoil it."

"It's had that much air on it since last year," she said, and put it back in the refrigerator.

At 12:40 Mrs. Kirby drained the whey off the curds completely. "If you let it cake, you have to shred it. It wants to cake, but I try to keep mine stirred up. If I had a big colander, it would save a whole lot of work. You see how it begins to look creamy. As it cools, some butterfat comes to the surface of the individual curds. It gets more yellow then, and it gets more oily."

She kept breaking up the curds as best she could, working

at one edge of a developing cheese mass, a spongy cake. "If I had a cheese mill, I could mill the curds. This is the hardest part of the process."

The curds were squeaky when chewed and had a dry, flat, uninteresting taste. They seemed to be matting rather severely, but Mrs. Kirby was unconcerned.

She broke up half the matting curds, enough for one cheese, broke them into grape-sized pieces. "I will use 2 level table-spoons of salt for this 5-pound cheese. I use more salt if the whey is heavy in the curds, because when it's pressed the whey carries some of the salt with it. For a 5-pound cheese I break up about 6 pounds of curds or more and mix 2 tablespoons of salt with it. You don't want to taste the salt much at this stage, because the cheese presses down."

Once salted, the curds began to sweat. They developed a creamy coating. There was only a slight taste of salt, too little in my opinion. The curds were even more squeaky than before. When Mrs. Kirby referred to the toughness of the curds, they were tough when compared to the initial custard consistency, but they were not "tough" in any pure meaning of the word; they were quite moist inside, actually.

Mrs. Kirby set the 6 pounds of salted curd aside and began to break up the matted cake that remained. "If I had a larger pan . . . This is the hardest work of all. My hands get so tired I have to slow down. If I had a shredder, I'd shred it. But then I would have to wash the shredder. When I eat cheese, this cheese right here is what I eat. Can't you eat another bite? If the curd is good, the cheese will be good."

By 1 o'clock Mrs. Kirby had two pans of salted curd. She got out two small presses, one metal, a cast-iron round sau-sage and lard press, and the other a rectangular wooden con-traption which she said had been made by the husband of a cheese lady who lived across the river. "I've got another little press that makes a 5-pound cheese, but its tin basket broke and I've not been able to get it fixed. I used it without the basket and the cheese cracked the metal side of the press, but I can still use it if I can get the basket fixed. Then outdoors I've got a little press that would make a 2-pound cheese that I bought in a junk shop up in Maryland. It's so little I don't know what it was made for, but it's all rusty. My dog likes this whey with the cream in it; the first whey to drain out of the salted cheese is creamy. I tried my dog on milk but she doesn't like milk."

She got out her cheese cloths, which she had made from feed bags and had washed in soda water, then had sunned. "I use the same cloths for three days, scalding them and washing them in soda water between times; then after three days I wash them in detergent. If the cloth is as closely woven as sheeting, the whey won't drain through it easily. If it is loosely woven, like cheesecloth, the cloth gets pressed into the sides of the cheese and won't pull away easily; it tears the cheese. That's why I never use a thin cheesecloth when I first press a cheese."

She brought the two followers for the presses in from the yard, where they had been warming in the sun; one was round, the other rectangular, and each fitted inside the basket of each press, to cover the contents. She lined the metal press with muslin and filled it with the dry curds. She put that press's follower in place and turned the handle until slight, very slight pressure was applied to the cheese. A spurt of whey came out of the press and fell into a pan, a trickle followed, and within a few seconds whey barely dripped from the press. "A lady over near here, her husband made her a press out of a pressure cooker. He drilled holes in the bottom and made a wooden follower to fit on top of the cheese. For weight she set a gallon jar on top of the follower and put a quart of water in it. Now and again she would pour a little bit more water in it, until at evening there was half a gallon. That's all the pressure she ever used, about 4 pounds. It seems to me her cheese would have too much whey left in it. She told me a press wasn't even needed, that you could let most of the whey drip out of the cheese when it was hung up in a bag. But I noticed she didn't hang hers up. Some of the old people hung their cheeses up and let the whey drip. Now and again they would take the bag of cheese down from the nail and break it up and hang it again, after an hour or so they simply let it hang and drip. What they had the next morning was a round cheese with a rind on it. They would sun it, let the sun draw the remaining whey out of it."

She set the wooden press on the table. It was rectangular. The box into which the cheese curds were to be placed was about 9 inches long, 4 or 5 inches wide, and 4 or 5 inches high. A wooden follower had been made to fit the box, and above the box was a frame which held a wooden hand screw. Mrs. Kirby did not line this press with muslin; instead, she put the remaining curds in a square of muslin, folded the ends over the top of them, and with her hands pushed the cheese, bag and all, into the rectangular hopper, into the wooden box, the spongy, springy cheese resisting and objecting and contorting itself. "If I had made the press, I would have designed it better," she said. "This top part ought to come off so you can get the cheese in the press. Look how I have to stuff cheese in." The top of the cheese bag stuck up above the press by a few inches. She perched the follower on it and turned the screw until the merest pressure was applied to the cheese, only enough to make the whey start dribbling out.

"The lady who used this press couldn't get her cows' milk taken across the river, so she made cheese out of the milk. Once every week or so she would bring the cheeses across the river on a barge. But now the state has built a bridge across the river, so she sells her milk and she let me have her cheese press. First cheeses I ever made, I didn't get the whey pressed out of them enough. A storekeeper sliced one of my cheeses and put each slice in a cellophane bag, and as the whey dripped out it settled to the bottom of each bag. I hadn't sunned the cheeses long enough."

She went upstairs to get her dog. Apparently she doesn't allow the dog in the kitchen when she is making cheese. She took the dog outdoors and chained him to the end of a long chain at what she told me was his favorite spot, where he could sun himself.

"This milk on the market, I don't think it would make good cheese, do you?" she said, once back in the kitchen. "It would taste processed, you know. I used to keep milk up to three days on occasion before making cheese out of it. I would keep it in the spring house for the first twelve hours, then put it in the refrigerator. The old people thought you shouldn't put milk in a cold place for the first twelve hours. They wanted to ripen it. The old people thought you had to have some morning's warm milk to mix with it, too. If I could get ripe evening's milk I would still make my cheese that way. Milk changes with the seasons, you know. Milk in fall gives the most and the best cheese."

Mrs. Kirby washed her enameled cookers in soda water and set them out in the sun. "Soda is one of the best disinfectants, and the sunlight will kill bacteria; bacteria in your vessels will make an off-flavor in cheese," she said. "I can take these cheeses out of the presses now and turn them if I want to.

They've taken shape now; they take shape in only five or ten minutes. I will keep adding pressure through the afternoon and will turn the cheeses in the presses tonight and add still more pressure, and I will take them out tomorrow morning. If they have overlaps on their rind, I will cut the defects off with a razor blade."

She was through now, I judged, and was mildly weary, yet satisfied, too.

"I once had a book that showed how to make a press. My husband and I made one. The book said to use bricks to weight down the follower. We would put on the bricks and would go upstairs, and then we would hear a brick hit the floor. New cheese is springy, and it would throw off a brick or two. We would go down and put the bricks back on the press, then go upstairs and hear another brick hit the floor. The next morning when we got up and looked at the cheese, it hadn't pressed properly. These two cheeses I'm making now, I can turn them if you want to watch me."

She released pressure from the presses and removed the cheeses, one of them circular and the other rectangular, each with a new, shiny rind. She put cloths on them again, being none too careful about it either, and put them back in their respective presses. "When it comes out of the press tomorrow, I will cut any rough places off and set it in the sun. The sun will draw the whey out and this will leave holes in it. One lady who used to make cheese made a lacy cheese. I believe she didn't press it much and let the sun draw the whey out of it. My cheese isn't lacy, but it does have holes in it. My mother would dry her cheeses on the roof, and my sister and I would climb out the window and gnaw the cheeses like a mouse. That's why I prefer the rinds. After three days of sunning it off and on, letting it be in the sun sometimes—you have to be careful to wipe the whey and fat off the cheese once or twice each day—after three days of sunning I put my cheeses in a cool room until somebody wants one."

I had with me a booklet printed in England, originally in 1909, and I showed her a recipe for a cheese. The recipe was almost identical to the one she had used: renneting at 90 degrees, cutting in half an hour, the slow gradual increase in temperature to 100–105 degrees or higher, the English process requiring about four hours to complete. Mrs. Kirby seemed to be quite impressed with the book and asked what name the English gave the cheese she made. Small Holder, I told her, named because of the small landholdings of the families who made it. They had not enough milk to make large cheeses.

Also in the booklet was another recipe, titled Small Holder's Cheese #2, and this process was quite different. But as we went through the recipe, Mrs. Kirby recognized it as one a few neighbors had used. "Yes, some of them would put curds on a bench with holes bored in the bench, and put a wooden hoop around it, or would fill in the hoop with curds, and they would press the cheese in the hoop, then take it out, break it up, and return it to the hoop and press it again, just as you say."

When I was preparing to leave, I asked her if she would let me buy two cheeses, which she did, two beautiful butter-moist cheeses, one round, and one, for reasons of the lady-across-the-river's husband, oblong. I asked her how I could get to the West Jefferson cheese plant, and she told me.

"Their presses have compression; they get all the whey out quickly," she said. "They can't sun them, you see," she said. "If the sun will draw it out, you'll have little holes. My brother-in-law told me his family's cheese was lacy because they didn't press the whey out so much."

I went down to my car, reluctant to leave a place I had for several hours visited so contentedly.

"When you get ready to eat those cheeses, wipe the butter off of them with a cloth," she called.

I stopped at the Kraft cheese factory in West Jefferson and bought a 22-pound cheese. I asked the foreman if I might talk to him about how cheeses were made in his factory. He said he would be happy to tell me, except that it was against company policy.

A quicker way to make Small Holder cheese can be found in old English books on cheesemaking, of which I have about twenty. They don't all have exactly the same recipe, but generally they require four hours.

To use an older recipe:

You will need a starter if the milk is absolutely fresh or has been kept in a cooler. In that case, begin as Mrs. Kirby did. You will not need a starter if you use evening's milk kept overnight at about 60 or 65 degrees, mixed evenly with fresh morning's milk, or allow milk from a farmer's cooler to cure at 60 to 65 degrees for 5 hours.

For 8 gallons of milk measure ⅓ ounce of full-strength rennet extract (or one-third more than that if you are using Guernsey or Jersey milk). Mix the rennet with six times its own amount of tap water.

With the milk at 90 degrees, add the rennet, noting the time. Stir for five minutes. Float a piece of toothpick or straw and note the time when it stops dead. The time taken can be multiplied by 2 ½ to find out how many *more* minutes you need to wait before cutting. While you wait, cover the pot and read a book—this one if you want to.

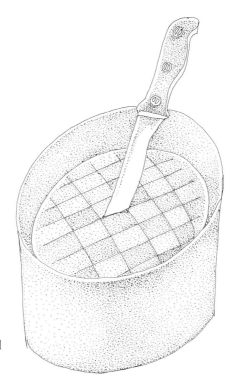

Cutting the curd

In about half an hour from renneting the milk will form a custard, firm and springy, which will break before your finger cleanly, as Mrs. Kirby said. At that time cut the custard into ½-inch cubes. Stir them gently for five minutes, gently loosening any milk curd adhering to the sides and bottom of the pot.

Increase the temperature of the bits of curd and their whey slowly to 106 degrees (or to 109 in the case of Jersey or Guernsey milk).

Leave all or most all of the whey in the pot meanwhile. Don't allow the temperature to rise more than 5 degrees in any twenty-five-minute period. Stir intermittently to keep the particles of curd separate. The curd should become firm, so that the particles will not crush when pressed together in the hand and will fall apart when the hand is opened. Remove the pot from the stove.

Next, pour off the whey all at once. Break the curds into small pieces and when they are no warmer than 80 degrees salt them, using 4 ounces of salt to the curds from 8 gallons of milk.

The old English recipes say the cheese mold should be 6 ½ inches in diameter by 6 ¼ inches deep. The size isn't critical, nor is the shape. Line the mold with muslin or some other loosely woven cloth.

Pack the curd into the cloth-lined mold. The mold, whatever its size, should have holes to permit the whey to drip out of it when pressure is applied. Lay the ends of the cloth over the top of the cheese, and put a metal or wood follower in place. Exert light pressure on the press, or set weights on the mold, 8 to 12 pounds. In half an hour take the cheese out of the press. It is by now a soft, whole cheese. Wring its cloth out, reapply the cloth, turn the cheese, and return it to the mold, to a slightly higher pressure, up to 20 pounds of weight, if possible. The pressure or weight should be increased that evening to about 28 pounds.

Next morning any whelps can be cut off the cheese with a razor, and, if you like, a neat bandage, a cloth wrapping, can be applied, in which case the cheese should be returned briefly to press. When the cheese is taken out of the mold, rub its surface with coarse, dry salt. Place the cheese in a relatively dry room and leave it there at 65 degrees for two or three days. It should be turned daily and lightly salted. Then, according to the old people's methods, a bandage, a cloth, is stitched on the outside of it, and it is left in a cool room to ripen for three to four weeks, or is eaten fresh.

For this cheese, by either recipe, if your milk comes from a farmer's dairy cooler, it is fresh enough. Let it set at room temperature for three hours to ripen, or, if you prefer, add a cup of buttermilk for every 5 gallons and leave it but half an hour at room temperature.

If you bought milk at a city dairy from its receiving room, it will not need further ripening or a starter.

If you want to, you can test your milk to see if it's ripe enough. Put a quart of it in a pot and heat it to 90 degrees. Float a piece of toothpick on top and add 5 drops of liquid rennet extract, first diluted in a spoonful of water. Stir this in for two or three minutes, making a note of the time from renneting to the time the toothpick stops dead. If nine minutes elapse, the milk is ripe enough. If seven minutes elapse, let the milk age at room temperature for about thirty minutes. If it takes eleven or twelve minutes, use one-quarter less rennet and proceed.

This recipe allows for some error incidentally, particularly on the longer-time side, so if your big lot of milk does take more than nine minutes to begin to coagulate, don't despair. You will, however, find that the other processes will and should go slower, too, proportionally. The cheese might be as good, or even better, but the making of it will be more trouble.

To make this cheese out of pasteurized milk, please see the section on pasteurization in Appendix 1.

Recently I visited Wisconsin expecting to seek out home cheesemakers and ask how they were getting on. I knew of one at Appleton, a gentleman named Herbert Mossholder. He and his brother and their two sons make cheese every day of the year. Mossholders have been doing so for over forty years now, making a Small Holder type of cheese, using a method they developed and which Mr. Mossholder says he will not divulge.

"Who are some of the other families who make cheeses at home in this state?" I asked him.

"Nobody," he said.

"Nobody?" I said. "Why, I am sure there are others."

"Nobody," he said. "The factories have taken over everything out here."

Next morning I visited and phoned several cheesemaking authorities and found that Mr. Mossholder was correct, except for Lester Kasper who for years had made an excellent Cheddar. "A very, very good cheese," one of the Wisconsin cheese experts told me. "Kasper is the winner of many blue ribbons." I drove the fifteen or twenty miles to his community and stopped to ask for directions to his house. I was told that there was no point in going on down the road, that Mr. Kasper had recently died.

So Mr. Mossholder was right in that his is the only small-family operation in his part of Wisconsin, and maybe in the whole state. I went back to see him, found him at work in his cellar making room, and told him I was going to write a book on cheesemaking and wanted his help.

"I read a book on cheesemaking once, and I never saw—I never knew cheesemaking had to be like that," he said. "My father began making cheeses forty years ago on the back of the kitchen range in a kettle."

I noticed that the Mossholders had since graduated to a vat with a firebox under it, heated every day by firewood.

"They had in the book about starters," he told me. "We ordered a starter years ago, put it in a bottle and let it work, and that culture we used in the making, except for a bit left in the bottle every day. We put fresh milk in with it, and so we have continued for seventeen years with that starter. It sets in the refrigerator without even a top on the bottle. The trouble with a cheesemaking book is that it makes it sound impossible to make cheese."

"How do you make cheese?" I asked him.

"My father brought in cheesemakers, one a day, to show him how, and then he combined three: the Swiss, the brick and the Cheddar, and I won't tell you how it's made."

Mr. Mossholder did tell me that he uses milk from his own dairy herd. He feeds the Holstein cows fodder year round. The evening's milk he pours in his vat in the cellar room where he works, and he leaves it at about 70 degrees overnight. Next morning he puts the fresh morning's milk in with it. The milk is not pasteurized. He uses a tiny amount of his special starter. He adds rennet. He uses enough rennet to bring about a firm state of coagulation in one hour. He stirs the rennet in, then waits an hour for the coagulum to be ready to cut. He tests to see if it breaks clean when he breaks it with his finger. He cuts with curd knives. He does not scald—that is, he does not increase the temperature. He stirs the bits of curd until they have established their independence one of another, then he attaches a strainer to the vat and allows the whey to flow out. He then fills up the vat with cold water. This cools the curd and the curd absorbs some of that water, and both help slow down the development of acidity.

He does not use a press as such. Instead he puts the bits of curd in a number of wooden, brick-shaped molds about the size of Mrs. Kirby's rectangular press. The size of each mold

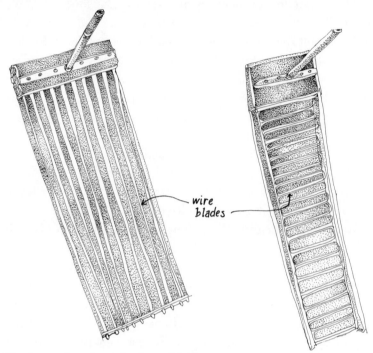

wire
blades

Horizontal and vertical curd knives

is 5 ¼ inches wide, 10 ¼ inches long and 5 ½ inches high. The molds are set on two thicknesses of plastic screening, and the screening is on a slightly tilted drainage table. Each mold holds the curd for a five-pound cheese. They are filled once and are not filled again even after drainage has reduced the height of the mass of curds. Each mold has vertical slits cut along its sides about every half inch, to help the whey drain. The mold has a follower, a piece of wood cut to fit it, to cap its contents. Mr. Mossholder puts the follower on top of the bits of curd, and on the follower he lays a single eight-pound brick. That's a heavy brick—not a regular-sized one. He turns the cheese every hour and a half or two hours, first loosening it in the mold by pressing it at one corner, then freeing it along one edge, then the other edges. He told me that before he turns a cheese, he pours warm water on it. That evening he removes each cheese from its mold and salts it. This is the first salt the cheese receives.

He keeps the cheese on a shelf in a 70-degree curing room, located beside the making room, and turns it and salts it from time to time. He says it takes five days for the salt to penetrate to the center of the cheese.

At the end of five days, he puts Saran Wrap around the cheese and touches the wrap's seams with a warm iron to seal them. The cheese is then put in a cool storage place to wait for a buyer. Mr. Mossholder sells fresh cheeses and also has cheeses aged two or three months. (He will ship to you from his Route 4, Appleton, Wisconsin, address, if you want to order a cheese from him.) But he will not, of course, tell you how he makes his cheeses.

I enjoyed talking with him. He is a man of considerable integrity, I felt, a likeable, helpful, dour man. He told me he does not use in any of his processes soap, detergents, or sprays; he uses only hot water to clean his utensils, molds, and vat. He has had trouble with his cheeses only when a relative scrubbed down his curing room and painted it; he had to wait a week or two for the friendly colonies of bacteria to re-establish themselves and once more begin to give his cheeses the mellow taste that he prefers. Now, if he paints his curing room, he paints one wall at a time.

He told me he has thus far had thirteen offers to sell out to factories. They couldn't conceivably want his old vat or his curd knives or his basement, and I don't think it would be difficult for them to find out his methods. I suppose they want him out of business because he makes an excellent cheese, setting a troublesome standard, and represents a way of making cheese which is anathema to them.

Mr. Mossholder gave me one of his wooden molds as I left and told me where he thought I could find curd knives. I loaned the mold to a cheesemakers' shop (Appendix 3) so copies could be made and gave the shop the address Mr. Mossholder had given me so the curd knives would be ordered for me. It is not unusual for a cheesemaker to give me a mold, or a net, or some other piece of his apparatus. There must be something in my character that brings this about.

If you don't have an 8-pound brick, pour a gallon of water in a plastic bag, tie the bag closed, and set that on the follower of the wooden box. It will do as well.

2

Cream Cheeses

My wife, Rosie, and I often make cream cheeses. They call for no special equipment, no endowment of luck. One needs fresh milk, rennet, and salt. That's all. And a quart of extra cream can be added to each gallon of milk if it is available.

We have a country house, about a mile from a farmer's milking barn, and from his cooler we get 2 or 3 gallons of milk on occasion, choosing a day just after the milk truck has taken most of it away, so that the milk in his cooler is of that day's milkings. He charges us less than half what milk sells for in the stores, and that milk, in addition to being too old, has had some of its cream removed. His herd is Holstein, and milk from Holsteins makes excellent cheeses of all types. Some cows, such as Jerseys or Guernseys, give more cream, but generally the leaner Holstein milk is better for cheeses.

The Holstein herd is tested regularly, so we don't pasteurize the milk. You might in different circumstances decide you need to, and in that case you should read the paragraph on pasteurization in Appendix 1.

We usually go get the milk for cream cheeses in the early evening, simply because a cream cheese must set for several hours at 60 to 65 degrees, and we prefer to let it set overnight. So about six or seven o'clock we drive down the road and return.

We pour the milk into a canning kettle, though any pot or vat will do. Let's say we decide on a small lot tonight and use 1 gallon of milk and a quart of cream. We stir the two together and heat the milk to 60 to 65 degrees. We measure ½ cc. of rennet and dilute it with a spoonful or two of tap water. We add the rennet to the milk and stir it in for three or four minutes, then in ten minutes we ripple the surface of the milk for a minute or so to help keep the cream from rising. We cover the pot and set it on a shelf and set the house thermostat at 60 to 65 degrees for the night, or in summer we set the pot in the bathtub, which we've partly filled with 60-degree water. Twice at thirty-minute intervals we ripple the milk's surface for a minute or two. Then we leave the pot undisturbed until morning. Usually about twelve hours is the time needed for the milk to become a custard thick enough for our purpose.

Next morning the custard will split before your finger if you run your finger one way, then another, through it. The whey which appears in the scar of the break will be limpid, clear with a greenish hue.

After breakfast my wife or I ladle the curd into yard-square clean cloths. The curd of 1 ½ gallons of milk needs only one such cloth. The cloth can be moist or dry. It must be clean and free from odors. Huckaback cloth is all right, sheeting or muslin is all right, a worn-smooth towel is all right.

We tie the four corners of the cloth together, once the curds are on it, and hang the bag from the ceiling or from the lintel of a closet doorway, where there are no drafts. We set a bowl on the floor to catch the dripping whey, and our dog Bella, a basset, laps up the whey as pleases her. Some people like whey—I do not, myself. Little Miss Muffet used to eat her curds and whey, you'll recall, and maybe she liked them.

When the drainage of whey slackens to a drip, in twenty or thirty minutes, we take the bag to the sink, open it, and with a spoon scrape the cheese off the cloth, where the drier cheese adheres, and mix it with the body of softer cheese. Then the bag is hung once more. We repeat this operation from time to time, every hour or so.

Once the cheese has a firm consistency, which is after six to twelve hours—anytime in there—we get out the small containers we use to mold the cheeses in, tiny wicker baskets, tin or aluminum cans we have cut both ends out of, or whatever. The cans we choose are about 2 or 2 ½ inches in diameter. We set the cans on a woven mat—actually a place mat.

We salt the cheese to taste, then spoon it into the molds, pressing the cheese into shape with our fingers or with the spoon, tasting more of it during the process than is in any way required. We make our cheeses about 2 inches thick.

When they are firm enough, and often they are at once, we push them from the molds onto a mat or a plate, and the cheeses are ready to eat, or to store.

To store them we wrap them in waxed paper or metal foil. They will keep for a long time in the refrigerator or on a cool shelf. They seem to me to be better when aged a week or so.

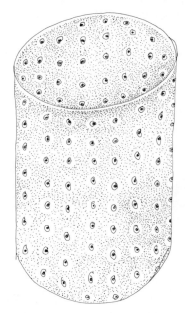

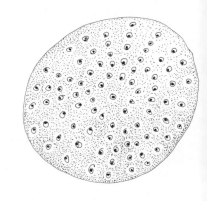

Small holder cheese mold

Gervais and Pommel

These two French cheeses are the same. They simply have two names. A M. Gervais and a M. Pommel divided France into two parts—Paris and the remainder. Some say this is the best cream cheese in the world.

Can you make it?

I think so. It is the cream cheese I have just described the making of. It couldn't be much easier, could it?

Only give it time, as I have indicated. A quicker cheese can be made by using more rennet, but at the expense of quality.

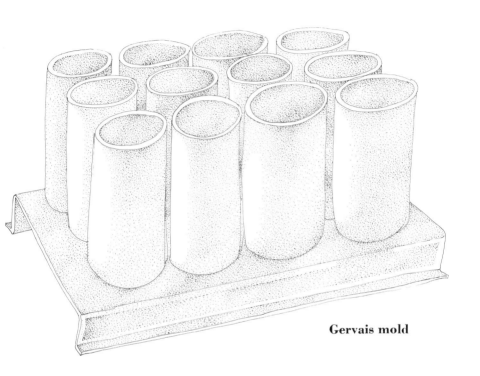

Gervais mold

Bondon

Bondon is another French cream cheese. It is made from whole fresh milk; cream need not be added. The cheese is drier in body and less rich in taste than is Gervais.

Two gallons of milk will produce twelve cheeses of the conventional size and shape: cylinders 2 ¼ inches across and 2 ¼ inches tall, or, if you prefer, 1 ¾ inches across and 2 ¾ inches deep.

The recipe is the same as that for Gervais. Traditionally Bondon molds—for our purposes tin cans or cardboard cylinders or whatever—are lined with waxed paper or muslin. Use enough lining, if you like, to cover the cheese once it has set, to wrap it in all around.

French Double-Cream

Basically the Gervais recipe is used, except that only half as much rennet is required. The cheese will, therefore, be ready for the cloth in twenty-four rather than twelve hours. Once in the cloth, the bag of cheese, rather than hung, is set on a draining board for an hour or so, then is weighed, salted (2 percent of its own weight of fine, dry salt being used), and ladled into large round molds, where it is allowed to continue draining for a few more hours. You can make such molds out of 1-pound coffee cans by cutting holes in one end, or by removing both ends and cutting drainage holes in the plastic cover supplied usually with American cans. The holes permit the whey to escape as it drains from the cheese curds.

A cheese of this type is likely to have 60 percent butterfat, more or less. Thick cream can be mixed in with the cheese to make it even richer, if you like. Cream cheeses rarely go over 70 percent butterfat, even so.

Neufchâtel (French Method)

To a gallon of fresh milk add ½ pint of cream. With the milk at 86 degrees, stir in rennet—only one or two drops of rennet are needed to bring about the desired firmness in eighteen to twenty-four hours. The molds traditionally used are cylinders open at both ends, and they can be set on straw mats for drainage. The usual weight for the individual cheese in France is 4.4 ounces.

This is the basic recipe for several French cheeses. Some require more or less time for coagulation—as little as three hours for those using more rennet. Some of them are molded in little baskets. Some are made in heart-shaped molds and are served with fresh cream and sweetened fresh fruit, a dessert called *coeur à la crème,* as you perhaps know.

Petit Suisse

Petit Suisse is made by combining the Neufchâtel and Gervais recipes. The milk used is enriched slightly, as in the case of Neufchâtel, but the renneting temperature is 65 degrees, the same as for Gervais. Slightly more rennet is used, 3.4 cc. liquid rennet extract for one gallon of enriched milk. In about eight hours the curd is ladled into cloths. During the next eight hours the cloths are untied and scraped from time to time, just as we described before.

Gournay

A Gournay is quite similar to an American cream cheese. The method of making it is yet another combination of Gervais and Neufchâtel recipes. It uses the same milk, but slightly more enriched, like the Neufchâtel. The renneting temperature is 77 degrees. One or two drops of rennet extract are used for a gallon of milk, and the milk requires up to thirty-six hours to reach coagulation. During that time it should be kept at 77 degrees or thereabouts.

The curing of Gournay is similar to that of the double-cream, in that the sack in which the curds are placed is not hung; to keep the cheese from becoming too dry during the long curing, the bag is set in a colander or strainer from which the whey can drain, or is laid on a draining board. Once the curd has achieved a firm consistency, it is removed from the bag, weighed, and salted, the amount of salt being 2 percent of the weight of the cheese. The salted curds are then pushed through a strainer with a wooden pestle or something similar. After being strained the cheese is put into molds which are 2 ⅓ inches square by ¾ inch thick. In France the cheeses are wrapped in tinfoil.

Coulommiers

Coulommiers is one of the best and easiest cheeses to make. It is a favorite French cheese and is eaten either when fresh or after ripening. I will give the recipe for the fresh cheese version.

In shape it is circular, 5 ½ inches in diameter, 2 ½ inches thick when three days to one week old. It is about the size of a Camembert and has the taste of a fresh Brie; it is, in fact, a small, fresh Brie, but less carefully made as a rule.

One gallon will make two cheeses. Milk should be quite fresh. The renneting temperature is 86 degrees, or a few degrees lower if the temperature of the making room is warmer than 65 degrees (so that in a room at 71 degrees you would rennet at 80). The amount of rennet used is ¼ cc.

for a gallon of milk, the rennet being diluted with tap water in proportions of one to six, as usual.

Stir the rennet into the milk for five minutes, then leave the milk alone for ten minutes, then ripple the surface with your finger or a spoon for a minute, then leave it alone for ten minutes before rippling the surface again. If coagulation has not set in, ripple the surface yet a third time before finally covering the milk and letting it be. Coagulation will require 2 ½ to 3 hours from renneting. During this time the vat or pot should be covered and an effort made to hold the temperature unchanged.

When the curds break cleanly over the finger and greenish whey is seen to separate from the cut curds, the curd is ready for the molds.

Coulommiers cheeses in France are formed in special molds, made of two metal pieces which fasten together, the lower being 3 inches high and the upper 2 inches. I have not been able to find any in the United States. Probably a more gifted man than I could make his own, but I have taken a more slovenly, though effective, way out. I use tin cans about 5 ½ inches in diameter, both ends cut out, and cut down to 3 inches high. I also have for each can a 2-inch tin collar extension, which will fit into the top of the mold. As the curds drain, they drop lower in my extension until at the first turning the extension isn't needed any longer and can simply be removed.

The mold is set on a straw mat—I use a table mat—and this is placed on a small board, each mold having its own. Once the curd is distinctly firm, it is ladled gently into the assembled mold. If you like, first slice off the smooth top curd in large pieces, to be used later for topping. Ladle the curd into the molds; the thinner the slices of curd, the quicker

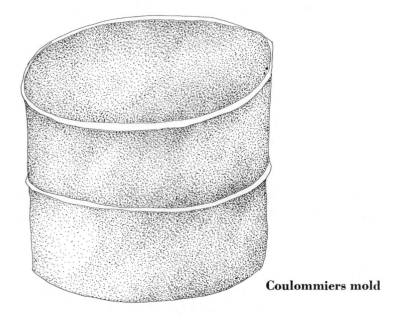

Coulommiers mold

the drainage. When the molds are filled, let the cheeses stand until the curd has shrunk enough so that the top half of the molds, or the extensions in my case, can be removed. This will take eight to ten hours for a cheese of ideal quality in a 65-degree room; in a warmer room drainage will take place in less time, but the cheese will not be as good.

On top of each remaining three-fifths of a mold, or the mold without its extension, put a straw mat, then a small board. Now turn the mold over, so the cheese can drain from the other side.

In a few hours, turn the cheese again. This time, despite your nervousness, the process will be easier, because by now the cheese will be firmer and better able to protect itself.

Just as soon as the cheese is firm, rub fine, dry salt on the two exposed surfaces.

The cheese can be taken from the mold by the morning of the third day.

The fresh cheeses—that is, three to seven days old—in France are wrapped in waxed paper and put in wood-chip or cardboard boxes. They can be held a week or two at a temperature of 52 to 60 degrees.

I toured a factory in France several years ago which made a Coulommiers type of cheese, marketed under its own trade name. The process was like the one I have given here, except that more rennet was used and the curd was cut sooner and cut into 1-inch to 1 ½-inch cubes. The cubes and the whey were poured into the molds together, none too gently either. Of course, the whey flowed on off. The only advantage to this method is that it allows for large-scale manufacture. Its disadvantage is in loss of quality compared to cheese made at home.

English Cream Cheeses

The English make a renneted cream cheese similar to Gervais, which they simply call cream cheese. They also make unrenneted cream cheeses.

The cream constitutes up to half, or even more on occasion, of the milk used. For a milk one-quarter to one-half cream, the setting temperature would be 60 to 65 degrees, and about 3 cc. of rennet would be needed for each American gallon.

The setting time is eight to twelve hours. The cheeses are cured as is a Gervais. When the cheese has attained a firm consistency, it is usually salted to taste, although salt is not always added, and put into molds. An English cream cheese usually weighs about 4 ounces.

We have two recipes for unrenneted cream cheese, one apparently the favorite of Mrs. Beeton, who wrote *Book of Household Management* in the mid-1880s, reissued in 1970, the book by which English ladies patterned their thinking for one or two generations. Mrs. Beeton wrote in an authoritative style though she was a slight, retiring young lady; we suspect her husband, who sold the book and doubtless kept the profits, had something to do with its sense of authority. According to Mrs. Beeton, cream cheese is not properly cheese; it is nothing more than cream which is dried sufficiently to be cut with a knife. There is an old English recipe for double-cream cheese which is perhaps what she referred to, and it goes this way:

English Double-Cream Cheese

Thick cream (which cannot be pasteurized if this recipe is to succeed) at 60 to 65 degrees is put in a fine linen cloth and hung to drain. No rennet is used. The draining process is the same as for English cream cheese. When the cream has a pasty consistency and is still moist, it is put in molds. In hot weather it is best to accelerate the process in order to prevent the cream from developing a sour taste and smell; this can be done by increasing the number of scrapings and by adding a slight amount of pressure. For instance, a board can be laid on top of the bag of cheese. Thus encouraged, the cheese can be molded in five to six hours.

The cheese is easily tainted by odors in the making room or by contamination of the cloths. The cloths can be cleaned with scalding soda water and aired in the sun—that is the old-fashioned way.

English double-cream cheese will keep one week without salting, but salting will increase its life expectancy. An over-ripe double-cream cheese has a fat-like flavor. If green mold appears on the cheese while it is being stored, this condition can be avoided in the future by wrapping the cheese in paper or muslin which has been soaked in salty water.

There is a very old recipe for this or a similar cheese; I will put it down for your amusement, and for the practical use of any of you who owns twelve cows.

Use the new milk of 12 cows in the morning and add the evening cream of 12 cows. Put in 3 spoonsful of rennet, and when it is come, break it, and whey it, and when it is well whey'd, break it again and work into the curd three pounds of fresh butter, and put it in your press, and turn it in the press very often for an hour or more, and change the cloths, and wash them every time you change them. You may put wet cloths to them, but toward the last put two or three fine dry cloths to them; let it lie thirty or forty hours in the press, according to the thickness of the cheese.

Old English Unrenneted Cream Cheese

An older recipe for an unrenneted cream cheese takes longer to make. Old recipes usually do take longer than newer ones. This one, from the nineteenth century, goes this way:

The cream (unpasteurized) should be thick and fresh. It should be mechanically separated if possible since that process yields a thicker cheese than does cream skimmed from milk. The thick cream is put in an earthenware or stoneware vessel and left in "pure air" at 60 degrees until the cream is thickened by natural fermentation, which will take about three days. It should then be poured into a deep linen bag with a fine texture, one that closes with a drawstring, and hung with a vessel under it to catch the whey. The bag should not be more than one-third full. In two days the cheese will become soft and comparatively dry. It will now need slight pressure, which can be supplied by two boards or a small press. (The recipe suggests twenty lead plates weighing 2 pounds each, but surely that isn't a practical instruction. The recommendation is to go from 2 pounds at first to 40 pounds in twenty-four hours.)

The curd is emptied from the bag, once pressed, and it "requires to be kneaded with a wooden knife until it is reduced to a uniform consistency." It is then ready for the mold, which can be of any convenient shape and any small size. The molds were lined with strips of butter muslin (cheese-cloth) or parchment in the old days, and the maker pressed the cheese into the mold with his fingers, folding the ends of the lining over the cheese; he either lifted the mold off the cheese or withdrew the cheese from the mold, and the cheese was ready.

This is a rich cheese. You can work a little salt into it or sprinkle a little salt on it to increase its keeping qualities.

Devonshire Cream

This isn't a cheese at all, but there will be other items in this book that have no better reason for being here. It is a cream, a magnificent cream.

It is made from unpasteurized whole milk, the fresher the better. The milk is poured about 6 inches deep in an open pot or pan. The container is put in a cool place until the cream rises to the top, which might take ten hours or even more.

Then one sets the pan on a stove and gradually increases the temperature, without stirring, to 175 degrees or thereabouts, at which point a wrinkled appearance will develop and spread over the surface of the cream. It is this wrinkling, not the exact temperature reached, which is consequential. In order to develop the burnt flavor characteristic of Devonshire cream, the heating must occupy not less than one-half hour.

Now the pan is set in a sink of cold running water. As it cools, the cream will become thick and clotted, and once cold, it can easily be removed with a slotted spoon. Some makers allow the pans to cool by themselves, but this is an inferior way.

The pans used in making Devonshire cream in the old days held 6 to 7 (American) quarts of milk and cream. They were 15 inches in diameter at the top, 11 inches in diameter at the bottom, and 7 inches high.

Devonshire cream is packed in widemouthed tins or pots. The tins have lids and are used for mailing the cream. In summer the cream will keep three or four days; in cold weather, for a week.

Cottage Cheeses

Cottage cheese—also called pot cheese, and if made from whole milk and pressed slightly, so it can be sliced, often called farmer's cheese—is a favorite in England, as well as in the United States. Its popularity in America reaches toward the mark of a national obsession.

The pieces of curd are distinct, giving it the appearance of popcorn. They are not rubbery. They are meaty and have a milky, slightly acid taste and a pleasant aroma.

Unrenneted Cottage Cheese

The recipe we give here calls for whole milk, unpasteurized.

In place of the rennet, cultured buttermilk is used, up to

12 ounces buttermilk per gallon, which will produce desired firmness of coagulation in four to five hours. The curd will be very soft. You will know that it is ready to be cut when it becomes jelly-like and shows clear whey when you break the curd with your finger (its acidity rating is 0.6 percent if you want to test it). Cut the curd gently into ½-inch cubes. Let them rest five to ten minutes. Increase the temperature very slowly and after five or ten minutes begin gently stirring the curds by hand. Continue this, raising the temperature but by only the slightest amount, say 1 degree every five minutes, until there is enough whey to float the curd; then increase the temperature somewhat faster and stir more vigorously in order to prevent the formation of lumps. Do not heat beyond 110 degrees; some makers do not heat beyond 95 degrees. The time allowed for reaching maximum temperature is forty to eighty minutes, and the curd is left in the hot whey for fifteen to thirty minutes longer, the shorter time being used for the hotter temperature. (A high temperature and prolonged heating will make the curd tougher and drier in the finished cheese; the lower temperature will make it smoother, but if it is too low or is increased too swiftly, the cheese might be mushy.)

The whey should be removed when the curd does not become milky when rubbed between the fingers; also, if you wash a bit of the curd in cold water, you will have an idea of its firmness once it is cold—it should have no soft centers. Remove the whey. Run a trench through the middle of the curd and remove more of the whey as it collects. Or, if you prefer, put the curd in a cloth and set it on a draining board, or hang it up.

When the whey stops leaving the curd, wash the curd with cold water, the first time at 70 degrees and the second at a cooler temperature, 55 or even lower. (If you plan to use only one washing, set the water temperature at 55 or lower, as the cooler water stops harmful bacterial action.)

When most all the moisture has drained away, salt the cheese to taste.

Renneted Cottage Cheese

This is an English recipe from the 1920s.

To a gallon of milk at 72 degrees, add 1 ½ ounces cultured buttermilk as a starter, stir well, and add a commercial rennet tablet (see Appendix 3 for markets). This amount of starter and rennet will result in a soft curd in about twelve hours. (The curd will be more solid than that produced without rennet as in the preceding recipe. The acidity in the whey will be 0.4 percent to 0.6 percent.)

Cut the cheese, remove the whey, and proceed as for unrenneted cottage cheese.

Creamed Cottage Cheese

To make creamed cottage cheese add a bit of cream at any time after draining the cottage cheese made by either recipe. Add enough cream to give the mixture a fat content of 2 to 4 percent, or to taste.

Colwick

I have had my troubles with Colwick, at least with the slipcote process I tried to use. Colwick is made in the counties of Nottinghamshire and Leicestershire, England, and its distribution is largely confined to these districts. The cheeses are round, cylindrical cakes, of about 1 ½ pounds. The cheese is quickly made; that is, a cheese you start to make in the morning can be eaten before you go to bed at night, if you like, the entire process requiring about twelve hours. Or, by putting slight pressure on the bag of cheese, you can have it ready for lunch, as we will explain.

Colwick is often made by Stilton makers; the curd used is the same one from which Stiltons are made.

Four gallons of milk, about 3.5 percent butterfat, such as Holstein milk, will make four cheeses of the usual size, about 1 ¼ pounds each when fresh. The milk should itself be fresh. To 4 gallons of milk, 3 pints of water are added.

Renneting temperature is 82 to 84 degrees. The amount of liquid rennet extract used is ¾ dram, the rennet being diluted with tap water, as usual. After renneting, stir the milk six minutes, then ripple the surface five or six minutes, using your finger or a spoon, then cover the pot and leave it alone for an hour.

The molds are ordinary cake tins in shape, circular, and the sides and bottom have rows of small holes to allow the whey to drain off. They should be lined with muslin or some open-texture cloth, and the cloth should be big enough to overlap the cheese on top. The curd is ready to be ladled into the molds, slice by slice, sixty to seventy-five minutes after renneting. Large, clean-cut slices are used. Some of the whey is allowed to drain off; then the extra curd is used to fill the molds again. Room temperature during this process ought to be about 65 degrees.

In half an hour fold the ends of the cloths over the tops of the molds, to help cause the curd to become concave as it drains. Some makers tie the cloth Stilton fashion; that is, they tie one corner of the cloth around the other three, and keep tightening the cloth to help the cheese drain. They are, therefore, ready to remove the cheese from the mold in a few hours, rather than in the ten or twelve hours which a system not exerting pressure requires.

As soon as the cheese is firm enough, the cloth is removed entirely and the cheese is put on the shelf. It can be eaten straightaway, which is what I would recommend, or can be kept several days to ripen. The traditional way to ripen it is to put the cheese between two tight-fitting dishes, which will exclude air, and pour off the whey as it accumulates. I did this, but my cheese soured. The whey soured, or the dishes soured; anyway, eventually the cheese soured. The cheese might develop a white mold, called *Oidium lactis*, and will in that case liquefy under the surface, developing a creamy consistency. Cheeses cured in this way are known as *Slipcote*. This is what I was after but did not attain. I understand now that the cheese, once the whey has drained away, should be put in a warm place, to encourage the mold.

Cambridge

Cambridge is also called York cheese, and is distinctly English. It is a delicate, soft, unsalted cheese and must be eaten when quite fresh. It used to be made only during the summer months, which is when the people of York demanded it.

The molds usually used in making Cambridge cheese are oblong and are in two pieces. They are not commercially available, so far as I can determine, so you will need to devise your own. The lower part is a bottomless wood frame about an inch high, and inside this frame a straw mat is placed; incidentally, the mat is permitted to adhere to the

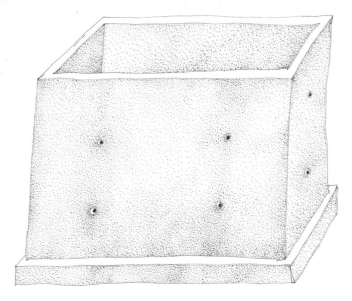

Cambridge mold

cheese and is sold with it in England. The upper part of the mold, which is 7 ½ inches long, 5 inches wide, and 6 inches deep, is pierced with sixteen drainage holes; this section rests within the bottom frame.

Cambridge cheese requires a gallon of whole fresh milk heated to 92 to 95 degrees. The amount of rennet used is ¼ dram, the rennet being diluted one to six with water, or thereabouts.

The rennet should be stirred into the milk for three or four minutes but no longer—not even the surface of the milk should be rippled—for some of the cream should be allowed to rise to the top.

In about an hour, when the curd will break clean over your finger, ladle off the upper, creamy surface and slide it bit by bit onto a plate, then fill the mold with the remaining curd. When the mold is nearly full, slide the creamy curd gently from the plate onto the top of the cheese, to give it a creamy topping. This is much less difficult to do than it sounds.

The mold should be kept out of drafts and at a temperature of 65 to 70 degrees. The cheese is not turned. It is left on the straw mat to drain for twenty-four hours, during which time it shrinks to one-third its original height. In another twenty-four hours it is ready for use. By that time the mold can be removed without damage to the cheese, which will weigh something over a pound. In wooden molds, the curd adheres to the wooden side, so that the edges curl in, improving the appearance of the cheese, but wooden molds are difficult to keep clean, fresh, and sanitary.

Should the cheese have a leathery consistency, the drainage has been too quick, perhaps because the room was too warm or the renneting temperature too high. If the cheese is spongy and lacks stability, the opposite of these conditions is in effect. If you had trouble getting the whey to drain properly from your cheese, you might at a future time add a small quantity of buttermilk before renneting. Given a try or two—maybe even on the first try—you can make this cheese nicely, and it is a superb treat, indeed.

Traditionally Cambridge cheeses were delivered in large wooden boxes, each holding several trays and each tray holding six to eight cheeses, but you need not concern yourself about that. I simply gathered that bit of information somewhere along the way and want to set it down.

These soft and cream cheeses are rather easy to make. With more rennet you can make them quicker, though not as well. If you use milk somewhat ripened, perhaps bought from a dairy, add less rennet. You can test a quart of the milk, as described in the first chapter, using the suggested portion of rennet and noticing the time needed for coagulation to begin. If the rennet is to produce a firm enough "custard" in one hour, the time to the first instant of coagulation will be about seventeen minutes.

The cheeses in these first two chapters are practical. For the novice they are quite enough. As experience with them leads you on, you will find ever increasing challenges and appetite in the chapters to follow.

This poem from nineteenth-century England, telling a dairymaid how to make a cream cheese, might amuse you. It uses the word *vat* where we usually use the word *mold*. Another meaning the same as these two is *hoop*.

> Would you make soft cheese? Then I'll tell you how,
> Take a gallon of milk quite fresh from the cow.
> Ere the rennet is added, the dairyman's daughter
> Must throw in a quart of the choicest spring water.
> When perfectly curdled, so white and so nice,
> You must take it all out of the dish with a slice.
> And put it 'thout breaking with ease in the vat,
> With a cheese-cloth at bottom, be sure to mind that.
> This delicate matter take care not to squeeze,
> But fill as the whey passes off by degrees.
> Next day you may turn it, and do not be loth
> To wipe it quite dry with a fine linen cloth.
> The cheese is now finished, and nice it will be
> If enveloped in leaves from the green ashen tree.

3

Actually, the kinship between fine cheese and good wine is so close that neglect of one encourages neglect of the other. What irony that, though England is not a country of the vine, our men of letters have kept the great literature of wine in full vigor; while the great cheeses that England still produces have inspired almost no literature in praise of them.

—Osbert Burdett, writing in 1937 in
Cheddar Gorge, a Book of English Cheeses, edited by John Squire

English Country Cheeses

All cheeses are, I suppose, provincial—even rural—at birth, but in the case of some of them, Cheddar and Cheshire, for instance, international and urban acceptance has followed. The cheeses in this chapter have not found such popularity, though each in the place of its making has its devotees. Some of the cheeses do not age long and in consequence are not shipped far from home, but all of them are available from time to time in London and even in New York, though not always exhibiting their best native dress and manners. You can order them, and you should order a pound or so of any cheese you plan to make. In Appendix 3 I will list a few mail-order markets in case your local cheese merchant looks startled when you ask for a piece of Dorset.

53

These are distinctive cheeses when properly made, each with its own body and soul, sense of pride and well-being, but sometimes their distinctions are modified by their makers, either out of economic callousness or on account of hopeful concessions to the more celebrated Cheddar and Cheshire. I recall that in a spanking new supermarket in London recently I bought packaged portions of four of these very cheeses, all vacuum-packaged alike. I took them home to have a little cheese-tasting session and discovered that they were identical in taste and texture, though not in coloring. The Leicester, Lancashire, the Wensleydale, and the Double Gloucester were the same cheese. The distributor had mischievously misappropriated four ancient names for his own skimpy purposes, which need not surprise us, though it did surprise me at the time, and the supermarket had nobody working inside its walls who knew anything about cheeses, which need not surprise us, either. Supermarket people know most about packaging and displaying, and as this cheese was neatly packaged, all was well.

That very afternoon I walked from our little mews house to a proper cheese shop and there bought portions of these same four cheeses. I brought them home, and my wife and a friend and I had our cheese tasting. My wife preferred the Wensleydale, our friend liked the Double Gloucester, and I was much taken that day with the Leicester, which goes to show why there are still available in proper cheese shops many different cheeses, and in ever so many other shops many different names of cheeses.

Of course, forty years ago the same four cheeses were even more different from one another than they are today. To look into this I have gone to the British Museum and done my homework in the Reading Room. Since the museum was bombed in World War II and lost many old books, I have also gone to Dublin—the Irish Republic sat out that war—and in the National Library and at Trinity College have fitted in the missing pieces. So the recipes I give here are sound and authentic, verified in various works, and the recipes I have used, two or three generations old, are themselves mature, traditional. Cheeses change—I know that. Tastes change. Recipes change, if they reflect all this. In a practical sense we all change, but this is no reason to insist that present-day versions be used, for they might prove to be the most impermanent of all. We will perhaps never again find in any shop a Lancashire made by its traditional recipe, but I present that recipe here because that is its native form and it offers a special set of challenges which interest me, and because the preservation of these particular recipes is one reason I am writing this book.

All these cheeses are pressed, though you need not have a brawny press or brawny arms. And all are called hard cheeses, though they are not in fact hard. They are in that respect, and often in many other respects, close kin to Cheshire and Cheddar. They do not require any elaborate curing room, though they need a clean place to cure in, and cool—60 degrees, more or less, will do. Or 50. Or 65. They are tolerant.

You will not, I trust, try to make all of them. Try one, and if you like it, stay with it for a while. You really should get to know any type of cheese you make, should at least try to know it intimately. Some of these are quite lonely cheeses and need your company.

By all means take advantage of the fact that these cheeses are not well known in the United States. If asked what you have made, you can say Derby with reasonable confidence that nobody present knows what a Derby is supposed to taste

like. Or say Danbury. That's better still, for if some wise
old fellow does say then, "Yes, I know that cheese," why,
you needn't worry a moment about him. Danbury dropped
from existence decades ago, as some of these will in time, and
nobody even knows how it was made.

Gloucester and Double Gloucester

My friend Jim Matthiason began working for the Milk Marketing Board of England as a teaboy; he is now, at about
fifty, in charge of Emberton Bros. Ltd., which is the Milk
Marketing Board's clearinghouse for all farmhouse cheeses
in England other than Cheddar. His office is in Crewe, a railroad and marketing center not far from the places in Cheshire
and Lancashire where most of his cheeses are made.

One of his own contributions to cheesemaking in England
has to do with saving the Double Gloucester, the great old
English cheese, perhaps with Cheshire the oldest cheese still
extant in England. A Single Gloucester weighs 15 pounds
and is 16 inches in diameter and between 2 and 3 inches
thick. A Double Gloucester, being twice as thick, weighs
twice as much; hence its name.

Traditionally Gloucester is straw colored. Some books
written by gourmets insist that it is red, and so it can be if
colored red, but this is not its nature. It was in olden times
colored a yellow butter color, or straw color, as I said, and a
ripened Double Gloucester will have a clouded reddish tint
on its variegated hide, but the hide (the rind) is blue. The
taste is mellow, delicate, pungent but not sharp, rich and long-
tasting on the palate. The Double is usually better than the
Single—it ages longer and more smoothly because of its

thicker body. The Single is softer, being fresher, more open of flesh, more mild; the Double is close and crumbly of texture and takes on qualities that can best be compared to those acquired by vintage wines.

In World War II the recipe for Double Gloucester disappeared; indeed, the manufacture of Double Gloucester might have disappeared from England except for Jim Matthiason and the Milk Marketing Board. As you might know, World War II disrupted all cheesemaking in England; the young men went off to war and milk was strictly rationed. The tight controls that the government had to exert did away with the random type of cheesemaking which had been one of England's finest achievements. Under the pressure of the war, England virtually abolished the manufacture of all cheese except two mousetrap types which they named Cheddar and Cheshire. There was practically no difference in the government's two recipes, and thus in one act the government put in jeopardy the reputations of two great English cheeses.

Each citizen was rationed 2 ounces of the mousetrap Cheddar-Cheshire per week.

It was, of course, a long war, and even when it ended, things being what they are with governments, no change was made in England's two mousetrap recipes. For ten years after the war, the Ministry of Food continued its routine limitations, and, as Jim Matthiason told me, the result was that many housewives in England had grown up without knowing what good cheese was. Meanwhile, the oldest and best cheesemakers had died, and their sons and daughters had taken up other occupations.

Jim Matthiason was operating one of the factories making mousetrap cheese when the government roused itself and decided to reactivate old-fashioned cheesemaking.

"A factory which for ten years had been forced to make a bastard Cheddar would receive a book in the post on how to make Lancashire, or Caerphilly, their new assignment," Jim Matthiason told me. "My book was Caerphilly. We were to convert to Caerphilly. We were given a recipe."

He began to make Caerphilly, learning what he could from books and from old people, and soon shipped a representative product to London on straw stacked on the floors of cattle trucks. At which point he received a book in the mail changing his assignment from Caerphilly to Double Gloucester. "We've come on a reference to it," the letter said, "but we can't find a recipe for it."

Matthiason tried to find out what he could about Double Gloucester from old people near his factory, but nobody close by knew more than a modicum about Double Gloucester, or any Gloucester at all. "The first lot we made, we buried it," he told me.

At this time anyone who could bring back old-time methods of making cheese was in good standing with the Milk Marketing Board. Matthiason's wrestlings with the mysteries of Double Gloucester became known generally, and one day an acquaintance phoned him. "Jim, we've found an old lady who actually can make it," he said.

"Get her down here. Any expense," Matthiason said.

She arrived. She was eighty if she was a day, feeble, prone to get cold in the slightest drafts. She hobbled about with difficulty on legs marked with dark-blue veins. "She looked at our cheese; she smelled it," Jim told me. "She tasted the tiniest bit of it and said, 'That's no good at all,' which was the truth, as I knew.

"The next day she helped us make it. She moved into the factory with the men and went through the entire process with them. Again the day after that she came in and worked with the men. Later a third time she came from her home and worked with the men, and this time she said, 'I think you're almost there.' Then she went home and died, and there but for the grace of God went Double Gloucester. I always told her that her reward would be in Heaven, but I didn't know it would come so soon."

The recipe we give, supplied by Jim Matthiason, is for Double Gloucester, so it can be halved for a Gloucester, or reduced still further, though a 5-pound cheese is the smallest recommended. The recipe includes the acidity percentages, and you might want to read the section on acidity testing in Appendix 1.

It is a factory type of recipe, involving pasteurization of the milk and a relatively short curing period; we give it just as Jim Matthiason wrote it out, developed in his factory with the old lady as they went along. The recipe subsequently was made available to the English cheesemaking industry. Jim wrote it up this way:

As for the Double Gloucester, in some senses it is made in a similar manner to Cheddar. The aim is to obtain a curd which is rather a cross between that of Cheshire and Cheddar and in the process, produce quite a distinctive flavor.

Milk is pasteurized by the H.T.S.T. method to 162°; 1 ½% by volume of starter is added and the mixture is allowed to ripen for about 45 minutes; the acidity then should reach .19% lactic acid. (In this country very few people use pH measurements due to the buffering effect of certain of the proteins which can mislead acidity measurements taken in this form.)

Rennet is added and the curd allowed to set for 40 minutes. The curd is then cut into pieces round about ¼″ cube. It is then stirred for about 10 minutes to free the particles and the temperature is slowly brought up from the renneting heat of 86° to between 94° and 96° Fahrenheit, depending on how the cheese is developing or on weather conditions. Stirring goes on after the desired heat has been reached; total stirring time would be about ¾ of an hour.

At this stage the acidity should be about .16% lactic acid and after about 10 minutes the whey is run off. The curd in the bottom of the vat is allowed to stand for a further period and is then cut into blocks about 18″ long by 6″ to 8″ wide and is then turned. At 2 ½ hours from renneting the acidity should be in the region of .35% lactic acid. The curd is turned at regular intervals to encourage drainage and by about 4 hours from renneting the curd should reach an acidity of .6 to .7% lactic acid. Then it is milled using a Cheshire peg mill which tends to tear the curd rather than cutting into chips; 2% of salt is added which is then mixed in the curd using stainless steel forks.

After a short period allowed for cooling, the curd is filled into moulds, either rectangular or cylindrical. It then undergoes pressing for 2 days before it is either, in the case of traditional, wrapped in cloth or, in the case of block, wrapped in heat sealed film and put into store for ripening.

We normally ripen at a temperature of 50° Fahrenheit for a period of 3 to 4 months. Traditional cheeses are waxed. The moisture should amount to 39.5%, the fat 32–33%, the average fat in the dry matter of finished cheese comes out at about 50%.

The body of the finished cheese should be firm but not so firm as a matured Cheddar. The texture should break down nicely to the touch having a silky finish and the flavor should be clean and distinctively mellow.

I first met Jim Matthiason early in 1971. I had just spent two weeks in the Reading Room of the British Museum, doing further research on English cheeses, and when I left him I returned to that same great room—surely the most beautifully designed reading room I have ever seen—and tried to find an old recipe for Double Gloucester. Not a one was there. By chance this recipe had not been recorded in any of the books. The cheese was often mentioned and discussed, but just as one author relied on the past authors (which I do, too, mind you), each one necessarily glossed over this particular recipe simply because all his predecessors had done so.

Several months later I went to Dublin, and in the wonderful Irish libraries, the National Library and Trinity College, tried to find the recipe for Double Gloucester, but none was to be found.

In January of 1972, in New York City, I went to the New York Public Library and found nothing on Gloucester cheeses. There was one book titled *The Rural Economy of Gloucestershire Including Its Dairy*, two volumes, published in 1796. This book was stored in an annex on West 43rd Street, near the river, and that building was closed for a week or so, for economy reasons. When the building reopened, I even went over there to look in that old book, which a Mr. Marshall had written—somebody has penciled in the word *William* before his name.

And near the close of Volume One, from almost two hundred years ago, preserved in a loft in New York City, was the detailed description of the making of this great English cheese.

I have asked Harper & Row to print the description pretty much in its entirety in Appendix 1. The reader will need to strain to read its old-fashioned language, but I don't intend to rewrite a description I feel so fortunate to have at long last found.

Does this old cheese resemble the cheese today known as Double Gloucester? Nobody knows, of course.

Little Wensleydale

Little Wensleydale, a small, creamy cheese, has elements of Reblochon in taste. It is easy to make, is only 1 ¼ to 1 ½ pounds in size, and has for a long while been extremely popular in Yorkshire and throughout much of the north of England. It has been sold under an assortment of trade names, Wensley, Cheeselet, and others. It is made, when best made, by makers of Wensleydale, the larger cheese that is discussed in Chapter 6.

Ripened evening's and fresh morning's milk are mixed. The renneting temperature is 80 to 84 degrees, depending on the acidity of the milk and the temperature of the day, the higher the temperature being for the warmer days. This is so the bits of curd will be tougher and better able to avoid too rapid fermentation. The amount of rennet used is 1 dram to 4 gallons of milk. If the milk is not ideally fresh, less rennet is used. Also, later in the year slightly more rennet normally is needed than is required by the lighter milk of spring and early summer.

Five gallons of milk make three cheeses.

Coagulation takes about sixty minutes. After that the curd is cut vertically, first back to front, then side to side, after which the maker waits three minutes before cutting horizontally. The pieces are small cubes, about ¾ of an inch in size.

Next the curds and whey are stirred for ten minutes; however, if the milk is not as fresh as it should have been, one dispenses with the stirring.

Now the temperature is slowly increased to 90 degrees. This scalding is done to firm the curd, but sometimes it isn't necessary; some of the old people insisted it wasn't needed except now and then in winter, though the majority of makers always scalded. (If the curds and whey, when cut, had less than 0.14 percent acidity, they needed to scald. We explain about acidity testing in Appendix 1 for those of you who are chemically minded, which they were not.)

As soon as the scalding is finished, the curd is removed from the whey and put on cloths, about a yard square, which are set on a rack in the warm whey; some of the whey should be removed, enough so that the pack of curds remains only partly immersed. In thirty minutes, the maker removes the whey entirely. Now the curd is cut into 6- to 10-inch squares and turned over. Ten minutes later they are turned again and piled in double layers. The curd is even now still soft and tender, yet much drier than before (and has an acidity of 0.25 percent, or just under that, if you are curious).

When it crumbles between the fingers, the curd is broken into small pieces, or the pieces are put into a curd mill and ground, if a mill is available. The pieces are salted, 1 ounce of salt to 5 pounds of curd. The curd is then gently pressed into tin or aluminum molds, each mold having two tin followers, the one for the bottom having been perforated to permit the whey to escape. A 1- or 2-pound coffee can will do. At once pressure is applied, but not much—5 or 6 pounds for a cheese. A gallon jug three-fifths full of water is about the proper weight.

In twelve hours the cheese is taken out of the mold, turned, and returned to the press.

Six hours later it is again removed, and, if one wants to be thoroughly traditional, a smooth cloth bandage is pasted on it with a flour paste. The bandage usually is stretched slightly, to make it snug about the cheese, which again is put to press, so that the bandage can be pressed onto it. This bandage helps protect the cheese in shipment and from mold. You don't have to have it.

In about six more hours the cheese is taken from the press and put in a well-ventilated ripening room to dry. In two days it ought to be dry, and it is put in a less airy room. If mold gets on it, a cloth dampened with salted water will wipe it clean. In two or three weeks it can be eaten, though it improves with longer curing, a month or two.

The Little Wensleydale can develop an interior blue mold, as often does the Blue Wensleydale, its big brother, but it is such a small cheese that by then it is likely to be rather hard and dry.

Leicester

Leicester is the brightest colored of English cheeses today, a brilliant orange. The flesh is firm and free from holes. The taste is mellow and creamy, with silkiness to it, and with a fresh tang, in no way bitter. Some of the cheeses are small, 7 pounds or so, and some are large, 40 pounds or so. All are about three times as large in diameter as they are high, so they are flat cakes in appearance, and the rind is thin and smooth.

The flagrant color in the old days was achieved by using extract of carrots, but annatto, which is tasteless while carrots are not, has succeeded it. Cheese annatto is readily available; butter annatto coloring will not do for cheeses and should be avoided.

The origin of Leicester cheese is unknown, but the cheese has been made for centuries in Hinckley, Lutterworth, Market Bosworth, and other such wondrously named neighboring places. The old cheeses were all farmhouse made and were a favorite exhibit in cheese fairs, which were held twice a year, in May and October. The best Leicester cheeses sold in those fairs were five or six months old, but we understand that young cheeses were sometimes sold, these to be aged at home. Some people would punch a hole into the top, pour a bit of old ale in, put a damp cloth over the cheese, and bide their time, or so the stories go. I think I would prefer a cheese aged naturally, but I like the story.

The cheese fairs are no longer held at Leicester, and there is nobody left alive, we suspect, who remembers the great farm wagons, loaded with cheese, moving through the early light of a May morning from as far as 20 miles away. Nor are the factory-made Leicesters of our day in the same delicious, rich, fat class as were most of these. As for the leaner ones, the dealers at the fair would come about and would bore samples from two or three of the cheeses stacked on a farmer's wagon, and if they were not "up to sample" they were all sent home, the whole wagon load, and the farmer and his distressed family. As for those who sought to sell a cheese not up to standard, or not of its reputed weight, they were subject to a long list of pains and penalties decreed by law, and on fair days the entire awful list was called out by the town crier.

The recipe I give here is the one in use generally in the 1920s.

The milk should have an acidity rating of 0.19 or 0.20 percent, which means that it should be, on average, only six or eight hours old, say a mixture of ripened evening's and fresh morning's milk. The ripening of the milk was sometimes assisted by adding 1 ⅓ ounces of starter, such as buttermilk, to 3 gallons of milk. Before the proper degree of maturity is reached, the maker adds cheese annatto coloring, 1 or 2 drams for 3 gallons, mixing it in well. One way to do this evenly is to immerse the bowl of coloring under the milk and release it while it is submerged.

The renneting temperature is 84 degrees. The amount of rennet is 1 dram to every 3 ½ (American) gallons.

In seventy-five minutes the curd should be ready to cut. It is cut into ⅜-inch cubes and is left for a few minutes before stirring begins, carefully, with the hands. Next comes the scalding, the temperature rising slowly so that forty-five minutes after cutting it reaches 92 degrees.

For ten minutes the maker continues stirring, letting the curd scald at 92 degrees, until it is firm and "shotty" enough to "pitch"; *shotty* is a cheesemaker's term and means the bits of curd settle like lead shot to the bottom (pitch). The curd is not like lead shot, mind you—it is not as hard or heavy— but it does exhibit a marked tendency to sink. Within fifteen minutes the curd will form a mass. With his hands the maker now presses the curds gently, compacting them and assisting them to help expel some of the whey they contain.

In another fifteen minutes the whey is removed from the vat, the mass of curd is cut into 6-inch blocks, which are piled up two or three deep, and the vat is covered. Every twenty minutes or so the curds are cut and turned (until the acid test reads 0.35 to 0.40 percent).

The curd, which is cooler now, perhaps 80 degrees, is torn into small pieces by hand or a mill. At this point it is dry and firm and velvety. The maker mixes with it 1 ounce of salt to 3 pounds of curd.

He spreads the curd and leaves it to cool to 75 degrees— better perhaps, on a cloth-covered rack than in the warm pot in which it was made. In any event, at 75 degrees, he puts the curd into a cloth-lined mold and applies moderate pressure, gradually increasing the pressure slightly. (A test of the whey from the press will likely show 0.60 percent acidity.) At evening the cheese is taken out of the mold, re-clothed, and put back in the mold bottom side up. A moderate to heavy pressure is now applied, as much as 600 or even 1,000 pounds for a large cheese, so you at home will need a press with a ratchet or screw head, a car jack, or whatever.

By morning the cheese is ready for new cloths and is returned to the press under increased weight, as much as 1,200 to 2,000 pounds, depending on the size of the cheese.

Twenty-four hours later the cheese can be bandaged, if one wants to bandage it. The traditional bandage is of gray calico. The cheese can then be taken to the storeroom, where it is kept at a temperature not exceeding 65 degrees, to age for six months. It should be turned now and again and wiped clean with a damp cloth when it needs it, or with salty water if the molds become a problem. A Leicester has excellent keeping qualities.

Today's Leicesters are hard and pasty, but a true farmhouse Leicester should be crumbly and soft and will leave a smudge on a knife.

It was a favorite with hunters, incidentally. It was said to be even better outdoors than in. I'm not surprised. Most cheeses are. Some preferred it with spring onions. Probably they were the same ones who aged it with old ale. More to my taste is the report that old farmhouse Leicester and water-cress are made for each other.

Caerphilly

My wife and I have a Welsh friend who sometimes enjoys taking lunch at the Connault on Sunday, the best place to eat just now in London, and when the cheese board is brought around she always asks for Caerphilly.

They never seem to have Caerphilly at the Connault, as she knows very well and doubtless is relieved each time to find out. She can then go ahead with a clear conscience and eat the Stilton. But being Welsh and being in England, she must ask.

Caerphilly is snow-white and flaky and has a taste of but-termilk in it. It used to be consumed in large quantities in the mining districts of southwestern England and of Wales. Some say it originated in Wales; others say it originated in England and was exported to Wales. Since it offers a high yield, a pound or more of cheese to every American gallon of milk, and needs no curing to speak of, the theory that England is its initial homeland and Wales its place of intended consumption might well be true.

The miners would wrap pieces of cheese in cabbage leaves and take them into the mines. They would eat the leaves as well as the cheese.

The cheese is ready for consumption in ten days or two weeks after making; it is highly perishable and begins to deteriorate in quality after three or four weeks because of its high moisture content. This is one reason a true Caerphilly is not likely to be found in most cheese shops. The flavor is clean and mild, somewhat salty. Even though the texture is extremely flaky, the cheese is firm, not spongy. When broken it appears granular; therefore, cheesemakers say that it "breaks short." It has no holes in it. The rind is thin and white and does not attract mold.

The cheese is flat, a quarter to a third as tall as its diameter, and it weighs 5 to 10 pounds.

The recipe given here for it is the one in common use in the 1920s.

The milk should be fresh morning's and properly aged evening's milk mixed. The acidity at renneting should not exceed 0.20 percent. Sometimes a little starter is used, as in the case of Leicester, sometimes none. The renneting temperature is 90 degrees. The amount of rennet extract is 1 ½ drams to 6 (American) gallons of milk, the rennet being diluted one to six, more or less, with water.

Stir the rennet in the milk for five minutes, then gently ripple the surface for three minutes. In forty minutes from renneting, the curd should break over the finger and be ready for cutting. The curd is cut into cubes ⅜ to ½ inch in size. Sometimes cutting is carried out in two stages, vertically in both directions and then, after a few minutes' rest, horizontally. The curds and whey are then stirred gently until the curds appear to want to settle to the bottom, to pitch, at which time the whey is removed.

The curds are tied in a cloth, and the bundle is hung to drain, as in the case of cream cheeses. After a few minutes the bundle is opened, and the curds are cut into 3-inch sections and are turned in the cloth. This process continues for an hour—the draining, cutting, turning, and draining. (When ripe enough, the acidity equals that of the milk when renneted.)

The curds are broken into small pieces and put into the mold as salt is dredged upon them in several layers, 1 ounce of salt to every 3 pounds of curd.

No pressure is applied for three or four hours. (By then the acid reading is 0.30 to 0.35 percent.) The cloths are then exchanged for dry ones, and the cheese is put to press, pressure being applied gently; 200 pounds of pressure is sufficient for the first night.

The next morning the cheese is removed. It will by now have taken on form and will have a rind; it can be handled by a gentle handler. It is put in a dry cloth and put to press, bottom side up, for the day. As much as 500 pounds of pressure is used. The next day the cheese is taken to the storeroom without bandages, and it is turned there daily for ten days.

Should the cheese become slimy in the storeroom, a cloth dipped in brine can be used to wipe it clean. Soon a thick, protective coat will form on the cheese.

In two weeks the rind might have a fine, white mold, which is desirable, and its development is encouraged by not turning the cheese daily after the tenth day. For such a mold to form, the storeroom must be quite cool, 55 to 60 degrees, and moist, 80 percent or more relative humidity.

A considerable amount of Caerphilly is made from part-skim milk with about 2 percent butterfat. Some makers maintained in the old days that this cheese actually was better, but remember what we suggested earlier about cheeses made by the English for consumption by the Welsh. I doubt if a skim-milk cheese is better.

There is today no Caerphilly cheese to be found in Caerphilly, which is situated on the marshes a twenty-minute drive north of the Welsh city of Cardiff. The waitresses in Caerphilly, if asked after dinner for Caerphilly cheese, respond with an offering of Danish blue and Cheddar, and perhaps a query as to just what you mean—"Is it a joke, sir? There are plenty of cheeses in Caerphilly shops, sir. You can get most any you want." They think you're joking.

From the waitress's tray take a piece of Swiss cheese, then wander on out to see Caerphilly Castle at night, about which Barrow wrote in a travel book, "I reached Caerfili at about seven o'clock, and went to The Boar's Head, near the ruins of a stupendous castle on which the beams of the moon were falling."

As they do most nights, as, if you are fortunate, you will someday see.

Derby Cheese

Derby cheese is white and is usually made as a flat, thin, cylindrical loaf. It is quite similar to Single Gloucester. In earlier days it was made in kitchens, as a rule, and since the kitchen was the warmest room in the house, the place of making probably contributed a special quality to the cheese. We know, too, that the best Derby cheeses were made during the summer months.

Since this cheese was made in hundreds of homes, it came to market in hundreds of sizes, tastes, colors, textures, and qualities. Not until about 1885 was an attempt made to standardize the Derby. In its standardized, or at least representative, form it is a mild, sound, useful cheese, once quite a favorite in its neighborhood. Today it is an ordinary, unimaginative cheese, perhaps because it is not made properly by the factories which bother with it, and because it wants to be aged three months to be at its best, and nobody honors its wishes any more. It is aged half as long at much too low a temperature, so it is aged a quarter of its allotted time.

I will give a recommended recipe used about 1885 in the best kitchens of the farmhouses of Derbyshire. I have no idea what this cheese, properly aged, tastes like, and I dare say nobody else alive does.

The Derby's flat, thin size was determined by the character of the curd, which in the Derby process is so soft it cannot safely be made into large forms lest the cheese break in two. The milk used was fresh, the fresher the better. The milk was about 3.5 percent butterfat. Renneting temperature was quite low; if the temperature of the kitchen was 65 degrees, which in an English house, particularly a farmhouse, is considered indiscreetly warm, the milk was heated, or, if fresh from the cows, cooled to 79 degrees. It was heated one degree warmer for each five degrees that the kitchen was colder than 65 degrees, one degree cooler for each five degrees that the kitchen was warmer than 65 degrees. This is quite a specific instruction for 1885, when I suspect the dairymen and maids usually tested the milk's temperature with their elbows, but it is the way the recipe was written down back in that day.

As you see, the milk is low in acidity, no starter is used, and the renneting temperature is low.

The amount of rennet varied but was intended to yield a firm curd in an hour. About 1 dram of rennet extract to 4 gallons of fresh milk will produce this result. After renneting, the milk was stirred for seven or eight minutes and the surface of the milk was then stirred gently for five minutes. The vat was covered, and insofar as possible the renneting temperature was retained.

In cutting, the curd was reduced to the size of horsebeans and was allowed to sink to the bottom of the pot. Fifteen or twenty minutes later, the bailing out of the whey began, proceeding quickly; however, before the last whey was removed, the curd was pressed, either by hand or by a wooden rack or metal perforated follower, to consolidate it. The last of the whey was then removed, and the curds were put immediately into the mold. As you see, there was no scalding of the curds and no lengthy waiting period during which they were encouraged to develop acidity and toughness, and you notice we are dealing here from the start with very fresh milk. Soft, mild, non-acidic bits of cheese is what we have just now in the mold. Please notice also that the cheese has not been salted, so it will be permitted to ferment, to develop tartness, in the pressing period.

The initial pressure of the press was slight; one method was to press with the hands on the follower and as the whey stopped running, to lean harder on the follower. When by that means no more whey was expelled, a dairymaid was asked to kneel on the follower. It was in Derbyshire, I imagine, that the saying arose: "The bigger the dairymaid, the better the cheese."

The pressure was increased slowly, steadily, the makers being careful not to seal the whey in the curd, which severe bursts of pressure here at the start can do.

Up to this point the fermentation had been slow, and the curd had still not been salted. Yet in this condition it was left overnight, with the pressure increased slightly on the press.

Next morning the cheese was ready for salting.

The method of salting practiced from time immemorial in Derbyshire is to rub salt on the outside of the cheese, or immerse it in brine strong enough actually to float an egg, or both. This preference for exterior salting also accounts in part for the thinness of these cheeses, for the salt does need to reach the center portion. Another method of salting is to break down the cheese at this point, after its first night in the press, break it into small pieces with one's hands or a mill, and salt the pieces at the rate of 4 ounces of salt to the curd from 12 ½ gallons of milk.

After salting, the cheese was returned to the mold and to the press. Pressure was increased day by day, sometimes for four or five days, reaching a ton for a cheese of 60 pounds or over and about 1,500 pounds for smaller cheeses. Ideally the pressing room would be kept at 60 to 65 degrees.

Derbys should be stored in a cool room (a conventional cellar will do) and turned now and again and wiped clean of mold on occasion, like the cheeses previously described. Traditionally bandages were cheese-gray in color and were put on with a flour paste, as was the case with the Leicester. The cheese matured by six weeks but improved for several weeks afterward. After three months it began to falter but was sufficiently dry and close in body to last well, even so.

When cut, it was close and smooth in body, firm and elastic, and when a slice or even a round bore was held to light, the cheese was translucent. That was a prided characteristic, of course, and no coloring was ever added to Derbyshire cheese.

Another method in Derbyshire until the end of the nineteenth century was to mix with curds of one day some curds from the previous day's making, which Derby makers, even the best of them, agreed worked a subtle improvement in the finished cheese.

Lancashire

Lancashire cheese is the best for cooking purposes, the English say, for toasting and rarebits and the like. When heated it becomes a thick, delicious, delicate custard, and if you like, will toast to a rich brown color. The cheese has a life expectancy of only three or four months, so it is not available in an authentic form in many places. At three months of age it will spread like butter.

Today the cheese is not made anywhere, as far as I can find out, by its older recipe, which is an impractical one for most people in that it requires a mixture of curds made on two or three successive days, preferably three. Admittedly, even before World War II most farmhouse Lancashire makers had begun to use a one-day, one-curd system, but authorities in that day decried this practice, complained bitterly about it, saying that the one-day system was not conducive to a typical texture and resulted in an inferior cheese. Expressers of this view included the Ministry of Agriculture and Fisheries of the government, but that body of opinion carried too little weight, it seems. If you want an old-fashioned Lancashire, you will have to make it for yourself.

When made by the old recipe, which is what I offer here, Lancashire is rather dry but not flaky. It is free of holes. It is white. The flavor is clean, mellow, mild, and slightly acid when the cheese is under two months old but not thereafter. The mixture of curds at different stages of acidity gives the cheese a loose and friable texture. Since the acidity of the three different curds and of the final combination is critical, the cheese should be made with an acidity tester on hand. Acidity tests are described in Appendix 1. The final one, that of the combined curds, is the most important, and fortunately is the easiest test to make.

A bit less than a pound of cheese for each American gallon can be expected.

Traditionally the cheese is made in three sizes: the 1 ½-

pound size, called Little Wensleydale; a 10-pound cheese, which is 8 inches in diameter and 6 inches high; and a 40- to 50-pound cheese, 14 inches in diameter and 6 inches high. Since they take different lengths of time to age, the Little Wensleydale taking less time, their tastes are different, but the process is the same.

The cheese was often made by small landholders, farmers who had only a little milk to spare each day and who could in the course of three days process one large cheese.

To make a 40-pound cheese over a three-day period—one might as well be shot for a major crime as a minor one—use 15 American gallons of absolutely fresh milk and add 5 ounces of buttermilk, to serve as a starter. Heat the milk to 84 degrees in summer or as high as 88 degrees in colder seasons and permit the milk to ripen for thirty minutes (until the acidity level is about 0.18 percent).

Measure the rennet, 5 drams for the 15 gallons. Dilute the rennet with a dash of cold water. Stir it into the milk for five minutes and afterward gently stir the surface of the milk for five minutes longer. Cover the vat.

The curd is ready for cutting in fifty to sixty minutes from the time of renneting. Test it in the customary Mrs. Kirby way; that is, it should break evenly before your finger. Cut it with a knife into cubes the size of small beans. On old Lancashire farms the curd was cut vertically—back to front, then side to side—so that inch-square bands were formed. These were gently stirred by the hand, and the sides and bottom of the vat were cleared of curd before the cutting proceeded, to make 1-inch cubes.

Allow the curd to rest about half an hour. Then remove the whey a little at a time, over a period of forty-five to sixty minutes. It helps to place a cloth over the curd and thus to encourage them to settle on the bottom.

When the whey has been completely removed, the matted curd will be in one piece and can be lifted without breaking. Gently tie it in a cloth, making a bundle. Five minutes later apply slight pressure to the bundle, about half the weight of the curds; one way is to put a small board on the bundle and rest weights on it, or a gallon jug of water.

In fifteen minutes untie the bundle and cut the cheese into blocks, then break these with your hands into 3-inch cubes. Don't squeeze them unduly. Put them in the bundle again and slightly increase the amount of pressure, but use no more weight than that of the cheese itself. Every twenty or thirty minutes repeat this process. (At the first breaking, the acidity should be 0.14 to 0.15 percent. By the third break, it might be about 0.175 percent, and by the fourth break it might be as high as 0.19 to 0.20 percent.)

The curd is now torn apart into small pieces by hand or a mill. It should be firm and fairly dry. If the curd is milled when too dry, the texture of the finished cheese will be too loose; if it is ground too wet, the taste of the cheese may be sour.

The curds can be saved for the next day by holding at 65 to 70 degrees. By the next day they will have become sour to the taste and smell.

The next two days' curds are made in the same way as this first batch.

On the third day the three curds are mixed in such a way that the average acidity of the mixture will be 0.99 percent in cold weather and 0.90 percent in summer. For instance, if whey from the forty-eight-hour curd is 1.6 percent acid, and from the twenty-four-hour curd is 1.2 percent (these are reasonable estimates), and if the new curd is 0.18 percent, an equal mixture of the three curds will produce 0.99 percent acidity.

Grind the curds finely until they have the appearance of chopped suet. Mix the ground curds and salt at the rate of 1 ounce of salt to 3 ½ pounds of curd. The mixture ought to be kept at a temperature of 70 degrees.

Loosely put the curd in a mold lined with fine muslin. Leave the cheese in the mold without pressure until evening, when a wooden follower should be put on the cheese. Turn the mold and allow the cheese to sit on the follower. Leave it there without pressure until the next morning.

Next morning turn the cheese again and put it to press at 1,200 to 1,500 pounds pressure for a large cheese, half that for a small one.

The following morning turn the cheese, bandage it with a clean cloth, and return it to the press for twelve hours. Then put it in an airy room to dry.

When the bandage is dry, the cheese traditionally is bathed in hot whey butter; whey butter, not generally available, has about the same consistency as regular butter or lard, which you can use; either forms a light coating on the cheese. In the old days the butter was colored with ½ dram of butter annatto to 1 pound of butter.

Put the cheese in a ripening room, 62 to 65 degrees, for three to five weeks. Turn it daily to ensure uniform distribution of moisture. If kept in a cooler room, say 55 degrees, the cheese can be aged over a longer period, even up to six months.

Lancashire cheese can be made with curds from two, rather than three, successive days; the same acidity, that is, 0.90 to 0.99 percent, still applies to the mixed curds.

Banbury

Banbury is the only cheese which is mentioned by name in Shakespeare. In *The Merry Wives of Windsor* Bardolph calls Slender a Banbury cheese because of his thinness. As of this moment no recipe for Banbury cheese survives. We know it was cylindrical in shape and about an inch thick; a thin pie.

Shakespeare's lack of interest in cheese is perhaps significant. By 1600 many cheeses were made in England, but not many were transported to London, and it may well be that he rarely risked his stomach on the local product, whatever that was. London is a favorite city of mine, but its charms are largely achieved because of what it imports from other places. To consider a London that must depend on its own products is depressing, and to consider any city which depends on foods that it makes is confusing anyway, for cities don't make the best foods; they make the best factories, and the best factories make the poorest foods. The cities then publicize them and wrap them nicely and distribute them widely.

Not in Shakespeare's day, of course. I am merely rambling, and not with distress, either, and certainly not with bitterness, for one comes finally to recognize the features of inevitability, even if he refuses to eat city cheeses.

Shakespeare did as much, as well.

Oxfordshire

Oxfordshire is no longer made and I have not been able to find a recipe for it either. Swift's *Polite Conversations* refers to it, indicating it had an assertive aroma. In one of the dialogues Lord Smart tells of a fellow who fainted, or pretended to faint, when an Oxfordshire was set on the table. This led a friend to ask that it be removed. "No, said I; take away the fool," Lord Smart said.

Among other English country cheeses which have faded away are Essex, Langtony, Kentish, Suffolk, of which we read: "Dogs bark at me, but can't eat me." Bath cheese was long popular in fashionable circles and could still be purchased in this century. It was originally 9 inches square and 1 inch deep. It was a soft cheese which ripened in a week, was white, was firm in texture, was creamy and had a piquant flavor. Among other cream cheeses that have been lost thus far are the Devon, the Cornwall, New Forest, Guildford, and Little Welshie.

4

French Semisoft Cheeses

English semisoft cheeses, such as Small Holder (Mrs. Kirby's cheese), are not often encountered, even in England, but French semisoft cheeses are world renowned.

Port du Salut

Perhaps 110 years ago, the Trappist monks happened upon a secret, or maybe two secrets. They came upon a helpful bacteria which has since been named *Brevibacterium linens*. It can do miracles with a cheese, softening and enriching it in taste, and a miracle is perhaps what the monks assumed their newfound process was. *B. linens* can be ordered today from supply houses (see Appendix 3) and can be rubbed on the shelves in a cheese curing room once a season, if needed. I say if needed because *B. linens* is likely to be naturally present in a curing room of a type it likes. Some authorities say it likes 60 degrees and 95 percent humidity. Others more democratically say 55 to 65 degrees and 85 to 90 percent humidity. In either case, we see that in cool, damp places, *B. linens* grows.

But so do other bacteria, and this brings us to the second part of the monks' secret: *B. linens* has a higher tolerance for salt than do its competitors. To help *B. linens*, the monks would rub their cheeses every day or so with a warm saline solution, thus ruining the societies of unwanted bacteria without hurting those of *B. linens* at all.

The monks guarded this secret, this miracle gift. I have a beautifully written French text on cheesemaking published in 1927, and in this text the monks' secrets were still secure in France; the recipe for Port du Salut in this text was authoritatively but erroneously given, the author had been misdirected, and the dear fellow went so far as to reverse the desirable processes in the curing room, recommending that no salt at all be used, claiming that salt was undesirable in curing a Port du Salut.

If you can arrange for a cheese curing room, or closet or cabinet or whatever, having suitable coolness and dampness, which many homes can, then steam-clean it or disinfect it and introduce *B. linens* to it by dabbing the culture on the shelves, and try making a Port du Salut. You need no press; you need no special cheesemaking equipment except easily contrived molds. As for your "cellar," a small humidifier can be used if the room needs more moisture, and an air-conditioner or refrigerator unit can be used if it needs cooling. An expensive hygrometer-thermometer is purchasable or borrowable almost anywhere, to tell you what the temperature and humidity are. You might refer to the section on cheese cellars in Appendix 1 for other suggestions.

Other bacterial surface ripened cheeses are the Bel Paese, the California-made Monterey, the Muenster (which is identical to the French Géromé except in size but which I will leave for a book on German cheeses), the so-called brick cheese of the United States, the Liederkranz of the United States, and the Limburger of Belgium. I have listed them in ascending order of pungency, the strongest at the end. In the middle would fall Port du Salut.

The mildness or strength of the cheese is determined by the amount of surface area the cheese exposes to the surface bacteria, *B. linens*. As you see, the strongest cheeses have flat sides all around, and each side is from time to time laid flat on the shelf where the bacteria have their master colonies. Knowing this, you can experiment with the creation of a cheese of your own. The Monterey, the brick, and the Liederkranz are America's three contributions to world cheeses, and they are quite similar except in the way I have just mentioned, the surface area exposed during curing, which makes them quite different.

Port du Salut is a new cheese, as cheese history goes. About 1865 the Trappist monks began making it at their abbey at Port du Salut, which is near Laval in the Department of Mayenne. Other abbeys in various parts of Europe began to make similar cheeses, the monks sharing the secrets among themselves and keeping the secrets from others. Trappists have indeed kept their exact process to themselves even to this day, refusing to admit visitors to their cellars, but com-

parable cheeses are now made outside their monasteries, and
the method I suggest here is accurate and authentic.

St. Paullin, Gautrias, and Rangiport, all of which resemble
Port du Salut, are made by similar methods.

As you know, Port du Salut cheeses are compact and elastic
and hold their shape when cut. Their flesh is soft, has no
holes, and is almost translucent. They taste something like
Gouda and have the aroma of all other bacteria-ripened soft
cheese, which, as I mentioned, approaches its strongest ele-
vations in Limburger.

The rind should be smooth, without cracks; it will have a
yellowish-gray color. The edge of the cheese should be quite
straight, without bulges, showing that the texture of the cheese
is not custardy.

The Port du Salut of France is flat and cylindrical, 8 to 10
inches in diameter and 1 ⅕ to 2 inches thick. (In Kentucky,
monks make one 7 inches in diameter and 2 inches thick,
weighing about 3 pounds.)

The cheeses are made from cow's milk with about 3.5 percent butterfat. No higher butterfat is desirable. The milk is
ripened slightly, but not past 0.20 percent acidity. If absolutely fresh milk is used, a small amount of starter is added,
up to 1 cup of buttermilk or sour milk for 5 gallons. Cheese
coloring (annatto) is often added.

For renneting, copper vats are used in France. They are
double-jacketed so that they can be heated with steam. The
smaller vats hold about 55 gallons of milk. Practically any
vat except a galvanized one will do for home manufacture—
a canning kettle is all right. I use the copper body of an old
washing machine.

The renneting temperature is 83 to 95 degrees, a wide latitude. The higher temperature is for warmer days. The hotter

the temperature of the room, the higher the renneting temperature, in order to develop a drier curd, which will withstand the inducement to ferment quickly. The amount of rennet needed in a 65-degree kitchen for 5 American gallons of milk at a renneting temperature of 89 degrees is 1 ⅓ drams. The rennet should be diluted one to six with tap water and stirred into the milk for three to five minutes. The pot should then be covered and left alone, absolutely still.

The curd will develop quickly; it should be ready for cutting in thirty-five to forty minutes. (If it takes longer, up to eighty minutes, no harm has been done; some makers prefer a slow coagulation and a proportionally slower process throughout.)

The curd is cut with a knife, first from back to front and then from side to side into strips about an inch square. It is then gently turned under from top to bottom with a scoop or ladle, and the strips are cut into 1-inch cubes.

The curd is allowed to rest for five minutes before the maker, using a Swiss cheese harp, though a whisk or knife will do, proceeds to cut and stir and generally mix the curds and whey until the curds are in tiny pieces the size of grains of rice, about ⅛ inch in diameter. This "harping" takes about fifteen minutes. So the cutting requires twenty-five minutes in all, and should take that long.

Some of the whey is removed, and over the next twenty minutes the temperature is slowly increased to 96 degrees. After the curds have cooked in the whey for three or four minutes at this temperature, the maker removes all of the whey except enough to cover the curds.

The curds are stirred for an additional five minutes. Then the whey is removed entirely, and at once the curds are put into metal molds. The molds are, on average, 10 ½ inches in diameter and 3 ⅕ inches high. They are perforated. The monks made for each mold a smooth, closely woven cloth bag which fits it without wrinkles.

The cloth-lined molds, set on small, individual draining boards, are filled, and the curds are mounded over the top half an inch or so. The cloth is pulled tight, and the corners are laid over the curd as smoothly as possible. At once a weighted disk is put on the cheese. Some makers use no additional weight. Others increase the weight gradually as the cheese drains, so that in eight to ten hours the weight is between 22 and 33 pounds, about the weight of 3 to 4 gallons of water. By then the cheese will have stopped dripping whey.

In either case the cheese must be turned often—every twenty minutes for the first hour, every thirty minutes for the second hour, and every hour thereafter. The cloths at the early turnings are merely wrung out and replaced on the cheese, but in the last turnings one must use dry cloths in order to assist the cheese to dry properly.

After this eight- to ten-hour pressing period the cheeses are taken out of their cloths and put on shelves in a drying room. The room should be ventilated in order to help dry the crusts; it should have a temperature of about 70 degrees. The time a cheese spends in this room is twenty hours.

Next the cheeses are taken to the curing cellar where they are salted with a fine salt, about 1 percent by weight. Each cheese is salted again in a day or so; at that time coarse salt, again about 1 percent by weight of the cheese, is dissolved in a small amount of water, and the brine is painted on the cheese with a brush or cloth.

Or, if you prefer, you can put your cheeses into salt brine, a 23 percent solution at 50 degrees, and let them float there for eight hours, turning them at least once. While they are floating in the brine, you can sprinkle dry salt on their exposed surfaces. When the cheeses have been removed from the brine, put them on a shelf and occasionally wash them lightly with a warm brine solution, containing *B. linens* if you have it.

A proper curing room is cool, about 55 degrees, and has about a 90 percent relative humidity, as was mentioned earlier. Every three or four days for two weeks you should rub the cheese's surface with a hand dipped in a warm, slightly saline solution and turn it. On the fourteenth day rub off any surface growth on the cheese.

Now put the cheese in a less humid room, one of about 60 degrees and with a relative humidity of about 70 percent for one day. Wrap it in parchment and box it.

After two weeks of further curing at 40 to 60 degrees, the cheese is ready to be used. It can be stored for about three more months at 40 degrees, and for a shorter period at higher temperatures.

If you make a Port du Salut, it will be, I suppose, the first ever made in your community.

Pont l'Evêque

Seven centuries old, from Normandy, where Camembert also is made, Pont l'Evêque is a soft, yellow, pungent cheese highly favored when bought in France. It is mold ripened. For centuries its recipe was kept secret, and traditionalists have claimed for centuries that it can be made only in Normandy. More accurately, I suspect, it could be made only where the cellar conditions were conducive to success. To help ensure success, I suggest you rub a bit of Pont l'Evêque on the shelf where you cure your cheese.

Six American gallons of milk will yield six oval cheeses, 1 ⅜ to 1 ½ inches tall, 4 ¼ inches square, weighing about 12 ounces each. When ripe they have a golden exterior with a brownish, reddish hue, and are pliant and yielding. The flavor is similar to that of Edam, though sweeter.

The cheese is made from whole cow's milk, about 3.7 percent fat, absolutely fresh; if there is much acidity in the milk at the first stage of making, the cheeses are likely to be hard and dry.

The milk is heated to 90 degrees in spring and as high as 94 degrees in summer and fall. An old practice was to heat the milk in a caldron over an open fire and to make the final adjustments after the caldron was removed from the fire by adding boiling water.

Rennet is added at the rate of 2 drams for 6 American gallons of milk. The rennet, as always, should be diluted with tap water. It is stirred into the milk for five or six minutes, after which the pot is covered.

In about fifty minutes the curd will be firm and will break clean over the finger. It is cut into 2-inch squares, and the squares are cut diagonally across. In five minutes much of the whey will have separated out, and at that time the curd is ladled onto coarse cloths about a yard square, which are laid over wooden lattices or other types of drains so the whey can flow off. Into each cloth goes the curd from about 2 gallons of milk. The cloth is tied Stilton fashion: Three corners are held in one hand and are bound around with the other corner, making a bundle.

Every ten minutes or so for two hours the cloths can be tightened. Some makers cut the curd repeatedly, about every twenty minutes, into chunks, but normally the curd drains well enough without the cutting. It is important in making Pont l'Evêque that the curd does not drain too much, for if it does, it might not mat together properly in the molds.

In the old days tin molds were used. They were open-ended and were placed on individual straw mats, a small board under each mat. Some were oblong and some were square. In all cases the corners were rounded off. (The oblong molds measured 5 ¾ inches by 3 ¾ inches and were 2 ½ inches deep.) The molds were not cloth lined. The firmest curd was piled at the middle of the mold, the moister curd on the outside, a technique which assisted the cheese to drain evenly. When a mold was filled, a straw mat was put on top and a small board was set on top of the mat. The cheese was then sandwiched between the mats and boards and was turned over, board, mat, mold, and all.

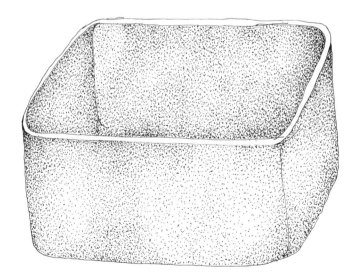

Pont l'Evêque

As the curd is ladled into the molds, it can be lightly sprinkled with salt, though some makers do not salt at all at this point. If the cheese has all along been developing faster than it should, if it has begun to dry out in the bags before the elapse of the two hours, a sprinkling of salt will help slow down its progress.

The cheese should be turned again in five or ten minutes. Before turning, the top straw mat should be given a quarter turn, so that the impressions made by the straw will form a latticed pattern. This should be done to both sides of the cheese during one turn or another, for old times' sake.

During the next few hours each cheese ought to be turned onto dry mats three or four times, about once every hour, and after that it should be turned every two hours.

Next day the cheeses are salted, ½ ounce of fine, dry salt for each cheese. The dry salt is rubbed onto the cheese surface.

The salted cheeses are dried in an airy room, about 65 degrees, on straw-covered shelves. They are turned twice a day. When they are firm enough to stand by themselves, after two or three days, the molds are dispensed with. When the mold is removed, the sides of the cheese are scraped lightly with a table knife in order to fill any crevices.

In the curing room the cheeses can be placed close together on lattice-work shelves or on straw, or they can be placed in a wooden box covered with a damp cloth for the first few days, then put on shelves. They are turned now and again, even daily, for three to four weeks, and are washed occasionally with salty water (two teaspoons of salt dissolved in a pint of water). They should occasionally be stacked two or three deep, with different sides on different days touching the other cheeses. A gray mold will cover the cheeses (or at least one hopes so, for it should), but in order to keep the cheeses from becoming too strong in taste the mold is not allowed to progress uninterrupted, as a similar, milder mold is, in making Camembert, for instance.

When the cheeses are ripe, in three or four weeks—though in the cooler cellars they might take six—they will feel like a ripe pear to the touch.

If the finished cheeses are greasy on the surface, the drying prior to ripening was not sufficient or the temperature of the room was too low. If the cheese is leathery and not mellow, the draining of the curd was too rapid in the cloth squares, which might mean that the room temperature was too high, or that the milk was not as fresh as it should have been, or that the renneting temperature was too high.

Traditionally, Pont l'Evêque cheeses were packed in chip or cardboard boxes, or were put in tinfoil.

5

Chèvre

Goat's-milk cheeses are soft and mild when young, hard and harsh and pungent and almost overpowering when three or four months old or older. Usually they are small, white cheeses, shaped in cubes (as is St. Maure) or pyramids (as is Valençay) or ovals (as is Le Banon, a 4-ounce cheese dipped in brandy). They all have the goat's-milk animal taste and aroma.

To make a goat's-milk cheese, use any soft or semisoft cheese recipe; the cheeses are made in the same way as cow's-milk cheeses. Gavot, for instance, is sometimes made from goat's, sometimes from cow's, and sometimes from ewe's milk. It's all the same recipe, even the same name for the cheese, but since goat's milk is far richer than cow's milk, more rennet

is needed, the amount determined by the butterfat involved;
either that, or the milk must be skimmed, and in France it
often is, so that a 3.5 percent butterfat is settled for in the
cheese milk—or whatever the maker wants.

A mixture of goat's and cow's milk, or goat's, ewe's, and
cow's milk, is often used.

To make a blue goat, you can use the *bleu* recipe. *Gex Bressons* is a blue goat's-milk cheese made that way.

Camembert de Chèvre is a goat Camembert.

St. Marcellin is made by the Brie-Coulommiers recipe and
can be used fresh, like a Coulommiers, or aged, like a Brie.
It can be made of goat's milk, of goat's and cow's milk mixed
(most frequently), or goat's, cow's, and sheep's milk mixed.

For those who want to experiment with a fairly representative goat's-milk cheese, I suggest the Coulommiers recipe in
Chapter 2, but use small molds and age the cheese in a cool,
damp place for four days to a week.

Or use this recipe for *Mont d'Or.* It has been made in Mont
d'Or in the Department of Rhône for over three hundred years
and is made in some other parts of France today. The old
people made it from goat's milk exclusively. Today usually
some cow's milk is mixed in. For the Mont d'Or:

Use either whole or part-skimmed goat's milk. Renneting
temperature is 90 degrees. Use enough rennet so that the curd
is ready in ninety minutes to be ladled into the molds. The
molds should be 4 ½ inches in diameter and about 3 inches
deep and are placed on straw, or mats, on individual draining
boards. In an hour turn the cheeses. Turn them thereafter
rather frequently until they are firm. Then salt them. They
can be eaten fresh or cured for three weeks or so. In the latter
case they are turned and washed with a light brine, in the
manner of Pont l'Evêque.

6

Blue Cheeses

If you have a room or closet or cabinet suitable for the making of Port du Salut, it will do for blue cheeses. As in the case of French semisoft cheeses, it must be controllable from 50 to 60 degrees, and from 80 to 95 percent relative humidity.

If you want doubly to ensure the growth of the blue mold—a blue cheese which does not have a blue mold might well be good cheese but is a disappointment anyway—you can inoculate your cheese with a piece of blue cheese you purchase in a shop, or you can order a supply of the mold and inoculate your cheese with that, by putting a bit of mold either in the milk or in the curd when you salt it. The mold generally used is *Penicillium roquefortii,* and is available for purchase (see Appendix 3). One pound is enough for about a hundred

5-pound French blue cheeses or thirty Stiltons. *Penicillium glaucum* is sometimes used but is inferior.

No equipment of consequence is called for to make these blue cheeses; no press is required, except for the Blue Wensleydale. You will need only a normal amount of luck and a full allotment of patience.

Stilton

The most seclusive company of cheesemakers in England historically, and the most exclusive as well, makes Stilton cheese.

The origin of Stilton is unknown, but we do know that Alexander Pope referred to the cheese by name in his "Imitation of Horace," in the course of a reference to Matthew Prior's story of the town mouse and the country mouse. This would establish the existence of the cheese by the 1730s. Also, in the eighteenth century, around Quenby Hall in Leicestershire, a cheese named "Lady Beaumont's Cheese" was made, and some believe it was a Stilton because, as it turned out, a housekeeper of Quenby Hall married a farmer at Dalby and bore a daughter who by marriage became a Mrs. Paulet, who made a cheese in the town of Stilton which she sold to a Mr. Cooper Thornhill, who ran the Bell Inn, and this was a true Stilton we know.

The Bell Inn, now closed, was located on the Great North Road and was one of the places the coaches stopped. The coach passengers came to like the white cheese with the blue-green mold in it.

My favorite maker of Stiltons is a Mrs. Musson, who won me over with her remark that Stiltons "with the exception that they make no noise, are more trouble than babies."

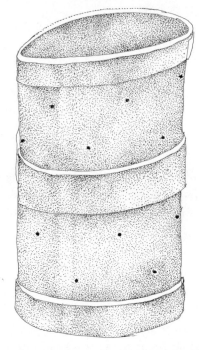

Stilton mold

A Stilton cheese is taller than it is wide, and its maker expects his cheese to weigh 16 pounds when ripe. The hoop or mold he uses measures 8 inches in diameter and 12 inches in height, and an 8- to 12-inch extension fits on top in order that sufficient amounts of curd can be put in the molds to yield a 12-inch cheese. A piece of tin or aluminum or heavy plastic tied in stovepipe shape will do as an extension. The hoops are open-ended, unperforated cylinders. The Stilton can be made in smaller sizes with equally excellent qualities. The smallest I have seen was 5 pounds. This cheese was 5 ¼ inches in diameter and 4 ¾ inches high.

Stilton cheese is white. It has a moderately soft, quite smooth, even velvety texture, which as the cheese ages gradually becomes open and flaky; however, it does not lose its silky consistency or the individual particles. Many Stilton cheeses are eaten fresh, though these do not have the mold, and I don't like them nearly as much.

In England aged Stilton cheese is in special demand at Christmastime, and since Stilton matures in less than four to six months, June and July have always been heavy months for making it in Leicestershire. In the old days few cheeses were made before April, when the cows first had plenty of green grass to eat, and Stilton making reached a peak in the summer and continued to late September or early October. Milk from cows fed in large part with hay does not make the best cheese of any type.

On the outside, the Stilton has a brownish, drab, wrinkled skin. Once it is dry, it needs to be brushed now and again lest cheese mites get on it and nibble through. I'm told in one or two of the great stores of London, which are great stores indeed, the vaulted cellar rooms have rows of aging Stiltons, and an attendant once or twice weekly picks each one up and brushes it, turns it over, and sets it back on a clean shelf until such time as "The Stiltons are ripe, sir."

A mature Stilton should be cut by one of two different methods, if tradition means as much to you as it does to me. One way is with a spoon—you dip down into the center of the cheese and in the course of weeks spoon out the cheese, leaving the hull, the rind to help conserve the moisture. You eat that last. The society of Stilton makers now frowns on this wasteful way, but I like it, and I like it no less for that reason. Their way is to cut 1-inch-deep, pie-shaped slices from the top of the cheese, removing a complete layer of cheese before proceeding to the next. I recommend the first way and suppose the second way is better. In either case a damp cloth should be kept over the cheese, and the cheese need not be stored in a refrigerator.

The present-day makers of Stilton cheese are associated; not just anybody can make and sell a cheese under this name. The recipe for Stilton was guarded in the early years, but through chinks in the cheesemakers' armor, recipes have appeared since the end of the nineteenth century. Back then Stiltons were sometimes made by the one-curd system, but the two-curd system, the older way, was believed to present the most favorable conditions for the cheese to establish its creviced texture, in which mold fungus could grow. By the 1920s this idea had lost many adherents, the amount of work required having worn away their loyalty to it. Not only was the work greater, but a two-curd cheese was sometimes uneven in body and color.

The One-Curd System

We will here give the one-curd recipe, then will tell you how to make a two-curd cheese. An acidimeter is most helpful in using these recipes. I am going to set down the acidity percentages and every other detail that you might need, for the Stilton is one of my two favorite cheeses, and I like to think each of us was meant before he dies to make his own, at least one.

Whole cow's milk is used. Some English makers prefer Shorthorn cow's milk to any other. That is likely to have 3.4 percent butterfat, more or less. Only fresh milk is used, fresh from the milking barn, because a low acidity is required at the initial stages, 0.18 to 0.19 percent, or 0.20 toward the end of the season when fresh milk normally has a higher acidity.

Fifteen American gallons of milk will make a 10- to 11-pound cheese when fully ripe; 20 gallons will make a cheese close to the conventional size. Renneting temperature is 82 degrees in summer and 84 degrees in cooler weather. The quantity of rennet is 2 drams to 10 American gallons of milk in spring, a bit more with the richer milk later in the season. The milk is stirred five or six minutes; then the surface is rippled for five or six more. The milk is expected to be well set in sixty to seventy-five minutes. The curd is tested in the customary ways to be sure it is firm enough.

The soft curd is ladled out in thin slices, and these are put in yard-square draining cloths. Each cloth will hold the curd from 3 or 4 gallons of milk. These bags are tied and are allowed to stand for half an hour in their own whey; that is, one sets the untied bags in a stoppered sink or pan and allows the whey as it drains off to stay with the curds. After half an hour the whey is removed and the bags are tied "Stilton fashion." As I said before, that means that three corners of the cloth are brought together and the fourth is bound around them. The bags are left in a sink to drain until evening. To increase the draining, one tightens the cloths every hour or so during the first eight hours. This might be done four, five, or even six times before the curd is firm (and an acid level of 0.18 to 0.20 percent is reached). If after seven or eight tightenings the curd is not matted, the bundles can be piled one on top of another to help expel more moisture.

The curd is then gently turned out of the cloth into a pan or sink and cut into 3- to 4-inch cubes. The cubes should be soft but have enough strength to stand by themselves (cubes of 0.20 percent acidity are more likely to stand firmly than cubes of 0.18 percent acidity). The curd at this point is fairly solid, quite tender and moist, and when torn apart should be flaky.

Some old makers leave the cubes to oxidize, turning them only once. Next morning the curd is flaky, acid to the taste, and free of sliminess or sponginess. (The acidity is 0.40 percent, more or less.) The blocks are broken by hand into pieces the size of walnuts and are salted, 1 ½ percent by weight of the curd, or 1 ounce of salt to the curd from every 2 ½ gallons of milk. Coarse salt is preferred to fine. The curds at 60 to 65 degrees are lightly packed into hoops, without cloths. The hoops have wooden bases, and on the base traditionally is placed a square of calico, cut to fit. The cloth keeps the cheese from sticking to the board while it drains.

When piling the curd in the hoops, the makers press the curds firmly at the bottom and lightly at the sides. They put the smaller pieces on the top and bottom and the larger pieces in the loosely filled middle of the hoop. The extra tin extension is attached to increase the capacity of the mold; this is removed when the curd sinks below it. Twenty American gallons of milk will produce about 30 pounds of curd ready for vatting, which will yield 14 pounds of cured cheese.

The cheese, on its board, is set to drain in a room with temperature of 65 degrees. After two or three hours the hoop and cheese should be turned. The cheese stays in the hoop six or seven days and is turned once a day, hoop and all. A wooden board, also covered with calico, is placed on top of the hoop and the whole thing is turned upside down, so that the cheese rests on the new board.

By the fifth day the cheese should appear somewhat slippery; if it does not, it should be turned more frequently. By the seventh, eighth, or ninth day it will have sunk into the hoop and pulled away from the sides of the hoop, enough so that it will easily slide out. If the cheese does not settle properly it should be skewered through the perforations in the hoop, and a little salt should be rubbed on each end.

The hoop is removed, and the cheese is scraped with a dinner knife in order to fill its surface crevices. The knife is frequently dipped in hot water to make this work go smoother. The cheese should be creamy on the outside and have an aroma similar to a ripe pear's.

A bandage of cheese-gray cloth, cut 2 inches wider than the cheese is high, is pinned tightly around the cheese, and the hoop is put around it again. The cheese is turned over onto a calico-covered board.

Next day the maker removes the hoop and bandage, scrapes the cheese, then lightly pins a clean bandage round the top. He allows the bandage to hang loosely down, inverts the cheese, pulls the bandage smooth, and loosely folds the bandage over the cheese. Presumably the cheese is sturdy enough to stand by itself; if it is not, it is returned to its hoop on a clean bandage, and one dispenses with the hoop next day.

The room in which the cheese is kept should be cool and well ventilated. Sixty degrees is ideal. At an early stage the cheese will begin to show signs of white mold, and dry patches will appear on the bandage. These are the first signs of the coat. During this period the loose bandage will need to be changed from time to time. Once a coat starts to develop over the cheese's surface, which will require at least eleven and might require as many as sixteen days, the bandage is dispensed with.

When its coat covers it completely, the unbandaged cheese is placed on a small cloth. It will need to be turned once a day onto a dry cloth, or onto a dry place on the shelf. The ventilation, temperature, and humidity of the curing room remain the same; that is, the room is airy, about 60 degrees and 90 percent relative humidity. If the temperature is too high, evaporation will be excessive, and as a consequence you will have a hard, dry cheese; if too low, the ripening of the cheese is retarded. A Stilton takes from four to six months to ripen when it is not skewered, less when it is.

As you see, the process involves patience, but it is not trying otherwise. One troublesome condition does occasionally arise during the coating period or shortly afterward, when moisture cannot flow from the cheese as readily as in the past; it may collect under the new coat, making the curd under the coat slimy and causing the skin to crack. To help guard against this, the cheese should be protected from drafts, and of course the temperature and humidity of the curing room must be kept within proper range. Should cracking occur, scrape away the defective coat and wait for the cheese to form a new one; it will do so, and the cheese will become perfect, without scars from its recent failing.

The conditions essential to the growth of blue mold are these: (1) The cheese must have the correct acidity and moisture content, and a somewhat porous, open texture which allows air to get into the cheese; (2) There must be access of fresh air to the drying room and proper temperature and humidity in the ripening room. The mold will develop without inoculation, conditions being ideal. Should you decide that a cheese has too close a texture, run a skewer with ⅛-inch diameter into the cheese in thirty or forty or even fifty places, about halfway through at a thrust, entering the cheese from each end, not at the sides; the ends of the skewers should pass each other, even if barely. Skewering should be done, if done at all, when the cheese is one month old. Makers usually skewer Stilton cheeses today, but the old people felt that the blue mold developed too quickly when it got too much air and did not create the enzymes which yielded the fine flavor they sought in their cheeses; some of them believed that artificially inseminated cheese tasted objectionably moldy, too.

A prime Stilton should have brown, uniform, crinkled, wrinkled skin, or coat, which should "give" when pressed. The wrinkling comes about because of the consolidating effect of the scraping on the surface of the cheese; this means that the skin will settle less than the internal portion of the cheese and will have to wrinkle. The cut surface should have veins of blue mold, numerous and distinct from the curd, and the curd should be creamy, not yellow in appearance. The flavor should be rich and mellow, without an acid or pungent taste, and without a predominance of the blue mold taste. The texture should be moist and creamy. A properly aged Stilton has long life-keeping qualities.

A Stilton can be eaten during its early ripening, at four to six weeks, or it can be left to ripen fully and develop the blue mold, at four to six months.

In ripening, the Stilton loses about 55 percent of its weight within four months: about 25 percent on the draining shelves during the first week of its life, 10 percent in the coating process, and about 20 percent in the ripening room.

The Two-Curd System

The morning's milk is converted into curds, as described above, and the curds are turned out of the cloths and cut into 4-inch squares. At this point, instead of salting the curds, one leaves them in draining tins overnight, a cloth lightly thrown across the tins to prevent the curds from suffering too much from oxidation and thus becoming discolored.

The evening's milk is made into curds and is allowed to drain during the night, a cloth loosely thrown over it. The next morning this second batch is cut and is turned hourly until about three or four o'clock (or until the acid rating is 0.20 percent).

The two batches of curd, one about thirty hours and the other about twenty-two hours old, are then broken up and mixed together, and salt is added. (The older curd will probably show acidity of 0.7 to 0.8 percent at the time of salting.) If the combined curd is soft and has a slightly acid taste, 1 ounce of salt to 3 pounds of curd is used; if it is firm and has a distinct acid taste, 1 ounce of salt to 4 pounds of curd is used. The salt is mixed in by stirring and turning the curd frequently.

The maker proceeds as in the recipe above with the curing of the cheese.

Unripe, a Stilton is white and dry. When ripe, it is creamy in color and creamy of flesh.

In a high-grade Stilton the blue mold ought to be well distributed but should not overpower the cheese; the blue is an enhancement. The cracks in the flesh should not be conspicuous, either.

A streak of brown just inside the crust is natural.

The cheese should be cut when just ripe and should be eaten up before it becomes too dry. With a damp cloth over it, a Stilton will stay moist at room temperature for several weeks. Some people pour wine or ale onto it, or into its husk once it begins to dry, but this is a messy habit.

Port wine often is served with Stilton in England. I think this is as good a way as any to try to make port drinkable, but I prefer Stilton without it—with a Burgundy or with an apple or grapes, or with all three.

Roquefort

Roquefort (pronounced *Rock fort*) is the king of cheeses in France, or so the French say, just as Stilton is said to be king in England, and both are protected by their respective organizations—even the names are protected in most countries. Anybody can make and sell a Cheddar or call almost anything a Cheddar, and people do just that, but not so with these two members of royalty.

You can perhaps make a Roquefort, though I doubt if it is a proper choice for home manufacture. You will need to gather your patience about you, and of course you must have a closet or cabinet or room which can be made cool and moist. The blue-green mold can be ordered; it is the same one used by the Stilton maker.

Veins of the mold make their way along fissures in the texture of the cheese's flesh during the months of curing.

Roquefort cheese, unlike Stilton, is made of ewe's milk, from which usually no cream has been taken, and ewe's milk has 8 percent butterfat, over twice that of most cow's milk. The sheep used in France are of four breeds, famous for their milk though not their wool, the Lacuane, Lorzac, Segola, and Causses. They graze by hundreds of thousands on valley and hill pastures near Roquefort, as they have since Roman days. As best anybody can judge, Roquefort cheese was cured in the Roquefort caves as early as 1070. It was once made from a mixture of goat's and ewe's milk, but this is no longer the custom. On occasion 10 percent cow's milk is mixed with ewe's milk.

The ewes are milked six months of the year. About 230

gallons of milk might be expected annually for each average ewe. Some makers claim to use only the best milk, the four months of the richest milk, for Roquefort.

The cheeses are made in small establishments located near the Roquefort caves, which caves harbor the cheese during its curing. For centuries the shepherds and their families made the cheeses themselves and took them to the caves for curing, but for the last forty or fifty years most of the cheeses have been made in little factories scattered about nearby. This is an indication of the difficulties involved in curing this cheese at home.

Roquefort is sharp, somewhat peppery, in taste. It is quite salty and is best, therefore, when eaten with a crust of bread or some other accompaniment. The flesh of the cheese between the blue veins is white; the cheese has holes and irregular cracks; it is firm and ought to be creamy, but often excessive drying in storage makes it crumbly. A typical cheese is 8 inches in diameter, 3 ½ to 4 inches high, 5 to 6 pounds in weight. It has no crust.

Modern makers use whole ewe's milk, as I said, but the farmhouse makers in the old days, some of them, would heat the evening's milk to 140 to 200 degrees and pour it into glazed milk crocks. Next morning they would remove much of the cream that had overnight risen to the top and would later make a white butter from it—a rather mediocre butter, actually. The skimmed milk was mixed with morning's milk still warm from the ewes.

The renneting temperature is 76 to 82 degrees. Some makers heat the fresh milk to 122 to 140 degrees, then add cold milk to it to arrive at the renneting temperature desired. The rennet usually used is taken from the stomachs of sacrificed lambs rather than from sacrificed calves. The amount needed depends on the amount of butterfat in the milk after the dilution. It also depends on the inclinations of the maker; some makers add enough rennet for coagulation to take place in ninety minutes, while others prefer to take half an hour longer.

When firm enough to cut, as tested in the conventional way, the top 4-inch portion in these big 100-gallon vats is removed from the curds and processed separately, since it has been changed somewhat in consistency by exposure to the air, and the remaining mass of curd is cut with a cheese harp into pieces the size of a walnut. These are carefully, gently reduced further; then the curd is allowed to rest for ten minutes.

After the ten-minute rest, the whey is drained off, and the curds are scooped out with a wide bucket and put in cloths to drain. The curds should be kept from chilling while draining, the room being ideally about 65 degrees. At the end of thirty minutes the cloths are untied and the curd is quickly transferred to molds by hand. These molds are 7 ½ by 6 inches, open ended, and they are set on drainage mats. They are usually filled in four layers, blue mold powder being sprinkled between each layer. Care is taken not to sprinkle the mold near the bottom or sides, since the blue mold is to develop only in the interior of the cheese.

This powder contains spores of *Penicillium roquefortii* and in France is prepared for use by inoculating loaves of French bread with it; the blue mold is permitted to inhabit the bread for four to six weeks. About 10 grams of mold powder is used for 100 grams of curds.

The last layer of curd is stacked about an inch above the top of the mold, in order to facilitate slight pressure on the curds when the molds are stacked. They are put in a cupboard, called a *trennel*, kept at 64 to 68 degrees, which has holes in its floor to allow whey to flow out as it drains from the cheeses.

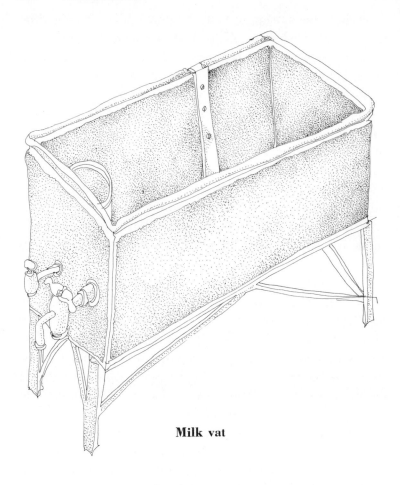

Milk vat

The molds are stacked two or three deep and are turned every hour or two, five or six times the first day. They are turned three times the second, and twice on the third, fourth, and fifth days.

The molds are washed in cool water in summer and tepid water in winter at least once a day.

By the fifth day the cheese can stand on its own and is freed from its hoop. The cheeses have not been pressed, and, you notice, they have not been salted.

On the fifth day, though some makers suggest the third or fourth day, the cheeses are washed, weighed, and marked. By now they no longer drip whey. In cellars they await shipment to the caves, such shipments being arranged by most makers two or three times a week.

The rapid shipments are made during the coolest hours of the day, and in summer it is preferable to travel at night. Twenty-four cheeses are shipped at a time, or so they were in the old days. In the caves, in salting chambers, the cheeses are salted, first on the top and bottom and later on the edges, with a fine, dry salt. They are stacked on the floor in stacks of two or three and turned three times each day. After three days the cheeses are once more salted and again stacked three deep. As an average, during the one-week salting period the amount of salt added is 10 percent of the weight of the cheese; the cheese loses slightly more than half of this quite soon. A finished Roquefort is 4 to 5 percent salt, over twice as salty as a cream cheese or a Cheddar.

During the salting and resting in the salt chamber of the cave, the cheeses become covered with a glazed coat, the *pegot*. This is brushed away.

The cheeses are then pierced by a special machine, needled on each end halfway through sixty times or more, so that air can reach the inner portions and the blue mold, already present there, can grow.

Now the cheeses are moved to a ripening chamber in the caves. The caves are a honeycomb of natural and excavated rooms connected with one another. The air inside is moist, 90 to 95 percent relative humidity, and as you would suspect a brisk breeze is blowing, the current reaching "three meters per second in summer," which is, I believe, about 6 miles an hour. The air is cool; the best temperature of an empty cellar is considered to be 41 degrees, and an effort is made when the chambers are full of fermenting cheeses not to allow it to rise above 47 degrees. The cellar temperature is sometimes regulated in summer with ice machines.

In the ripening chamber the cheeses are stacked one on top of another, three deep, for a week, then placed one beside another without touching for a week. In two weeks they are scraped by women using triangular, short-handled knives. The scraping, an operation called *rebirage*, frees them from a constantly forming coat and permits the air to reach the body of the cheese.

Now, about forty-five days after renneting, they can be sold; however, it is sixty days from making, after the third *rebirage*, that they are actually ripe. If left to their fourth *rebirage*, they become strong and piquant.

When ready to be sold, they are salted rather severely and are then graded as to their ripeness and quality. The saltier cheeses are marked for export to countries which are thought to prefer them, the United States, for instance. The cheeses are packaged in crates of six or twelve cheeses, separated one from another by wooden partitions. The finest cheeses, however, are packaged individually, wrapped in tinfoil. The inferior cheeses are sold in the Roquefort region. The best cheeses are marked, as a rule, for export.

If stored, the cheeses are kept at 40 degrees.

In general, cheeses made in May and June are the best; they are released to the market from September to December.

In curing, the cheeses lose 5 to 6 percent weight per month; even so, the weight of the cured cheeses represents 20 percent of the weight of the whole ewe's milk used in them.

The first Roquefort, according to folk history, was made by a shepherd—some say a shepherd boy—who left a crude cheese in a cave and sometime later came across it. A green mold had developed, but being hungry, he tasted it. It had a different and delicious flavor, so he told others about his discovery.

You might be curious about the bread used to house the *P. roquefortii* spores. It is made of one-third wheat flour and two-thirds barley flour. A heavy dose of yeast is added and the dough ferments, then is baked. The dough must be porous, more so than most, and the texture of the bread must be open. The baked loaves are taken to the caves, to a cool, damp room about 55 degrees and with 85 percent relative humidity, where many other loaves of bread are stored, nurturing the spores. At the end of five or six weeks in the room, the crusts of the leaves are removed and the bread is sliced, ground, and sieved. The crumbs are then ready for use.

Blue Wensleydale

This recipe for Blue Wensleydale appears to have been brought to England by the Normans. The monks introduced it to other monks, chiefly the abbots of Jervaulx Abbey, and it was passed on by word of mouth from generation to generation. It produces one of the world's great cheeses.

Originally the cheese was made of ewe's milk, but cow's milk had taken over by the eighteenth century, and factories had begun to take over by the twentieth. Today some Blue Wensleydale is still made by the monks, but not much, and when last I was in England I was told that they were having trouble getting it to turn blue. I suspect that problem has been corrected.

The white Wensleydale is soft and flaky and acidic to the tongue, but the blue cheese has a creamy, sweet, rich, endearing taste, and often its texture is so soft that the cheese can be spread like butter. The cheese is milder than is Stilton, its only rival in England; they are often linked in friendly comparison, just as Bordeaux and Burgundy are compared among the wines of France. Of these, Blue Wensleydale would be the Bordeaux—or the claret as the English call it.

And claret is wonderful with Blue Wensleydale, and so, for that matter, is English ale.

In the early twentieth century the Blue Wensleydale was made from June to the end of September. I have seen reports in cheese books that cream was added to the milk, but I believe this is not correct. Whole cow's milk was used. Mixed milk was used, the evening's milk having been kept at about 70 degrees; the dairymaid would stand the evening's milk in a bucket of cold water on warm nights. By my recipe, a recipe from 1918, only 1 ½ gallons of evening's milk was mixed with 2 ½ gallons of morning's milk, in order to ensure low acidity, no more than 0.19 percent at any season.

Old Wensleydale makers renneted at 86 degrees in spring and a degree or two cooler in summer and autumn. Usually no starter was used; however, if the milk was not acid enough, an ounce or two of starter to 4 gallons of milk was added, or ½ pint of sour milk, or ¼ pint of ripened cream, or ½ pint of good whey from the previous cheesemaking. The starter was left to ripen the milk for fifteen minutes in winter, five minutes in summer, at which time 1 dram of rennet diluted with ten times its amount of water was stirred into the milk. The milk was stirred well from the bottom of the tub for seven minutes, then lightly on the surface for five more. The tub was then covered and left for fifty to sixty minutes longer, the temperature being maintained as nearly as possible to rennet-ing temperature.

The 1918 Blue Wensleydale cheesemaker used this method to test the curd's consistency: "Dip the finger into water, allowing a large drop to cling to the finger's end. Allow this drop to rest on the surface of the curd, and if the curd is in proper condition, the drop of water will appear to form for itself a small hole in the surface of the curd, but if not, the water will mix and disappear."

When the curd was ready, it was cut into cubes ½ inch square, with a three-minute rest after cutting in one direction before cutting in another. The curd was then left for ten minutes to allow some of the whey to escape and rise. After ten minutes the curd was stirred gently with the hand for one-half hour, at a temperature as close as possible to that of renneting. The curd was left for another half hour, to settle to the bottom of the tub until the acidity reached 0.15 to 0.16 percent, which came between 1 and 1 ½ hours after cutting.

Meanwhile the Blue Wensleydale makers cut a yard-square piece of coarse muslin, which was placed over an empty bucket. Into this cloth the curds and whey were poured when the ripening was completed. The corners of the cloth were gathered, and the bundle of curd was hung to drain, or was set on a draining board. Or it might be laid on the floor of the tub with a slight weight on it, no heavier than the weight of the intended cheese.

In a short time, when the whey stopped running, the curd was cut into 3-inch blocks and retied. This process was repeated three times at intervals of twenty minutes until the curd began to show some flakiness (its acidity was 0.30 percent). It should by then be free of whey. The curd was broken with the fingers into pieces about the size of walnuts, and salt was mixed with it, 1 ounce of salt for the curd from 5 American gallons of milk. The curd was put into a cloth-lined mold, where it was left without pressure for an hour. Then the follower of the press was set in place and pushed down slightly with the hands. The cheese was left for another hour, taken out of the press, and turned over. Once more in the press, a little more pressure was applied for a few hours; then the cheese was turned and was left overnight, in the press and under about 400 pounds pressure.

In the morning the cheese was removed and rubbed with salt. A piece of muslin was sewn around it to keep it from breaking, and it was set on a shelf to dry. The cheese was not capped with circular cloths, but the side bandage did overlap at top and bottom and was fixed on by single-tied stitches at 2-inch intervals; that is, the free ends of the bandage were pleated over the ends of the cheese and kept in place by a lacing of twine.

A recipe I have from the 1920s uses a different pressing procedure. The walnut-sized pieces were not salted; they were put into a cloth-lined mold and left to stand in the mold without pressure all night, the mold being protected from cool night drafts. The next morning very light pressure was applied and was gradually increased, amounting to 300 to 500 pounds on the second day. Two days' pressure was sufficient.

As a variation, some cheeses are salted by being immersed in salt brine—a brine strong enough to float an egg, and made with water sterilized by having been boiled. In suitable storage conditions, the blue mold develops in five months. Inoculation of the milk or curd with the spores, and skewering, as with Stilton, help to hasten and assure this.

Blue Vinny

Of English cheeses this has always been the most difficult to find, either in shops or restaurants or clubs. You aren't going to find it anywhere today, even in Dorset, where the Dorset Blue—its other name, for it is a blue cheese—once was the pride of the farms. By 1935 the cheese was rare. Soon after that only one dairy in Dorset made it regularly and the makers admitted to a wastage of three cheeses in four. Today the cheese isn't made, so far as I can learn, in Dorset or anywhere.

There is some reason to accept the notion that it can't be made anywhere else. The reason is that it never has been. Perhaps the soil of Dorset contains, as André L. Simon has suggested, "infinitesimal quantities of various mineral salts which make all the difference to the texture and flavor of the grass in the first place and of the milk and its cheese later. This is the reason the Blue Vinny has always been a rare cheese and always will be. It can only be made from the milk of a very limited number of herds, those privileged to enjoy the rich pasture lands in the immediate vicinity of Sherborne. . . ." (From *Cheddar Gorge, A Book of English Cheeses,* p. 174.)

Mr. Simon goes on to wonder why not all the cheeses made from the best milk, from the best herds, and at the best time of the year will necessarily show any "blue." They obstinately remain white as chalk.

It seems that every blue cheese has a tradition of secrecy and aloofness and obstinacy, and I would disagree here even with as informed a man as Simon if he were speaking of Stilton, which is being made in several places today and for decades has been, or Cheshire, whose makers once claimed to have exceptionally salty pastureland and said nobody else could equal their product, or Port du Salut, or French blue, or whatever, for in these cases we have practical experience to lay bare the mysticism. Not so with Blue Vinny. Why then not believe in miracles? I do. I think we should, and I am prepared to say that Blue Vinny can be made only in Dorset, and I am sorry to have to say that it isn't, and that when it was, it was made successfully in Dorset less than half the time.

In case you ever get to Dorset and want to make a Blue Vinny, you can take this recipe along, for I do plan to set down the recipe if only for the record. The name is perhaps better than was the cheese; it is a catchy name, isn't it? The West Country people call any bread or cheese that is spoiled by mold *vinny*, and the word doubtless does come from their word *vinewed*, which means moldy and which they pronounce *vinny*.

The cheese is hard, crumbly. Its flesh is white and has blue-green veins. If the cheese does not develop the blue veins, it is virtually worthless—dry and chalky and lacking any mellowness at all, and with "a dirty, earthy taste," as one disappointed observer discovered. The mold is more needed to enhance a Vinny than any other of this family of cheeses.

This is simply because Blue Vinny is a lean cheese made from skim milk to start with. The Dorset farmers are famous for their butter. They took the cream off the top—or their wives did, cream separation being a woman's duty on farms almost everywhere—and out of the skim milk they made buttermilk, or they fed it to the pigs, or they made cheese. So long as the cheese turned blue, they had a profitable business going. Their cheeses had only a brief life-span; once they were ripe they had to be eaten at once, for soon they would harden like cobblestones. That handicapped them in the trade, of course. But what probably dealt them a deathblow was cleanliness, which became more and more fashionable as the twentieth century got into swing, and the old dusty shoes and saddles and harnesses were taken out of the Dorset cheese-making rooms, and the makers sterilized their floors and walls, and the blue mold became difficult to find.

They blamed fate. They had come to believe the blue mold was a gift from heaven, so they blamed heaven, or their own Dorset sinfulness. Little did they know that their late Uncle Harold, who had the funny habit of dipping the harness leathers in the milk when his carters brought it in each night, was wiser than disciples of dairy cleanliness knew.

But when it did turn blue, the cheese was as good as in the old days, sharper than other blues, leaving a long-lasting sensation on the tongue. It was dry and crumbly. The rind was hard and "wasteful." We are told by early writers that its taste was a male taste, and that "no man with a relishing palate should die without tasting the Vinny." The cheese was 6 inches high, 8 inches in diameter, and 10 to 12 pounds in weight, though cheeses half that size were made. An analysis of several Blue Vinnys before the cheese's extinction showed a moisture content of 41.5 percent, fat content ranging from 8.8 to 27.6 percent, and salt 2.9 percent. When compared to a Stilton or Blue Wensleydale, this cheese actually was significantly more moist, and much less fat, and much more salty.

One very old recipe for Blue Vinny says that the cheese was made by a two-curd system, perhaps similar to the Blue Cheshire system which I will describe in a little while. I think this is very likely, although no recipe—only one brief mention in an old book—refers to it.

None of the recipes mention skewering.

The milk was hand skimmed. Mechanical separation was likely to remove too much cream. The Dorset makers sometimes left as little as 1 percent fat, but they did leave that—and usually a beggar's mite more. Evening's and morning's milks were mixed.

The skimmed milk was allowed to develop a rather high acidity. Of course, skim milk rushes faster than does whole milk to sourness anyway. An acidity percentage of 0.24 was not unusual. A starter was not ordinarily used, but in spring (when milk is low in acidity) one sometimes was—buttermilk as a rule, or a commercially prepared starter in the Blue Vinny's final, antiseptic days.

The milk was warmed to 80 degrees, never more, and 1 dram of rennet was added, after being diluted, for every 3 ½ gallons of milk.

When quite firm, the curd was cut into ½-inch cubes. The curds and whey were gently stirred for five minutes in order to mix the whole and bring it all to an even temperature. It was allowed to rest for fifteen minutes, then was stirred again for five. (The acidity during this process should reach 0.17 percent.)

The whey was removed and the curd was cut into 2- to 3-inch blocks, which were tied in a cloth one yard square and hung to drain, or were placed as a bundle on a draining board. The main problems of the Blue Vinny maker at this point were to keep the curd from draining too freely and to keep it from becoming chilled.

The curd was turned out of the cloth and repacked frequently until it was quite flaky. Then it was ground and salted, 1 ounce of coarse salt to 2 ½ pounds of curd. Skimmed milk does not produce much curd, let me warn any of you Dorset cheesemakers who try this recipe.

The pieces of curd were next put into a cloth-lined mold, and sufficient pressure was exerted to make the whey run. For half an hour, whenever the whey stopped running the pressure was increased just enough to make it run again, and at the end of that time the cheese was left in the press until the next morning.

Next morning, if the rind had any cracks, the maker put a new cloth on the cheese and scalded the whole thing, both cheese and cloth, with hot water, then returned it to the press. In any case, he returned the cheese to the press under pressure of 200 to 300 pounds for another day, then put it in the storeroom.

Blue Vinnys were not usually bandaged, but some were before they were put in the curing room. A few were put in stockinette bags.

I have not as yet been able to find out exactly how the cheese was cured in Dorset. Those who have written about Blue Vinny in the past have not bothered with this aspect of its preparation, which is like going to church and not entering the nave. One chap tells us that he was told by "Dorset folk" that the best Blue Vinny was matured "for eighteen months, often, for a third of that time at the bottom of a vat of cider—which cleared the cider and ripened the cheese." That is a marvelous idea and I pass it along enthusiastically, but such scientific mind as I have requires that I admit puzzlement as to how blue mold is to grow while the cheese is immersed in an alcoholic beverage. I mean that as no criticism of alcohol.

The more usual way of curing the cheeses would need to follow the Blue Wensleydale pattern, I imagine, and I leave the matter there and turn over Blue Vinny's resurrection to you, and maybe to me some year in my old age when I have a little time to invest in devious, various ways. I might try

the Blue Vinny on a two-curd system, as Blue Cheshire used
to use.

Blue Cheshire

Blue Cheshire in the 1890s was promoted as a Cheshire
Stilton. The blue mold first came about by accident, perhaps
because makers of Cheshire cheeses often skewered them. To
improve the chance of getting a blue cheese, the makers
would use the old-fashioned recipe I give in Chapter 7 up to
the skewering process; they would not use their cheese ovens,
would not press heavily, and would ripen the cheese in a
humid room.

To help ensure an open texture for the blue mold, some
curd from the previous day's making was kept in a stone jar,
left partially covered to prevent its drying out. (The mold
spores were doubtless in this jar, as well as in the curing
room.) This day-old curd was mixed with the present day's
at salting time in the proportion of one to seven, or sometimes
one to five or six.

Factory-made Blue

This recipe is particularly good. It will produce a cheese that
will compare favorably with any blue, or French *bleu*. It
recommends low curing temperatures, which means much
time waiting for the cheese to ripen, but the cheese is virtually
no trouble during that period and the taste and quality of the
finished cheese are superior.

Use fresh whole milk. Adjust the milk's temperature to 88
to 90 degrees. Should the milk be less than 0.16 percent acid,

which freshly milked milk in the spring of the year might be, add lactic acid starter at the rate of 2 percent of the milk you have. If the milk is more than 0.16 percent acid, add 1 percent starter; in this latter case, to 5 gallons of milk you would add ⅘ ounce of starter.

Let the milk ripen for sixty minutes or so at about 86 degrees, or until it reaches 0.19 percent acidity.

Add rennet at the rate of 1 dram for 5 gallons of milk. Dilute the rennet in half a cup of tap water and stir it into the milk for five minutes, then ripple the surface for three or four minutes.

Allow the milk to coagulate. In forty-five to sixty minutes the curd will be firm enough to cut, as tested in the usual way. Cut it into ½-inch to ⅝-inch cubes, cutting front to back, then side to side, then into cubes by cutting downward at a diagonal if you need to. Let the curds rest in the whey for five minutes.

Stir the cubes gently every ten or fifteen minutes, only enough to prevent matting. Do this off and on for two hours.

By then the cubes should be round and firm enough so they show little tendency to mat. If you press a handful of them in your hand, then release them, they will tend to break apart.

Transfer the curds to molds, cylindrical, open-ended drums set on mats or draining boards, so that the whey can escape. The molds can be of just about any size. I suggest 7 inches in diameter and 10 inches in height. Use an extension for part of this height. Such a mold will accept the curd from 5 gallons of milk.

Add *P. roquefortii* spore powder, ¹⁄₁₂ ounce, to the curds as they are put in the mold. *P. glaucum* is usable as a substitute but is not as good. Flakes of any good blue cheese are usable but are not as dependable.

Turn the mold at twenty- to thirty-minute intervals during

the first two hours. Keep it out of drafts and covered with a cloth. Don't let it cool quickly.

Turn it twice more at two-hour intervals, then leave the cheese at room temperature, 65 to 68 degrees, overnight.

Next day take the mold to a room 50 degrees in temperature and remove the cheese from the mold. Simply run a knife around the edge and tap the mold and the cheese will fall out. Place the cheese on a flat board. Rub fine salt heavily on all surfaces. Three applications of salt, over a five-day period, are required. In all, use 3 ⅓ ounces of salt for the cheese from 5 gallons of milk.

When all the salt has dissolved, which will take five to seven days in the salt room, prepare a bath of molten wax. Melt paraffin in the top of a double boiler—I would use a double boiler to avoid the danger of explosive wax splattering. With the wax at 190 degrees, immerse the cheese for three seconds, then seal any cracks that are left, using a brush.

The next duty is to skewer the cheese. You will need to use a needle that will reach halfway through the cheese, or perhaps a bit more. A factory has a punching machine with stainless steel needles mounted randomly. You can use a household needle about ⅛ inch in diameter and should skewer the 7-inch cheese about twenty times on one flat side, then turn it over and skewer it twenty times on the other.

Put the cheese in a ripening cellar, one with 50 degrees temperature and relative humidity of 87 to 93 percent. Stand it on edge, not on a flat side. It is best to turn the cheese a third of a turn clockwise every three or four days, to help it keep its shape.

After six weeks in the curing room, remove the wax and surface growth, clean the cheese, and fill in the surfaces of the holes with cheese. Rewax it, but do not skewer it again.

Store it at a low temperature, 35 to 40 degrees, for four more months, until at about six months of age it is ready for cutting, wrapping, giving away to friends, and eating. A long process, but an excellent one, and much of it can take place in a refrigerator. A wine takes longer.

To make this cheese even better, separate the cream from the milk the night before the renneting and homogenize the cream; breaking down the fat globules helps make the cheese all the creamier. If you have the equipment, separate the raw milk at 40 degrees. Store the raw skim milk at 35 degrees overnight and pasteurize the cream, which ought to be 35 to 40 percent butterfat, at 170 degrees for nineteen seconds. Homogenize the cream at 500 pounds pressure and 140 degrees. Store the cream in a milk can at 35 degrees overnight. Next morning add enough cream to the skim milk to yield a 3.8 percent milk. This will require about ½ gallon of the homogenized cream to about five gallons of skim milk.

This recipe has been developed over the years by the people at Clemson University. They used to age the experimental cheeses in a cave, but now they use refrigerated rooms. If you can visit them, they make this cheese on most Tuesdays and will allow you to watch. And they will advise you, if you write them at Clemson, S.C.

The French make several blue cheeses out of cow's milk, and they are the *bleu* cheeses which this Clemson recipe seeks to duplicate. Gex is one of them, a famous French *bleu* which has been made for over a hundred years in the Department of Ain, and in more recent times has also been made in the departments of Jura and Isère in southeastern France. A Gex cheese weighs 14 to 15 pounds. Cow's milk is used. It is fresh; in fact, it is brought directly from the milking barn. *P. roquefortii* spores are added and enough rennet is used for coagulation to be finished in 1 ½ to 2 hours. The curd is broken up and stirred, then allowed to settle to the bottom of the vat. Ten minutes later the whey is removed and the curd is salted lightly and put into molds, which are 12 inches across and 5 inches high, open-ended, cylindrical. In an hour the cheeses are turned and a light disk is placed on them to press them slightly. The cheeses are turned three or four times the first day, after which the molds are removed and the cheeses are salted on their surfaces and taken to the curing room. The cheeses are cured over a period of three or four months, some of the curing done in caves.

Ambert, also known as Fourmé d'Ambert, differs from Gex in its making, in that the salt is mixed with the curd instead of being rubbed on the surface of the cheese.

7

Cheshire

Cheshire Cheese

Cheshire cheese, the favorite cheese of England until recent years and the oldest, so far as can be judged, is known as Chester in France and is the only English cheese ever to become popular with Continentals. Much of the rest of the world has taken Cheddar to its heart and table, rather than Cheshire.

Lewis Carroll named his Cheshire cat after Cheshire cheese. The vanishing smile that enchanted Alice had its birth in Cheshire curds and whey.

As you know from the section on Double Gloucester, before World War II there were hundreds of farmhouse cheese-

125

makers in England; son and daughter often followed father and mother in the tradition. But after the war and its consequent rationing and disruptions, most of these families had stopped cheesemaking. Today there are only a few farmhouse cheesemakers in England, most of whom have had to enlarge and generally change their style of operation in order to meet the competition of factories. The Milk Marketing Board, a federation of dairy farmers, in effect assigns milk to them for their use, and grades their product, and helps market it for them, so this has become a regulated style of family, farmhouse operation. Perhaps as a consequence there is at the moment minimal experimentation in England in cheesemaking, nothing like the excitement attending home winemaking, for instance, or ale or meadmaking.

Be all that as it may, recently when I was in England I asked an official of the Milk Marketing Board which of the Cheshire makers was the best. I was told that one farmhouse maker, Mr. Ferris Wild, who markets his Cheshire cheeses under the name William Wild, Ltd., has won many awards, including four recent first awards for the best cheese entered of any type in the London Dairy Show, virtually the national championship of England. I asked if I might visit Mr. Wild, to see him make cheeses, and an appointment was arranged for me for the next morning.

It is always a pleasure to travel the English countryside roads, and it was a special pleasure to visit Cheshire, my third time there. The pastures rose gently on either side of the road, and the fields were green, even in January. In the 1600s a historian named John Speed wrote this of Cheshire, which I suggest should be read aloud in a big voice: "The champion grounds make glad the hearts of their tillers; the meadows embroidered with divers sweet-smelling flowers; and the pasture makes the kines udders to strout to the paile, from whoem and wherein the best cheese in all of Europe is made." He must have been quite a historian, to have seen places and to have written about them with a storm of poetry and marvelous exaggeration. Imagine what he could do with wars and assassinations.

I traveled at dawn. Cheese can be made at night as well as day, but farmers always seem to make it of a morning, early. The gray sky was marked off sharply by the black limbs of the trees, close by, overhanging. I went through a few towns named Wordle and the like, where children were getting ready to go to school. I drove along past great houses, all of them old, some of them walled, my car warm and a cricket game from Australia on the car radio, believe it or not. My belly was full; I had had an English breakfast of eggs, kippers, York ham, toast, marmalade, and two cups of strong coffee. I had every right to feel privileged.

I drove through Chester, surely one of the most beautiful towns in the world, with second-floor balconies overlooking the main street, and a main-street clock housed to match the half-timbered buildings. I was in good spirits as I reached Mollington and Mr. Wild's farm.

The farmhouse was a long, low building, two stories, ancient if judged by its surfaces and crevices. It lent the impression of heaviness, of immense weight on the earth. The bushes and hedges were massive and were neatly tended.

I was admitted to the house. The main room was long and low ceilinged and opened out onto a rear garden with a large pond. To the left of that were the old farm buildings, and beyond them the pastures for the 4,000 pigs and 140 milch cows. Mr. Ferris Wild, himself a scrubbed, bright, hefty man, about fifty years of age, was a pleasant, hospitable person who seemed to be particularly conscious of the fact that I was an American. Americans are more of a novelty in Cheshire than London, and are likely to visit the country only to trade and scrounge.

"My father built this, all this," he told me. "My father told me he had put these timbers together and all I had to do was keep it afloat."

He had kept it afloat twenty-one years, he said.

As if testing me, a greedy American longing to own English antiques, which of course I am, he showed me a clock that had been in his family for three hundred years. I admired it. He called attention to a table, the main table in his dining room, which had been in his family for two hundred years.

I admired that, too. They were wonderful pieces.

As if coaxed along by what I had not said, rather than what I had, he said, "Americans keep bidding me for them."

"Do they really?" I said.

"Last time one offered seven hundred quid for the table."

"I'm not surprised," I said. "What did you tell him?"

"Of course, I said no. It won't go to America."

"Of course," I said.

We walked together toward the cheese house, which was joined to the dwelling house by walls and buildings. Mr. Wild's master cheesemaker, as he told me, was a Miss Ethel Davis, a hardworking foreman who would even boss the cowmen if they needed it. Miss Davis I knew to be one of the two or three most famous cheesemakers of Cheshire today. She was, Mr. Wild told me, the daughter and granddaughter of famous Cheshire cheesemakers.

"The work goes on every day of the year," he said. "I hire seven workers, so each can have a day off every week. Miss

Davis can have a day off, but she never takes hers. Use to, there was a three-month break from cheesemaking each year, when the grass wasn't plentiful and during calving time, but today, with your staffs and everything, you couldn't possibly have a three-month break. Now they've all gone to having their cows calve all year round, that is, some cows one time, some another."

We stopped at the starter room, a small, sparklingly clean place where commercially prepared starter is kept in a freezer. The batch for each day's use is thawed under water, to keep alien bacteria from invading it. "This is one of the most important changes in farmhouse cheesemaking," Mr. Wild said. "A definite improvement, for now we can be certain of the starter and what it will do."

The batch of starter for the next day was being thawed out.

"You have to be clean to make good cheese," Mr. Wild said. "Miss Davis, if she thought there was dirt under the tiles, would have them up and washed and would put them back again. Cheesemaking is 10 percent making cheese and 90 percent washing up."

He led the way into the tiled cheesemaking room; a small press and bandaging room lay beyond. Near the main door was a big vat. I suppose it would hold 1,200 gallons of milk, and it was equipped with rockers and paddles and knives and steam jets, a beautiful piece of modern sculpture, actually. It was full of milk.

Eight o'clock, by my watch.

I met Miss Davis, a slight, lean woman in her thirties or maybe early forties—I am not able to judge women's ages and know better than to try. Admittedly she was intense, concentrating on her business, yet she smiled easily and honestly. As we talked I noticed that she remained conscious of the work going on in the other room which consisted just now of bandaging the cheeses which had been made three days ago, and that she was watching over, hovering over, the sea of coagulating milk in the vast tub beside us.

"What time did you put the starter in?" I asked her.

"Six o'clock," she said.

"What time did you put the rennet in?"

"Seven forty-five."

"How much?"

"Forty ounces, mixed one to six with water."

"How much milk?"

"Eight hundred and eighty gallons," she said.

British imperial gallons are 160 ounces, larger than American gallons, so she was using over 4 tons of milk, 1,100 American gallons. A long way from the old days of farmhouse cheesemaking.

The milk had a butterfat rating of 3.6 percent, she told me. "You really don't want it any richer than that for cheesemaking." The acidity rating at the time of renneting had been 0.22 percent. The milk had not been pasteurized; it never is in farmhouse Cheshire making. Sometimes she and Mr. Wild color their cheese; this morning she had not colored it. The milk was mixed from last night's and this morning's milkings.

Mr. Wild was obviously proud of the room, of the equipment, of the precise activity of the six workers as each readied himself or herself for the more active assignments soon to begin.

At 8:23, with the milk's acidity rating at 0.15 percent, Miss Davis ordered the cutting to begin, and the machine's horizontal and vertical knives moved through the white curd, cutting it into small pieces, then cutting them into cubes of less than ½ inch in size.

This done to Miss Davis's satisfaction, the machine began to stir the curds and whey, and to heat them to 93 degrees, 1 degree increase every three minutes.

At 9:09 with an acidity rating of 0.18 percent, the curds pitched—that is, they began to seek the bottom of the liquid bath, even when stirred. "The snow pitches to the ground," Mr. Wild told me, trying to explain the derivation of the term, an old one in cheesemaking yet never clear to me as to origin.

One of Miss Davis's workers began to shove the curds toward one end of the vat, preparatory to letting the whey off at the other.

At 9:35 the whey was drawn off. The acidity reading was 0.25 percent.

At 9:40, the curds having begun to mat in a spongy mass, two of Miss Davis's male assistants, using stainless steel shovels, cut the mass into chunks, brick-sized or larger; they turned these over every five or ten minutes, moved them about, to help keep the whey draining. The acidity was increasing rapidly now. The workers with their shovels kept a channel open down the middle of the vat to assist the draining of the whey. The acidity increased to 0.4, to 0.5, to 0.6 percent.

At 0.69 percent acidity, Miss Davis ordered that the blocks of curd be salted. They were at once sprinkled with dry salt and the blocks were then cut and stacked in about one-third their former floor space in the vat.

When the acidity was between 0.7 and 0.8 percent, the tough, sweet blocks of curd, dry-tasting now, were shoveled into a mill, which tore them into pieces. These pieces in turn were shoveled into metal molds, each of which had a cloth-bag lining. The hoops were cylindrical, open ended. The curds were punched down into them, as more curds were added, and finally the curds were mounded above the top and the top of the bag was closed loosely, folded over.

"Cheshire cheese should be as tall as it is wide across, when cured," Mr. Wild told me. "These molds each hold 56 pounds of curd and after pressing will produce 50-pound cheeses."

When seventeen hoops were filled, a second group of small steel hoops, twenty in all, were brought forward and their cloth bags were filled; they would make 4-pound cheeses. "The smallest we make is a 4-pound cheese," Mr. Wild said. "They're dearer, when priced by the pound, mind you, because they're about as much work; it takes as long really to bandage one of those as the other size. But some people say they're cheaper in the long run, because you can make better use of the cheese, once cut, and its size does enable a person to age his cheeses, too, in a small space. If he likes a mature cheese, he should keep these three months each."

The thirty-seven big and little cheeses were allowed to sweat in their molds while the vat was washed. They were too warm as yet to put to press.

Mr. Wild uses horizontal hydraulic presses. The big cheeses were put to press at about 600 pounds weight, the little ones at about 100 pounds. After two or three hours they were taken out of the press and stripped of their rough-cloth bags. They had already taken on solid form. Given a smoother cloth bandage, they were reversed in the hoop and returned to the press, this time at 1,700 pounds for the big ones, 300 for the small. "We used to change the cloth twice," Mr. Wild said, "but we have stopped this because of the labor situation."

Come next morning, I was told, the cheeses would be unbandaged, any rough edges would be sliced off with razor blades, and they would be rebandaged and returned to the press, this time at 1,700 to 2,200 pounds for the large, 400 for the small. They would be left under pressure all day. The following day they would receive their final bandage and be set on a drying shelf. Several hours later they would be turned onto a clean shelf, the old shelf probably having acquired a flour paste from the bandage. They would be turned every day. Those not waxed would begin to have a mold form on them after five or six days, which would be wiped or brushed off. Most of Mr. Wild's cheeses are waxed now, however, waxing being done after the fifth day. The waxing prevents shrinkage and mold growth, and, although it delays ripening, it does not, Mr. Wild told me, delay it by much.

At fourteen days of age the cheeses will be delivered to the Milk Marketing Board's company, Emberton Bros. Ltd., and after a day or two of rest in the warehouse, they will be graded as superfine or fine or graded. Mr. Wild gets a 75 percent superfine rating consistently, which is considered excellent performance.

At twenty-one days, the cheeses are offered for sale; merchants frequently age them after purchase in their own storerooms.

"I personally don't like any cheese until it's three months old," Mr. Wild told me.

I asked him what effects changing seasons had on his cheeses.

"The best cheeses are made in September, October, and November," he said. "They will keep a long, long time, too. A May cheese isn't a good cheese. It doesn't have a nutty flavor."

We watched one of the workers bandage a cheese that had been made three days earlier. He first put on the round end

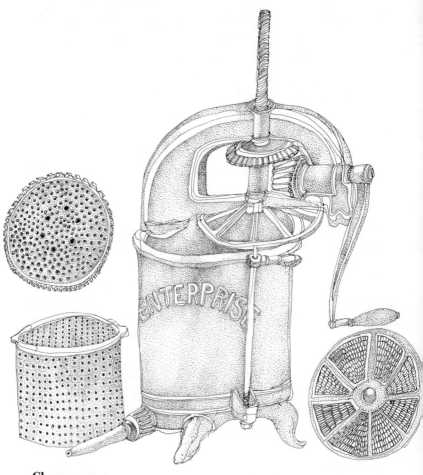

Cheese press

pieces, pasted them on with flour paste, then wound the side
bandages around the cheese, pasting them on. There was a
1-inch overlap at top and bottom, which he pasted over the
end pieces, working proficiently, quickly. The side bandage
also overlapped itself by several inches; he pasted this over-

lap in place, then set the Wm. Wild, Ltd. stamp on this double
thickness, as well as the date the cheese was made.

"If I make poor cheese," Mr. Wild told me, "I don't put
my name on it. If you get a bad day, you get all sorts of
things happening to you. Some cheeses won't even stand up.
Some days nothing seems to go right. I know a fellow who
tells me he doesn't care what the quality of his cheese is so
long as he has got his name on it."

I asked him if mechanization had affected the quality of
his cheese.

"In farmhouse making, if we knew a way to make cheese
better, we would use it, but we'll modernize if it doesn't make
the cheese worse. Waxing is one example of an improvement.
It has been a boon, a big help to the grocer and to us. The
cheese keeps longer. A cheese used to have mold; he had to
brush the mold off. Now that's no longer needed."

I asked the ever-busy Miss Davis what she thought about
changes from the old days. "The whole thing is different,"
she said. "The taste is different. They sell it too soon for one
thing. They sell it in four weeks instead of four months—
some people sell it in two weeks. I think some make it in two
hours forty minutes now, while used to be we took three hours
or more."

"How did your father make Cheshire?" I asked her.

"He would judge by the feel and the taste, and sometimes he
would put curd against the boiler door. If it drew threads so
long, it was ready for one stage, then longer threads."

"What starter did he use?"

"Buttermilk. He took more than four hours to make cheese.
I've often seen my father put an open cream stain—that's a
big, fancy mold—before the fire if the curd wasn't ready and

let it set for hours, while we waited. If we did that today, we'd never make cheese."

Which I suspect is so. Both individuals' comments are doubtless so. And honestly expressed.

Cheshire, an Old Recipe

We today have no idea when Cheshire was first made or by whom, or what it tasted like centuries ago. According to one edition of the *Encyclopaedia Britannica,* writers in the twelfth century referred to the excellence of Cheshire cheese; unfortunately the encyclopedia neither says who those writers were nor gives any details about their descriptions.

I do have descriptions of Cheshire cheese from the 1800s, which tell us that Cheshire had a more pungent and distinctive flavor and aroma than had Cheddar. "One peculiarity of the flavor deserves special mention, a sugary sweetness, very pleasing to the average palate, and due to the high proportion of sugar; this is not to be confounded with the nutty flavor of Cheddar, being very distinct from it."

The texture was loose and flaky, strikingly unlike Cheddar's smooth solidity. Cheshire had a softness to it, much appreciated.

The cheese in the 1800s was usually a brick red, made so by the use of annatto "to the point of positive disfigurement." This gave the makers considerable difficulty with uniform coloring, and in time many of them began to prefer a regular, dependable paleness to their cheese.

The size and shape of Cheshire were similar to those of Cheddar, though the Cheshire cheese was not usually as large. The largest Cheshire I have notes on weighed 300 pounds.

This was made in 1909 by Mr. Percey Cooke of Tattenhall Farm, near Chester. In fact, he made twenty such cheeses, one a day for twenty consecutive days on order from a gentleman who was writing a book on the makers of Cheshire cheese. This author set a standard for publicity which no writer could hope to equal today, short of television appearances. At the time these twenty cheeses were made, there was a question as to whether they would mature to the center, and before they were cut considerable expectancy was generated—I dare say for the book as well as the cheeses. Each of them was found to be cured throughout.

Prior to this twenty-cheese achievement, the largest Cheshire on record weighed 149 pounds and was presented to H.R.H. the Duke of York in 1825. Nobody seems to have recorded just why.

We are unable to give weight or dimensions for the smallest Cheshire cheese ever made, smallness not being as interesting. Cheshires can be made 4 pounds in weight, we know from Mr. Wild's experience.

A method in general use in the nineteenth century, one which helped Cheshire cheese attain its reputation in England and France, is as follows:

The evening's milk was kept overnight at 60 to 70 degrees, the aim being to secure the desired milk ripeness without use of a starter. The morning's milk was added to it. The acidity of the mixed milk was, when ideal conditions prevailed, 0.19 percent, quite low, much less ripe than the 0.22 percent of the milk Mr. Wild uses.

The temperature for renneting ranged from 75 to 90 degrees. It was believed that the lower temperatures produced a higher standard in the ripened cheese, but the general custom was to rennet at 90 degrees. The rennet was briskly stirred in for three minutes; then the vat was covered. A soft curd, firm enough to break over the finger, was desired, and was attained in about sixty minutes from the time of renneting. The amount of liquid rennet extract needed for ten American gallons was ½ ounce, much less than is used in today's Cheshire process.

In cutting, normally the horizontal cut was made first and vertical cutting was done ten minutes later—because the curd was quite soft. The final size of the cut curd was that of large peas.

The curds were intermittently stirred until small enough and tough enough to want to pitch, which took thirty to sixty minutes. The bits of curd in this state feel quite "shotty." They were then allowed to pack at one end of the vat or one side of a circular vat (the old vats were usually circular). The packing was often done by hand, the matted curd from one end of the vat being doubled over upon that at the other end; sometimes it was done by a curd-gatherer, a perforated tinned sheet stretched on a light iron frame, having projections which rested on the vat's top edge and thumbscrews which would secure it in place. Since the vats were large, two workers were usually required to operate a curd-gatherer. Once the curd was about doubled in the pack, the curd-gatherer would be fixed in place by the screws and a wooden rack would be lightly pressed on the curd's surface to settle it in place. Here the packed curd remained in the whey for an hour or so, until it felt quite firm. Then the whey was drawn. Notice that no scalding has been done.

The curd was cut into chunks and piled up, sometimes on a cloth-covered rack to facilitate draining, sometimes on the floor of the vat. The pile was covered again. This process was repeated, the curd blocks being turned every ten minutes over a sixty- to ninety-minute period until it had a slightly leathery feel and a distinctly acid taste and smell.

Now the curd was torn apart for grinding. It was still white and comparatively soft—soft, that is, when compared to Cheddar. If the ripening had been carried further, the curd would have had a tendency to hardness and firmness, to a shot-like toughness. The teeth of the grinding mill were constructed to tear the curd rather than to cut it, as are those used today. The curd was fed to the mill in 3-inch cubes. For small lots a mill is not needed; the curd can be broken apart by hand.

The milled curd was salted; the amount of salt varied with makers, in most cases being 1 pound to 40 gallons of milk used. The softer the curd, the greater amount of whey lost in the final stages of processing, and therefore the more salt required, since much of the salt would be carried off by escaping whey. Dry, coarsely ground salt was used.

The curd was next put into a cloth-lined hoop, a deep mold with numerous perforations in its sides. The perforations permitted skewers to be thrust into the cheese to assist in removing whey trapped in its crevices. This skewering was done at the start, after which the hoop was put into a small cupboard, called an oven, large enough to contain one or two cheeses. The oven had a gutter for collection of whey as it drained. These ovens generally measured 80 degrees in temperature, but some were as low as 70, others as high as 90 degrees. Some of them had hot-water pipes for heating; others shared the heat from the kitchen stove or a flue. Very little pressure, if any, was applied to the cheese, no more than 50 pounds for a large cheese. Some makers contended that a well-made Cheshire should go together without any pressure at all.

In the evening the cloth was changed and the cheese, which had taken on its form, was returned to the hoop. Again only slight pressure was applied, if any, and the hoop was returned to the oven. In the morning it was removed, re-clothed, and now put under pressure of about 100 pounds for a 50-pound cheese, half that for small ones. The pressure was increased steadily during this and the successive three or four days, finally reaching 2,200 pounds for a cheese of 60 pounds, or 1,700 pounds for a 30- or 40-pound cheese. It was believed that a greater pressure—for instance, as much as is used in Cheddar cheesemaking—and a more rapid increase of the pressure would cause retention of excess whey in the cheese, which would in the course of time lead to irregular and excessive fermentation.

A steady dripping of whey continued during the pressing, barely ceasing by the end of it. This steady draining of whey made it necessary to change the cloth daily; otherwise the outside of the cheese would become sodden, and the flowing of the whey would be hindered.

A cheese which was slightly concave at its top and bottom was judged to have been successfully pressed. One which became convex had not been, because unwanted gases had been trapped inside the cheese to cause the bulging.

The whole matter of pressing avoided haste and excess. It was believed that the time of pressing could not be shortened without risk of loss of quality.

Cheshire makers laid on their bandages with flour paste— most cheesemakers elsewhere sewed on the bandages. A few hours before the cheese finally was to leave the press, the bandage was applied, and it helped give support to the cheese. Often the cheeses were greased at both ends to prevent cracking. Butter or whey butter was used.

The cheeses were sometimes left in an airy room for a day or two, to dry, before they were taken to the curing room. There they were laid on shelves or on the floor and were turned daily for the first month, on alternate days for the next month, and twice weekly thereafter. Often straw was put under the cheese, once the cheese had become fairly dry. The curing room was 55 to 65 degrees, and a reading of moisture in selected Cheshire storing rooms before the turn of the century gave a range of 4 to 6 percent in the hygrometer, 60 to 70 percent relative humidity at 55 degrees cellar temperature. A wide latitude in cellar temperatures and humidity was tolerated, but if the air was too warm or too dry, the cheeses might crack.

The cheeses were kept by many makers for three to four months, and it was believed that the cheeses would improve for as many more. There was, however, a loss of weight during the curing process, and many of the makers did sell their cheeses "as early as they can be carried safely." If kept longer than twelve months, the cheeses were liable to become dry, crumbly, somewhat bitter.

Before the turn of the century new practices arose in Cheshire. The oblong metal vat, for instance, with its facility for heating milk, was introduced, and some of the makers began to scald the curd in the whey, as did the Cheddar makers in Somerset, and obtained by this method a contraction of the curd and a dryness by the time it was ready for salting that were equal to the contraction and dryness of the oven-dried curd when it was ready for pressing. This resulted in a saving of time. It is interesting that a few makers, willing to embrace change but unwilling to embrace it in its entirety, scalded the curd slightly, to 90 degrees, then used the oven at a low temperature, 70 to 74 degrees, to complete the work, thus having what we suspect was the worst of two possible worlds.

By the 1920s and 1930s in England there were three different types of Cheshire cheeses, one a semisoft cheese made only in the spring for use while fresh, one a long-keeping cheese made in July and August, and the third a medium-ripening cheese made in spring and fall.

I will record here briefly the recipes for the fresh cheese, which is an excellent one and a variation of Mrs. Kirby's.

Early-ripening Cheshire

Last night's and this morning's milk was mixed, and sour cream was used as a starter, 1 quart of sour though not coagulated cream to 10 gallons of milk. The milk was heated to 82 degrees. Annatto was added as a rule, ⅕ ounce to 10 gallons of milk, and the milk was stirred for five minutes.

When the milk was 0.21 to 0.22 percent acid, rennet was added, ½ ounce to 10 American gallons. The milk was briskly stirred with the hands for fifteen minutes. It was then allowed to settle on the bottom of the vat for another fifteen minutes before the whey was drawn off.

Traditionally, cheesemakers would at this point put the curd on wooden racks which they had covered with cloth; they would cut the curd into blocks and would turn the blocks three times at intervals of ten minutes. By then the curd, if all went according to schedule, should be wet, soft, velvety to touch, and should have a slightly acid taste and smell. (Its acidity rating was 0.50 percent.)

The curd was milled—that is, was torn into small pieces—and salt was added, 3 ounces of salt to 10 pounds of curd.

The salted curd was put in a mold from which the whey could drain and was placed in a cupboard, called an oven, and held at a temperature of 75 to 78 degrees.

The process to this point took about three hours.

Several hours later the cheese was turned and was returned to the cupboard. No pressure was applied until the second day, and then only enough to shape and consolidate the cheese.

For five days it was kept under light, gradually increasing pressure, just enough for the whey to drip out of it. Then it was bandaged, greased on both ends to help prevent cracking, and stored in a cool room where it was turned each day for fourteen days. It was now ready for sale.

The cheese thus produced was a meaty, fat, tart cheese, and was awaited in early spring by hungry Cheshire families; eating it was an annual tradition. The cheese was prized by the consumers because of its mellow taste and was prized by the cheesemakers because of its high yield—more than a pound of cheese per imperial gallon of milk, a higher yield than they could get by almost any other system. The cheese would not keep long without developing an acid, bitter taste and becoming dry.

The early-ripening Cheshire was not often made after the middle of May, simply as a matter of habit. It can be made at any season. I find that winter milk, even from cows fed only on hay, makes a good cheese by this method.

8

Gruyère and Cantal

Gruyère and Cantal are France's two famous hard cheeses, both old in time, both large enough to hold down the table of any feast or gathering.

Both are pressed cheeses. I will set down farmhouse recipes for them.

Gruyère

To make Gruyère is one of the higher challenges in cheese-making and needs to be considered as such, but Gruyère is also one of the most stable and dependable of cheeses. It is a longtime proposition because of its curing, and you might decide to make a less demanding cheese.

Many think of Gruyère as a Swiss cheese, and it's true that the inhabitants of the district of Gruyère, in the Swiss canton of Fribourg, were making a renowned cheese by the twelfth century, presumably Gruyère, but we also know that Gruyère cheese was being made nearby in Doubs, France, as early as 1288. Today Gruyère is made in many places in both Switzerland and France, with France the main producer.

It is a relative of Emmenthal, called "Swiss cheese" throughout most of the English-speaking world and "Emmentaler" in Germany. Emmenthal is made in France as well. The Gruyère, however, is more firm, more nutty, is slightly sharper in taste, and has smaller "eyes." A Gruyère's eyes are about the size of small cherries if made in France, of green peas if made in Switzerland.

Also unlike Emmenthal, the skin of a Gruyère is encrusted with the work of aerobic bacteria and enzymes, which over an eight- to twelve-month curing period help to develop the flavor, giving it a unique pungency.

Gruyère is not exported to the United States except in a heat-processed form.

Traditionally a Gruyère cheese weighs about 125 pounds, but smaller cheeses are made. A cheese made from 20 American gallons of milk will weigh approximately 16 pounds when ripe.

Gruyère is processed at a higher temperature than most other cheese, which helps it develop a special elasticity; the high temperature also helps the development of bacteria within the cheese which produce the carbon dioxide that makes the characteristic eyes. The milk used is cow's milk, 3.0 to 3.5 percent butterfat. It should be reasonably fresh, such as evening's and morning's milk mixed. The milk should come from cows which have been pasture-fed and have not been eating grass silage; this is a desirable factor in terms of all cheeses but is required here. The milk must be absolutely clean; otherwise in curing the cheese might develop gases which affect its eyes as well as its taste. As a rule, Gruyère cheeses are not colored. The milk is not pasteurized; the process and the long aging of the cheese make pasteurization unnecessary, assuming the milk comes from tested cows.

I visited a farmhouse operation in France on a bright, pretty autumn day, and I will tell you how cheese was made by the *patron* and his two helpers in a room adjoining his house. The three of them made four cheeses a day, about 400 pounds of cheese in all. They used jacketed copper vats, which are traditional; the old makers thought that copper gave a special characteristic taste to the cheese, a notion sometimes negated and sometimes confirmed by recent scientific research. The *patron* did not use a starter in his milk. He used last evening's milk curd at about 65 degrees overnight and this morning's milk, the mixture adjusted to 3.3 percent butterfat. The rennet he added was commercially purchased, but for many years Gruyère and Emmenthal makers preferred to use strips of a calf's stomach rather than the rennet removed from the stomach, insisting that this produced a better-flavored cheese. Contemporary research has found that such strips did indeed contain not only milk-clotting enzymes but also bacteria that were particularly helpful in the ripening of this type of cheese. Today when Gruyère and Emmenthal makers use commercial rennet, they add appropriate cultures of bacteria to the milk: for 20 gallons of milk, ⅘ ounce of *Streptococcus thermophilus*, ⅘ ounce of *Lactobacillus bulgaricus*, and 1 dram of *Propionibacterium shermanii*, which is called the eye-former. All these are available (see Appendix 3), and they are needed by the home maker. Yogurt contains the first two and can be used as a source of them, if necessary.

The amount of rennet used varies from one maker to another. Since Gruyère making has remained a family operation, the makers decide for themselves such details of manufacture. The temperature at renneting also varies. Some makers in spring rennet at 83 to 89 degrees, in summer at 77 to 80 degrees, and in winter at 95 to 104 degrees, which shows the extreme variation possible in the procedure. The renneting temperature obviously is not a critical consideration in making Gruyère. Some cut in thirty minutes, others in forty-five. Some contend thirty-five minutes is ideal. These variations are perhaps important, but since the cheeses produced by the differing methods are similar we are going to assume that the differences are provincial idiosyncrasies. For the purposes of our recipe, ½ ounce of rennet extract will, mixed with 20 gallons of milk, generally produce in thirty-five minutes at 90 degrees a curd which is firm enough.

The rennet is mixed with a glass of water and stirred into the milk for five minutes; should scum rise to the surface, it is removed. The vat is covered, and the milk is left to coagulate for another twenty-five minutes. The *patron* I visited stirred the top of the milk occasionally before coagulation began and turned the top milk into the main body of the milk, to keep the cream from rising.

When the curd could hold up a wooden stirrer—a "wooden hand" shaped like a grain shovel—he cut the curd both ways, using a Swiss cheese harp, which made a battery of 1-inch cuts; he cut the 1-inch cubes using a figure-eight pattern in the cutting. Some makers cut the curd much smaller, as small as ¼- or even ⅛-inch cubes, particularly in the spring, this variation having to do with the effects of warm weather on the curing of the cheeses. Also, if the milk is not quite fresh enough, the curds are cut smaller.

The curds were left in the warm whey for five minutes;

some makers remove part of the whey as a matter of convenience. After these five minutes—with some makers four, some ten—stirring was commenced, and it continued, slowly at first, then more quickly, for twenty to thirty minutes, as the curd acquired a mild firmness.

The curd was then heated during a thirty-minute period to 127 degrees for a 3 percent milk, higher for a 3.3 percent milk, and up to 139 degrees for a 3.5 percent milk. Cooking is done in two stages, the first stage to 104 degrees, and the second stage, the last fifteen minutes, to the peak temperature. The curds and whey are stirred during the heating process.

The curds will squeak between the teeth. They are left in the whey to scald, the stirring continuing occasionally for ten to sixty minutes, until they no longer squeak. They are quite firm. This is called "stirring out." (If you have a pH tester, the pH of the hot whey at completion will be between 6.3 and 6.4.) The curds will be dry when a handful are pressed together, and the grains will separate easily when rubbed. The curds that I have tasted at this stage of processing were rubbery and nearly tasteless.

The *patron,* once he was satisfied with the curd's maturity, dumped a bucketful of cold whey into the big vat and stopped the stirring. The bucket of whey is not a requirement—it serves to lower the temperature quickly and therefore give respite to the fermenting, scalding process. The curds were allowed to settle to the bottom, to form a cohesive mass. The vats used are actually kettles and are round at the bottom, and the shape assists the curds in forming the mass.

After five to ten minutes the mass of curds was gathered in a large dripping cloth, which was hoisted above the kettle to drip; in a few seconds it was brought to the press, where the curds were released into a hoop, a shallow, open-ended cylinder with metal clamps on the sides to tighten or release the sides. The mass had been removed from the vat unbroken, in a single piece. The hoop, set on a draining board, was lined with coarse cloth, and the steaming curds were allowed to pile above the top of the hoop 2 or 3 inches; that is, the hoop was about 8 inches tall, and the clothed bag of curds was about 10 inches deep. Wet, warm cloths were put over the top of the pasty, steaming mass. The *patron* put a second and third cloth on and tucked them into the hoop. He tightened and secured the hoop's own band. On top he put the wooden follower, a wooden plate which fit the mold. Then he activated his press, gently forcing the mass down to within an inch of the top of the hoop.

A few minutes later the pressure was eased and the top cloths were removed; two freshly wet cloths were put on to replace them. The heavy cheese was turned, still in its hoop. Already it had a rind, and its own body was set. The hoop was loosened, and the ends of the cloths, those just applied to the other side, were pulled through and folded over the cheese, but not before a clean damp cloth was laid across the top and wedged down neatly into the hoop with the heel of the hand. The ends of the other cloths were then folded over, the hoop was tightened, the follower was set on top, and pressure was once more applied, this time until the cheese sank to the hoop's top.

The cheese was to be turned five times during the first twenty-four hours of its life, but its size was set during the first and second pressings. The first turning came in fifteen minutes, the second in thirty minutes more, the third after an hour more. Some makers use six or seven, rather than five, turnings, and if the milk is less than ideally fresh, a maker is likely to turn the cheese more often at the beginning of the pressing process.

The pressure needed is not as great for a Gruyère as for

an Emmenthal. About 18 to 22 pounds is enough initially
even for a large cheese. It is important with Gruyère to press
while the cheese is warm and to keep it from cooling too
quickly. Lukewarm cloths help. Even so, during the first several hours in the press the cheese will fall from 125 degrees
or so to about 86 degrees.

The process sounds difficult, I realize. It is, but with a small
Gruyère it is less so.

The hoop for a 16-pound finished cheese would be 15 by 5
inches, or thereabouts. The pressure would be less than for a
large cheese.

A chart for pressing goes like this:

Cheese's Weight	Pressure at First	Pressure at Last
16–35 lbs.	1–2 lbs. per lb.	3–5 lbs. per lb.
35–55 lbs.	2–3 lbs. per lb.	5–6 lbs. per lb.
55–75 lbs.	3–5 lbs. per lb.	6–8 lbs. per lb.
75–90 lbs.	3–5 lbs. per lb.	8–10 lbs. per lb.
90–105 lbs.	3–5 lbs. per lb.	10–12 lbs. per lb.

At the end of twenty-four hours, after its several cloth
changes, the Gruyère cheese is taken from the press and moved
to the salting room. (Some makers use an intermediate step;
they put the cheese in a salt brine for twelve hours—or twenty-
four or even longer—turning it either once or three times and
sprinkling dry salt on its exposed surface, to toughen its rind,
but this is not necessary.) The salting room's temperature
should be 52 to 55 degrees and its relative humidity 80 to 85
percent.

In the low-temperature salting room, the cheese is sprinkled
liberally with salt on the top and edge by means of a slotted
ladle or spoon. After several hours, when the salt has dissolved, the cheese is rubbed vigorously with a towel on the top

and edge, on the salted surfaces. Two days later it is turned and salted on the other side and again on its edge and, once the salt has dissolved, is rubbed vigorously with a towel. This process is repeated every second day for a week. The amount of salt used for a cheese is 2 percent of the weight of the cheese, on average; up to twice that much salt is used in rooms warmer than the ideal, in order to slow the curing process. The salt should not be kept in a metal container, for the metal contamination is said to cause the cheese's curd to turn blue.

You notice that Gruyère cheeses are wiped but not brushed. The reason is that the bacteria of the cheese are important to its ripening, this being the chief difference between a Gruyère and an Emmenthal, and the colonies of bacteria are unable to survive brushing as well as they can rubbing.

The Gruyère cheeses are moved on their shelves occasionally. Otherwise the rind remains too damp and spots of mold will appear. In warm seasons the more diligent makers also lift the cheeses once or twice daily to cool and air the undersides.

After a week in the salting room, the cheeses are taken to a warmer room, 58 to 65 degrees, with humidity of 85 to 90 percent, in order to permit a faster curing. There should be still air, no drafts in this room. Sweaty walls and damp floors are to be avoided, however, since they lead to the development of black mold. At temperatures higher than 65 degrees, the cheese is likely to develop larger eyes and a taste like that of Emmenthal, so the temperature should be controlled. Mild salting continues for two months and a half. At the end of three months, the cheeses are washed, two or three times in succession, for two or three days.

Some makers rub a white wine into the cheese in order to attain additional flavor.

As you see, the primary curing requires three to four months. At this age frequently the cheeses are taken to market in France, but they are not ready to be eaten until nine to twelve months old. After twelve months of age, the rind is likely to become noticeably heavier, and over the following two months the cheese usually will become too ripe, the rind getting crusty and the flesh becoming too sharp.

The Gruyère gains 2 percent in weight because of the salting, but it loses 6 to 10 percent of its weight in the total curing process.

Gruyère in France is likely to have sharp edges. Rounded edges can be achieved by using a shallower hoop, so that at the first pressing the cloth-wrapped mass of curds will stand as much as 5 inches above the hoop, at the second, 2 to 3 inches above, and at the third, within an inch or two of the top. An Emmenthal, whether made in France or Switzerland, always has rounded edges. The larger the cheese, the more important the rounded edges become, being less likely to chip during the many turnings.

The Gruyère rind assumes a color from yellow to deep red. It has the texture of the wrapping cloths, which usually are somewhat rough. The cheese is light colored and has a soft flesh which melts, or at least leaves the impression of melting, on the tongue. The taste is nut-like.

The *patron* I visited in France had three copper kettles. As he finished renneting in kettle number 1, he would proceed to heat and rennet in kettle number 2, then later in kettle number 3, finishing in time to start the cutting at kettle number 1. The three men worked together without instructions one to the other. There was no need. Together they made fourteen hundred cheeses a year.

They also made cream cheeses from the cream removed from the milk, a soft cheese of which they spoke disparagingly. The soft cheese was excellent, but these were makers of hard cheeses and were proud only of the big cheeses, ones they could depend on, even lean on, which they wrestled in and out of the house cellar, which would not turn sour because of changing weather or something unknown and unknowable.

The net used to remove the curd from the kettles was on a metal frame made to fit the kettles being used. The net was linen, and the circular metal frame had a long handle; the hoop was moved down along the side of the kettle, went under the mass of curd, then up the other side of the kettle, capturing the whole lot. The net was transported by a pulley to the hoop, the process of capture and delivery to the hoop taking less than a minute. With 20 gallons of milk, the cheesemaker might not need so elaborate a system, but it is desirable that the curd be out of the whey only briefly before pressing.

A small amount of curd, two handfuls, had been lost in the vat when the body of curd was removed. These bits were pressed together by the *patron* in his hands, and at the second pressing the ball was laid against the side of the cheese, where it was to be incorporated. Later that clot of cheese would be used to receive the date the cheese was made.

As my wife and I were leaving, the *patron* gave us a few soft-cheese molds, which I wanted and which he seemed to think little of. He also gave us one of the big nets used to capture the curds in, and he did seem to think a good deal of that, and so did—so do—we.

We drove out into the French countryside, I recall, and came upon a little restaurant near the railroad tracks, at a crossing and gatehouse. We thought we might get a bowl of soup. The only other people in the place were farm workers, two long tables of them, and two French countrywomen, the cooks. There was one menu and no soup, only a fixed lunch. Very well, we said, bring us what the others are eating.

We were served a four-course meal, requiring over an hour to eat. First came for each of us a baked bowl of macaroni, then for each of us a fish, fried with a delicate lemon-flavored crust. The salad course was excellent. The bread had been baked that morning by the two women. The wine was a respectable *vin ordinaire* served in carafes. The dessert and coffee were delicious. You might want to contrast this restaurant with places farm workers eat in near your town.

Cantal

The French have not given much emphasis to hard cheeses. Among the few they make are the Cantal, also called Fourmé, a delicious yellow cheese, quite firm, made for centuries in the region of the Auvergne Mountains in the Department of Cantal. Some say it is the oldest cheese of France. Made by farmers to this day, it is a pressed cheese, not unlike Cheshire or Cheddar in manufacture and shape. Its flesh is smooth and firm and pale yellow. The taste is piquant. Most of my friends find it mild enough for their liking, and many prefer it to Cheddar. There is no distinctive aroma to a Cantal. Its shape is cylindrical. Its size as a rule is 12 to 14 inches in diameter and about the same height. Its weight can be as much as 120 pounds; a more usual weight is 75 pounds, and the smallest Cantals made are 40 pounds. I suppose a 5- or 10-pound cheese is possible.

For the Cantal, the cows are milked in the fields, and the milk is taken directly to the cheesemaking room, traditionally in 4-gallon wooden buckets. The cheesemakers for decades have been advised to use metal cans, but some still retain the wooden ones, tradition obviously being of more consequence to them than sterility or convenience.

Fifty gallons of milk will make a 40-pound Cantal cheese. The milk is about 3.5 percent butterfat. It is filtered through cloth directly into the vats, and since it is fresh from the udders of the cows, it arrives while still warm, often at the renneting temperature, 86 degrees.

Natural lamb's rennet, actually strips of lamb's stomach, was used in the old days, but that has given way over the past fifty years to commercially prepared rennet extract. The amount of rennet is measured to yield a cuttable curd in one hour, about 2 drams to 5 ½ gallons. A coagulation more rapid than that will make a curd which will become too dry for this particular cheese. A coagulation that is too slow, that takes too long, results in a curd that lacks the necessary consistency to meld as a cheese unless the maker waits patiently for the curd to ripen in the vat before cutting begins. The moment for cutting is determined by two means. One is the time-honored way: insertion of a forefinger to see whether the cheese makes a break before it and closes after it, leaving in the scar a little river of clear whey. The whey should not be white. As a second test, the Cantal maker cuts a gash in the custardy mass with a razor or sharp, thin knife, and if the coagulation is at the proper stage, this cut will remain open and will fill with clear whey, showing that the curd is firm enough.

During the hour or more of coagulation, care should be taken to keep the curds and whey at about 86 degrees.

The Cantal maker cuts the coagulate into cubes not much

larger than pea size. The bits of curd are gathered at the bottom of the vat and pressed together. When they have matted, the whey is removed.

The matted cake of curd is transferred to shallow dishes to drain. The whey runs off through holes in the dishes. A cloth or bag will do as well. The cake is pressed with the hands, gently kneaded in order to assist it to drain. Then slight pressure is applied to it—in olden days a milkmaid would kneel on a board set on top of it, much as the Derby maids used to do.

The cakes of curds, once pressed, are called *tones*. Several *tones* are combined to make a cheese.

The *tones* are now placed in a wooden vat into which an older *tone*, one which has already undergone a few days' fermentation, has been left. A cover is put on the vat, and the vat is carried to a room 50 to 65 degrees in temperature.

In a day or two the *tones* take on a yellowish color. By then the fermentation gases have made holes in the cheese. The *tones* are now crumbled up on a three-legged table, and the pieces are ground, usually by a mill. The crumbled *tones* are then mixed, *tones* of different ages often being combined, and salted. The amount of salt is 3 to 4 percent salt by weight of the cheese.

The Cantal maker now prepares to press the cheese. He puts the crumbled, salted pieces into a cloth-lined wooden hoop, a mold, similar to that used by Gruyère makers. The pressing requires thirty-six to forty-eight hours. In the first twenty-four hours the cheese is turned three or four times, its wet cloths being changed for dry ones each time.

After the cheese is removed from the press, it is left in an airy room to dry. When dry on its rind, it is taken to the cellar, where it ripens for three or four months, or sometimes a month or so longer, now and again being washed with slightly salty water and turned, much like a Gruyère. The rind of a ripe Cantal is gray, and the gray deepens with age. If over-aged the cheese will become hard and soapy.

9

Cheddar—Two Ways to Make It

Cheddar

In his *Brittania*, written in 1586, William Camden said that the Romans taught the Britons to make cheese. Later in the book he writes, "West of Wells, just under Mendippe Hills lies Cheddar, famous for excellent and prodigious cheese made there, some of which require more than a man's strength to put them on the table. They have a delicate taste, equalling if not excelling Parmesan."

The largest Cheddar ever made in England weighed 1,100 pounds; it stood 20 inches tall and had a 9-foot, 4-inch diameter. It was presented as a gift to Queen Victoria, who sent it away on a tour of England and refused once the tour was over to have it back. The largest practical size for Cheddar is 80 pounds, and from time immemorial Cheddar makers in Somerset have made small 7- to 10-pound cheeses, which they call "truckles," and which are about equal in quality to large Cheddar, though, of course, they cure quicker and have less longevity.

Cheddar today constitutes over half the cheese made in England, and various versions of it are made in the United States, Canada, Australia, and other countries, sometimes commendably, sometimes with bitter or soapy results. The quantity of farmhouse Cheddar made in England today will not meet the market demands of that country, and the cheese cannot legally be imported into the United States because of a shameful law passed to protect our own cheesemaking industry.

The best Cheddars are made in the six-month period after April 1, when the pastures are richest. May and June are perhaps the best time of all. The old makers used Frisian-Holsteins or Shorthorn cows, preferring the latter because they gave slightly richer milk. A milk having about 3.5 percent butterfat is best.

I will give two recipes, one in use in Cheddar factories today, and the other employed in the nineteenth century in Somerset.

Dunlop cheese, made in Ayrshire, is a Scotch type of Cheddar, farmhouse-made in the old days. It was a useful, dependable cheese, sweeter than Cheddar and with less bite to its flavor. It is the only Scotch cheese to become generally known. No doubt local cheeses survive even today, in certain isolated valleys in Aberdeenshire and Orkney.

Incidentally, there is nothing wrong with the word *Scotch* when used in connection with food and drink. To refer to a

"Scottish" cheese is as ludicrous as a "Scotch" lass would be—if a Scottish lass could ever be ludicrous.

The factory method usually involves vast quantities of milk, but I will translate it into 10-gallon terms, which will make one truckle.

The milk can be pasteurized, but unless you suspect the milk's health there is no reason to pasteurize a cheese you plan to age more than three months, and certainly you will want to age a Cheddar. A cheese made from milk that isn't clean and pure will be ruined in a three-month curing process and nobody will eat it. Of course, you lose the cheese that way. If you do decide to pasteurize the milk, see the comment at the end of this recipe, as well as the section on pasteurization in Appendix 1.

A starter is added, about 1 percent active lactic starter in summer and fall, up to 2 percent active lactic starter in May and June, when the cow's milk is less acid. This starter can be ordered (see Appendix 3), or buttermilk can be substituted. Factories usually color the cheese, and you can, too, if you like, using 2 ½ ml. annatto cheese color for 10 American gallons, which will make a straw-colored cheese, or more if you choose.

Whole milk testing about 3.5 percent butterfat is used.

Rennet is added, 3 ½ drams for 10 gallons of milk. Dilute it with water before pouring it into the milk. Stir the mixture for five minutes, then cover the vat and let it stand for twenty-five minutes.

Test the curd with your finger to be sure it breaks evenly. When it does, cut it into small cubes, as small as ¼ inch if possible. Gently stir them for five minutes, then slowly increase the heat for half an hour, no more than 2 degrees increase in five minutes, stirring steadily, until 100 degrees is attained. For the next forty-five minutes, stir the curds and whey occasionally.

At the end of that period, allow the curds to settle on the bottom of the vat and take off some of the whey, which will have a greenish color; remove the whey until the curds are 1 inch below the surface. Make a trench down the center of the vat—that is, stack the curd on opposite sides of the vat, leaving a river of whey between them. Remove the whey and allow the two piles of curds to become cohesive. If your vat has a plug to facilitate drainage, all the better. If not, you will have to devise another way to remove the whey—cups or towels or a bulb baster, I imagine.

Cut the two mounds of matted curds into blocks, making three or four blocks out of each, and leave them on the bottom of the vat about an inch apart. You will want to tilt the vat slightly so that the whey will gather at one end and can be removed. Try to maintain the temperature at 100 degrees; one way to help do this is to put damp cloths, wet with warm whey, over the vat. Another way is to set the vat in a bathtub containing 100-degree water, if you and a friend can lift it.

Twice, at approximately fifteen-minute intervals, turn the curd blocks over. Any loose curds can be swept under the blocks.

Next, pile the blocks two deep. In fifteen minutes turn these double blocks, and repeat the turning every fifteen minutes for between one and two hours, exposing new surfaces of the blocks. (The acidity rating will come to read 0.6 percent.) Toward the end of the process, you can stack the blocks three deep. If gas holes or unclean flavor are detected, continue with this cheddaring period until the curd becomes quite firm (0.8 percent titratable acidity); if no such defects occur, proceed at once to tear the curd into small pieces, using your hands or a mill, then into yet smaller pieces, and salt them with a coarse, dry salt, 4 to 4 ½ ounces of salt to 12 pounds of curd. Simply sprinkle the salt on the pieces of curd as you stir them, and it is best to apply the salt in three batches, with five to ten minutes elapsing between applications. The salting and stirring process should take about thirty minutes.

Put the pieces of curds in a cloth-lined hoop. The cloth might well be a muslin bag. Close the cloth or bag over the top, put the hoop in a press, and apply pressure. Pressure is comparatively heavy from the start, calculated on a hydraulic press at 20 pounds per square inch of surface measurement of the top of the cheese.

In thirty to sixty minutes, take the cheese out of the press and straighten its bandage. You might want to use a smoother bandage now, in order to keep deep wrinkles from forming, and it is helpful to dampen the bandage with warm salt water. Reverse the cheese and return it to press, applying heavy pressure overnight, 20 to 25 pounds per square inch. The next morning you will have a Cheddar, hopefully neatly clothed in its bandage, ready to be dried in an airy room for a day or two before it is taken to the cellar.

If the cloth has gone awry, you can straighten it or apply a new one. Then dip the clothed cheese in hot water and return it briefly to the press.

When the cloth is dry, write the date of manufacture on it. Write your name on it too, if the process seemed to go all right. For three or four days it ought to be kept at 60 degrees and about 60 percent relative humidity; variations are permitted, however. On the fourth or fifth day, the cheese can be coated with paraffin. Factories heat the paraffin to 245 degrees and apply it to the cheese in six seconds; they can dip a cheese all at once. You might need to dip half the cheese at a time. The paraffin ought to be heated in a double boiler and not beyond 245 degrees, if that hot. Color the wax with non-toxic crayons or colorings if you like.

When the paraffin has hardened on the cheese, you can put the cheese in a box and set it in the curing room. The cheese should be turned daily for seven days and occasionally thereafter. Wipe it, if necessary, with a damp cloth. A factory in England cures Cheddar at 46 to 50 degrees. An American factory is likely to cure it at 36 degrees. At that temperature the flavor of a large cheese matures in twelve months—though there is scarcely a factory that would think of keeping many cheeses twelve months; also the flavor would not fully develop at such a low temperature even if they did. At home your cheese will do well, do better, at a temperature of 55 to 60 degrees, and it will mature much sooner. A large unpasteurized Cheddar will achieve its best flavor and texture in six months at about 58 degrees average temperature, a truckle in four or five months.

If you would like to make a washed-curd Cheddar, after milling the curd cover the curd with 60-degree water, hold the curd under water without stirring for fifteen minutes, remove it, and proceed with salting.

Should you want to use this recipe and pasteurize the milk, do so, then cool the milk to renneting temperature. Use half as much starter and mill the curd when an acidity rating of 0.6 percent is present.

Cheddar—Nineteenth-century Method

This is a detailed account. It might bore you unless you are as interested in the matter at hand as I am. My aim is to set down as closely as I can just how the best Cheddar makers made Cheddar cheese in Somerset, England, in the nineteenth century. I realize nobody makes them that way today, maybe nobody ever will make them that way again, but I am unwilling to assume that or to leave such important matters to our dairying industry, which explains all too succinctly that the public's tastes change, that mild foods now are the ones in demand. Perhaps so, but I suspect the public is fleeing the bitterness the makers so often get in their cheeses. It is striking that each change in the public's taste is one that makes manufacture easier and cheaper and more profitable.

I will set down now the old description that I have assembled, admitting it is impractical—I know some impractical people read books. With cheeses made in this impractical way, the reputation of English Cheddar was established.

The Somerset makers used last evening's and this morning's milk, last evening's milk having been kept at a temperature of 50 degrees in 70-degree weather, 63 degrees in 50-degree weather. The morning milk was mixed with it as soon as it came in from the milkers. The ideal ripeness was indicated by an acidity reading of 0.21 percent. If the mixed milk was short of that, the makers waited for it to mature, or heated the mixed milk slightly to encourage ripeness, or added starter, which usually was whey saved from the previous day's cheesemaking.

The starter was stirrred into the milk only three to five minutes before renneting. It was not necessary to wait for the milk to reach the state of desired ripeness; the amount of starter was determined as the amount required to bring about ripeness during the process itself. If the milk was absolutely fresh, was morning's milk only, the makers would add about a quart of whey or buttermilk for every 12 ½ American gallons of milk. If the milk was ripe but not quite ripe enough,

they would add half a pint of starter for 12 ½ gallons. They had no way to make acidity tests until late in the century, and a fair amount of guesswork was involved.

Somerset makers had found that, with higher temperature of renneting, the cheese was not as fine as with lower temperature; also, the cheese did not keep so well, nor did it have the mellowness which they considered one of the glories of Cheddar cheese. Furthermore, the renneting temperature was gauged by air temperature, and by the quantity of the milk to be used. The amount of rennet used was sufficient to produce the start of coagulation in twenty minutes and a curd of proper firmness in about an hour. "It is found that, as that is departed from, whatever the other advantages gained, mildness, long-keeping qualities, and fine flavor are lost in proportion," says one of the old books, written by a Somerset cheesemaker and dairy school principal, John Oliver. The following chart gives the renneting temperatures as he listed them.

MILK RENNETING TEMPERATURES

Air Temperature	200 Gallons	100 Gallons	50 Gallons
65°	80°	81°	82°
60°	82°	83°	84°
55°	84°	85°	86°

The milk was stirred three to five minutes, then gently stirred, mostly on the surface, for five to ten more minutes; then stirring was gradually decreased until coagulation began. Most of the cheese vats were cylindrical, and in order to keep the milk from swinging whirlpool fashion, which might produce a severe loss of fat should coagulation unexpectedly set in, a stirring motion across the vat in various directions was used.

If coagulation required more or less than twenty minutes to begin, it was assumed that the rest of the work would proceed with more or less speed throughout, accordingly. A toothpick floating on top of the milk will stop moving at the point of initial coagulation, as by now you know.

Once coagulation began, the vat was covered, usually with wooden boards, although some small oblong vats had an entire cover with a hinged flap. A cloth covering was not believed to be sufficient. The intent of the additional insulation was to keep the upper 2 or 3 inches of curd from maturing at a cooler temperature than the rest, which would give the cheese a tougher body.

To test the curd before cutting, a finger was stuck into it, then lifted out to see whether a clean break was made—also to see whether part of the curd remained on the finger, in which case the curd was thought to be too weak for cutting. This is, of course, the standard test of almost all cheese-makers.

The curd was first cut into 6- to 8-inch squares by a knife. These blocks were then reduced by cutting and splitting, often by a skimmer. A skimmer was a perforated spoon which had a handle 1 to 1 ½ feet long, depending on the depth of the vat, the skimmer at times having to reach the bottom. It was sunk into the vat edgewise and was brought up under a block, raising it so that the block split into two or three parts. The skimmer was then returned, to get under another block and break it. The movement was kept slow and steady. Sometimes the skimmer entered at the middle of a block, dividing it on the way down. Use of the skimmer permitted the curd to split along its grain, irregularly, forming irregular pieces. It would cut through larger pieces in its downward movement and would exert upward pressure on both the small and larger pieces as it came up under them. Its work was done when all the pieces were 3 to 4 inches across. By this time fragments of the proper size were floating in whey, hopefully clear whey, for the splitting of the curd along its seams permitted the curd to retain a higher percentage of its butterfat than would any other method.

At this point, as a further step, the curd was split by a breaker, a frame with wires stretched across it, the wires varying from ⅛ to ¹⁄₁₀ inch in diameter and set 1 to 1 ¼ inches apart. The breaker had a long handle so that both hands could be used to push it through the curds and whey, causing the curds to split along the grain. The object was to break them into ³⁄₁₆-inch cubes. If the breaker moved too fast, the whey became white with fat globules; however, the process had to be done expeditiously in order not to permit the curds to harden before the splitting was completed, in which case the breaker would simply be stirring curds and whey. At first the breaker's passes were slow, but the speed increased steadily and in a large vat became quite fast ultimately. Instructions given for breaking include this comment from Mr. Oliver: "Mind must dismiss all other matters for the short time devoted to it and give the best attention to the work in hand, just as a painter on an exhibition painting or a musician in solo performance before a large audience must do." We understand that a skilled Somerset Cheddar maker was able to break a vat of curds uniformly, with so little loss of fat that, at the finish, the whey was almost as clear as wine.

In a large vat, the breaking took from one-half to one hour, which is why Somerset makers learned to break left as well as right handed.

Once the curds were uniform in size, the curds and whey were scalded. The temperature ranged from 95 to 100 degrees according to the temperature of the air and the quantity of milk. A temperature of 97 degrees was believed to be ideal. A chart for scalding temperatures is as follows:

MILK SCALDING TEMPERATURES

Air	200 Gallons	100 Gallons
65°	96°	98°
60°	97°	99°
55°	98°	100°

It was believed that the scalding temperature should never exceed 102 degrees. The scalding temperature was achieved

slowly, fifteen to twenty minutes being required. The amount
of time the curds were left at scalding temperature was not
constant. Mr. Oliver writes concerning this:

> It is wise to cast time out of the reckoning; and having
> chosen a proper scalding temperature, to carry on the
> work until the desired hardness is obtained, however long
> it may take. Only in this way can a regular result be
> secured, for curds differ from day to day. . . .

Stirring was continued, but more slowly, until the curd
had reached a certain hardness, which

> cannot easily be described. If before that some be
> squeezed in the hand, it clings together and mashes upon
> being pressed by the thumb; but when it is firm enough
> it will, under like treatment, rub abroad into its original
> particles. The actual point at which the stirring should
> cease occurs a little later, generally within a few minutes;
> and as it offers no evidence excepting a slightly greater
> firmness, it can only be learned by direct teaching or ex-
> perience. It is often described as "shotty" but this conveys
> an impression of a greater hardness than is desirable, and
> is likely to mislead. The stopping point also depends
> somewhat on the size of the cheese, for a small one needs
> a fraction more moisture than a large one, because it
> loses proportionately more in curing. The difference is
> from one to five percent, as shown by experience, but this
> cannot be calculated by any rule, and there is no test by
> which the amount present can be determined at the mo-
> ment when it must be known.

Once the curd had reached the desired hardness, it was
allowed to sink and pack, or mat together in a solid body.

The purpose of the matting was to get the curd into a form that could retain heat. A properly made curd would mat solid in thirty minutes, more or less. In large vats with 100 gallons or more, the curd was allowed to sink evenly over the bottom; with small quantities of milk the curd was drawn up at one end in a pile.

Many makers removed the whey with a siphon made of tinned steel and having a strainer made of perforated brass. Other makers released the whey through a tap.

Once the whey was removed, the curd was divided into two parts by a knife. The halves were drawn toward the sides of the vat, leaving a gutter between, so that the whey as it freed itself could flow out.

The curd was cut into squares, and a scoop about the size of these squares was used to lift them one by one, to turn each one over, and to stack them on top of one another, two or three deep, the two stacks occupying finally one-fourth to one-third of the bottom of the vat. The loose particles were then brushed out of the gutter with a hairbrush or a yellow whisk broom. Since a whisk broom might scatter the curd, the fibers of the broom were tied lower than usual, until such time as they had been shortened by wear.

Once the curd was piled and the drainage channel was cleared, the curd was covered with strainer cloths, which had been wrung out in warm whey just before use, and their ends were tucked under the lower edges of the piles of curds. The vat was then covered and left until the curd had become solid, usually fifteen to twenty-five minutes. In this way the curd would dry, changing from being slightly harsh and gritty to the touch to being softer, and from a crumbly texture to a stringy one. The temperature of the curd at this point was between 90 and 95 degrees.

The depth of the piles of curd diminished as the whey flowed out. The curd was cut again and restacked, the previously exposed edges of the old blocks being turned away from the air. The cutting was generally done in halves or quarters in order to facilitate repiling. One or two damp cloths were put over the piles of curd.

Some makers after the first cutting piled the curd on a wooden rack rather than on the vat bottom; the rack had a cloth cover laid over it, and the curd was put on the cloth. The older method was to use the bottom of the vat without the wooden racks.

As the curd was divided at intervals and restacked, the temperature was slowly reduced, and the progress of fermentation became steadily slower. At the end of the process, the curd was in pieces about 4 inches square by 2 or 3 inches thick, the pieces being uniform insofar as possible. At each cutting, or tearing, the curds were turned over from their previous position. The time at which any division ought to take place was determined by the drying, the slight yellowing of the surfaces that were in contact with the air. Before the desired dryness of the curds was obtained, care was taken that the temperature did not fall below 78 degrees in 55-degree weather, 74 degrees in 60-degree weather and 70 degrees in 65-degree weather. The air in the making room, of course, was helping to bring about this dryness; the maker had to worry about the temperature, humidity, and circulation of the air. A dry air would dry the curd quicker than a moist one, but a moist one would dry it more quickly if passing rapidly over it. Also, if the air was warm, whether dry or moist, the curds were cut into somewhat smaller pieces, and if the air was cold, they were cut into somewhat larger pieces. It sounds complex, but in most cases it meant only that the windows and doors were open, or that an exhaust fan was put into operation, such fans being installed in some Somerset cheesemakers' rooms by the 1890s.

Proper dryness had been reached when the curd was flaky and was capable of being stripped into thin sheets of a few inches in length, like boiled chicken breasts. If dried too far, the curd's sheets became too thin, drew out too long, and were porous and even slimy.

The dried curd was milled; that is, it was torn into ragged pieces. The best form of mill neither cut nor ground, but "tore the curd asunder." When fragments of about ¼ inch in size were achieved, should any ill odor be noticed, the curds were aired by "shaking them abroad" with a scoop, 1 to 2 feet above the bottom of the vat. They were then salted at the rate of 1 pound to the curd from 50 gallons of milk.

The curds were not put into the cloth-lined hoops until they had reached the desired temperature: in a 65-degree room this was 60 degrees for the curd; in a 60-degree room, 62 degrees for the curd; in a 55-degree room, 64 degrees for the curd; and in a 50-degree room, 66 degrees for the curd. In summertime, when the makers could not cool the curd to these temperatures, some of them would leave the salted pieces in the mold, with no covering but a cloth, until the cooler night air reduced the temperature to the point at which the pressure would not cause the cheese to exude fat unduly.

In general, the old Cheddar shapes were cylindrical, as they still are, with diameter and depth about equal. Tradesmen preferred the larger cheeses, about 80 to 100 pounds, because they retained moisture better than the smaller ones. Some makers used double hoops and produced what was known as a Cheddar Double.

The larger the cheese, the more pressure it needed. However, for the first hour, only a pressure sufficient to cause dripping of the free whey was used. One maker wrote,

> Excess does mischief, especially at the outset, when it brings together the outer part too quickly, enclosing the air and free whey of the innerpart, and making the latter of a loose texture, or full of "eyes," as the case may be.

If heavy presses were used, the weight was increased next morning and again the evening of the same day, and the cheeses were ready for the curing room the day following. With light presses, the time the cheese was in the press was longer, three or four days.

If we think of the pressing in terms of its three stages, and if we also consider the different-sized cheeses, we can make a chart (but please remember that an English hundredweight —cwt.—is 112 lbs.):

	PRESSURE IN CWTS.		
Cheeses	*Stage 1*	*Stage 2*	*Stage 3*
14 lbs. or less	2	5	10
28 lbs. or less	3	7	15
40 lbs. or less	5	10	20
60 lbs. or less	7	14	25
80 lbs. or less	10	18	30

On the following morning after pressing, "as early as may be," the cheese was removed from the press and bandaged in a gray calico bandage, as described later. The cheese was marked with its date and was without delay taken to the curing room, where it was stored at 60 to 68 degrees, with 65 being ideal. Humidity was 78 to 88 percent.

For several weeks, the Cheddar cheese made by this recipe was practically tasteless. It began to develop its nutty flavor in two months, and by the third month had reached the first level of maturity. By then it was firm enough to be shipped, but if made by this recipe, it would, we are told by the old Somerset cheesemakers, be at its best when it was eighteen to twenty-four months old.

One variation of this old process replaces the breakers with cutting knives. Obviously that would be a much easier procedure, but concerning it we have severe remarks from our Somerset friend of the nineteenth century, Mr. Oliver:

> If the use of cutting tools tends to leave a larger proportion of whey in the curd, it also manifestly leads to more fermentation, a flavour earlier and stronger, and a shorter lease of good quality, and therefore violates the first essential of the system. It may be answered that there is an evident gain in weight by the larger proportion of whey secured by cutting implements. We admit it, but the Cheddar system does not seek quantity so much as quality; and when any dairyer takes to cutting tools in order to gain that advantage, he forsakes the Cheddar system and has no longer a right to call his product Cheddar cheese. Our forefathers knew better. In the middle years of the century an apparatus was brought out for breaking, to be worked by a revolving handle; this has disappeared because it could not bear the test of use— but it was consistent, for it presented only rounded surfaces to the curd. But in these latter days there have been brought into western dairies "cutting breakers," easier to use, quicker in action, etc., with sideblades of metal and flat or diamond-shaped wires; and these are the curse of those dairies, not only interfering with the integrity of the system, but also bringing about the cause for the

complaint that modern Cheddars (such have no right to
the name) do not keep as those did which made the system famous. The pastures of Somersetshire cannot save
cheeses which are so made. We are not concerned to dis-
pute the claim to superiority according to the standards
of this market or that show, where quick-ripening goods,
the product of cutting tools, are encouraged. They may
be more profitable to their makers, more pleasing to the
modern merchant and grocer, they may be the cheeses of
the future for all we know, but they simply are not Cheddars—any more than they are Cheshires or Stiltons.

To bandage one of the old type of Cheddars, a band was
sewn to fit the side of the cheese and to leave 1 ½ to 2 inches
of edges to overlap at top and bottom. The bandage was
slipped down over the cheese ½ to 1 inch at a time, an effort
being made to keep the bandage from twisting, which would
cause the seam of the bandage to leave an irregular mark on
the finished cheese. Once the cloth had been slipped around
the cheese, a circular piece of cloth was laid on the cheese,
and the overlapping edges were turned down upon it. Then
the follower of the hoop was laid on top of the cheese. The
cheese was turned over, hoop and all, and the other end of
the cheese was covered with a circular piece of cloth and the
edges of the side bandage were folded over.

The cheese was returned briefly to the press for consolida-
tion of the bandage.

When removed from the press, the overlapping borders of
the bandage on each end were sewn with double thread so as
to leave two free ends which could be drawn tight and tied.

Cheeses were stored on wooden shelves, 2 inches left between cheeses. The cheeses "will have need to be turned daily

(excepting on Sundays) for the first month, on alternate days during the second month, and afterwards twice weekly," Mr. Oliver tells us.

Cheeses up to 80 pounds were turned as follows: The right hand was slipped under the cheese and the left hand was placed at the top of the back of the cheese. The cheese was drawn from the shelf, the right hand supporting it, and it was turned over quickly toward the operator, so that the left hand then supported it, and was carefully slid back onto the shelf. Cheeses over 80 pounds were turned as they were lowered onto the operator's knee, then were lifted back onto the shelf.

Some makers greased their cheeses with whey butter in order to keep them from becoming too dry and cracking, but greasing was unnecessary when the proper humidity was maintained. The humidity was increased by watering the floor and decreased by opening ventilation windows or doors of the cellar.

I talked recently with Lester Kasper's son in Clintonville, Wisconsin. For seventeen years he helped his father make great Cheddar cheeses. "There isn't much to it," he told me.

"I know, I know that's so. Every cheese process is simple, once it's mastered," I said.

He told me his father did not pasteurize the milk. He used a process similar to the older one described in this book, but he did not use a breaker; he used curd knives, and he made acidity tests frequently during the process. He aged his cloth-dressed cheeses for up to two years.

Lester Kasper and his father before him won many blue ribbons in Wisconsin. Today I know of nobody in this country who makes cheeses with the method he used. I would be pleased to hear from anybody who does.

10

Camembert and Brie

We are now on holy ground. Or unholy. Yes unholy, I decide, for it is populated with black and green molds and spoil bacteria, as well as hungry, ambitious cheesemakers. You will not have much trouble making Camembert or Brie up to the curing stage, but that, I suggest, is prayerful business. You will not want to venture into its trembling set of challenges until you have a feel for cheesemaking and, along a more practical line, a curing room with temperature and humidity control. Your cheeses will need inoculation with the proper mold, but this is no longer a problem and is described in the recipes.

No presses are used.

Many people prefer Camembert or Brie to any other cheese

in the world, and the cheeses, properly made, are difficult to find in many places; especially scarce are the tan cheeses, which have taste characteristics more complex than the white. The making of either is worth the attention it requires, and I will give you the recipes for both.

A Camembert or Brie is a living being, and once cut it will not mature any more, not properly. If cut at the right time, all is well; if not, the cheese is handicapped.

A frozen or canned Brie or Camembert is an inferior product and ought to be named something else, if named at all. These two cheeses are like flowers that bloom in their own time and for a short time only, and they cannot be treated callously—at any rate, not at this time.

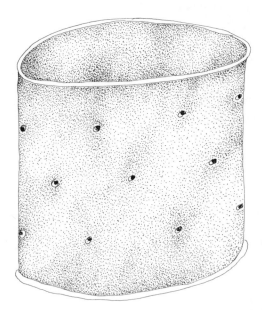

Camembert mold

French Camembert

I have several recipes for making Camembert, some of them dating back to early in this century, others contemporary. I also have a number of factory recipes. One factory maker told me when I toured his plant, "Anybody can make Camembert by a factory recipe, but the trouble is making it taste like Camembert." I suspect that one of the old makers in Normandy would say that not just anybody can make a Camembert, but if he does make one it will certainly taste like Camembert, maybe quite soon too much like Camembert.

When mature, Camembert is creamy and its flavor is delicate. When young, it is waxy and yellow. When overripe, it is runny and soon develops strong flavors.

A statue has been raised in Camembert, Normandy, to Marie Harel, a farmer's wife, who about 1790 supposedly invented the cheese. Actually, similar cheeses were made as early as the thirteenth century in France. I suspect Camembert was, but perhaps Mrs. Harel had a special knack with it. It is true to this day, as it was in hers, that excellent Camembert is made at Camembert, a village of the Orne Department, and it is made also in Normandy and Calvados.

Supposedly the cheese was named by Napoleon, who was first served it in Camembert.

Camembert is a mold-ripened cheese with a varicolored skin, white with tan variations, which must indicate a mixed bacterial growth. This would account for the richer taste, the creamier consistency, and the shorter life that the French cheese has when compared to any other country's imitations and even to the white-rind factory Camemberts now being turned out in France itself.

Camembert is usually made from whole cow's milk. Some people say cream is added, but this is not the case. In fact, often skimmed milk is added in proportions of one part skim to five parts whole. The cheeses are 4 ½ to 5 inches in diameter and weigh 8 to 12 ounces when cured. A suitable Camembert hoop or mold is 5 ½ inches in diameter and 5 inches high. If you want to get your own ready, coffee cans or any tin cans with nail-holes punched in them, from the inside out, will do.

I will give two methods of making this great cheese, the old home method and a new, factory way.

An Old Method of Camembert Making

Camembert was usually made only in autumn and spring, since the hot summer months imposed difficulties during the curing process. The milk was received uncooled from the milking barn and was strained into a wooden tub, the tub holding 7 ½ American gallons (6 imperial gallons). It was adjusted to 3.5 percent butterfat by addition, if necessary, of fresh skim milk. The milk was not pasteurized. The old people did not use metal tubs because the coagulation period was lengthy and, should the curd on the outside of the vessel get chilled, mixing it with the warmer, softer curd would cause irregularities in the finished cheeses.

The 7 ½ gallons made a dozen cheeses if a one-curd system was to be used or supplied half the curd for two dozen if the two-curd system was to be used, the latter system being preferred. In the two-curd system, the morning's milk was made up, and the curd was put in hoops to drain. Next morning the morning's milk was made into curds and these were added, the curds made on two successive days forming a cheese. This system had obvious time disadvantages, but it had three advantages: It permitted the cheese to drain with less loss through the oozing of the curd from the hoops; it exerted less weight on fresh curd at the bottom of the hoop, so that irregularities in the cheese were avoided; and the cheese was more evenly salted. As to the last point, in the one-curd system each cheese was salted on one side, and six to eight hours later on the other, simply because the cheese could not be turned over any sooner; salting the cheese at these two different times resulted in different mold developments on its two sides.

The mold which helped mature the cheese was introduced to the cheeses during the process of making them, at least for the first several makings in a new building, until the mold was well established on the shelves and walls of the curing room. To introduce the mold in the old-fashioned way, you will need to find a type of Camembert cheese you like, preferably one with a brownish cast to its crust, and from just below the crust of the cheese, which should be about half ripe, take half an ounce of curd and macerate it in a cup, adding to it about half a pint of pure 80-degree water. Thoroughly dissolve the cheese in the water, then strain it, and add what comes through the strainer to the milk you are using to make your Camemberts. A newer way is to order *Penicillium camemberti*, a mold culture, from a supplier and inoculate the cheese with it; this will tend to give you a white factory type of cheese, described in this chapter in detail.

In the old recipes, the renneting temperature for the milk was 80 to 82 degrees, the higher temperature being used in autumn. Rennet was added at the rate of ½ cc. liquid extract for each gallon of milk, the rennet being measured and then diluted one to six with water.

The rennet was poured into the milk and stirred into it for six minutes. Over the next twenty minutes the surface was rippled from time to time with a spoon, but not after coagulation set it. It was known that the cream, if allowed to rise, would interfere with the curing, the temperamental mold being unwilling to grow evenly on a surface which had bits of a creamy substance on it.

About 2 to 2 ½ hours after renneting, the curd was fully formed, as tested by the usual method, and it was ladled into hoops placed on mats and draining boards. A small board was set down first, a straw mat was put on top of it, and on that were placed the perforated, circular, open-ended molds, 5 ½ inches in diameter and 5 inches deep. The Camembert molds were made of one piece.

The hoops often had warm water poured over them before the curd was ladled into them, which helped to make the sides of the cheeses smooth.

The cheeses were left overnight in their hoops at about 65 degrees. Next morning they were about two-thirds their original height.

The following morning a similar quantity of milk was treated exactly as described above. Before it was added to the hoops, the top surface of yesterday's portions was carefully broken up with a wooden spoon or spatula to permit the two curds to join and to avoid the possibility of their later breaking apart. In ladling the second morning's milk, the maker often took nice-sized slices from the top of the vat, one for each hoop, and saved them for use later as a smooth top dressing. The hoops were filled and were left to drain at a temperature of about 65 degrees, not less than that. As the whey dripped out, the curds compacted forming a mass lower and lower in the mold.

When the two curds were approximately twenty-four and thirty-six hours old, the curds occupied the lower half of the mold and were firm enough to permit turning. To turn them, the cheesemaker put his left hand under the cheese, under the board or mat without removing the hoop, then inverted the hoop, steadying the cheese with his right hand as the cheese dropped a few inches in the hoop, and placed the hoop face down upon a fresh straw mat. This was risky, but not difficult for practiced hands, and one of the joys of Camembert making, then and now, is to be able to look down after such a maneuver and see that the cheese did survive the operation, and that its upturned surface has accepted the outline of the straw mat on which it had been resting.

(Should your cheeses settle in the hoop too rapidly, the milk used was not fresh enough or the temperature was higher than 65 degrees. If your cheeses did not drain sufficiently in the molds, the renneting temperature was probably too low or the temperature of the room in which the cheese was drained was under 65 degrees. A Camembert which drained too slowly was, the old makers knew, not going to be a good cheese and might as well be eaten fresh—it is delicious when fresh; they knew that in curing such a cheese it would become slimy on the outside, and the cheese could not ripen properly.)

When the cheese separated slightly from the sides of the hoop, the upper and old surfaces of the cheese were heavily salted, as much as ½ ounce of salt for each cheese. Six to eight hours later, the cheeses were taken out of the hoops and their other surfaces and their sides were salted with the same amount of salt.

The salted cheeses were placed on latticed shelves, usually in the same room in which they were made, and were turned twice a day. When they began to show a white, hairy mold, they were taken to the drying room, which was well ventilated. In order that currents of air could touch the cheese from all directions, the shelves for Camembert were often placed in the center of the room rather than along the walls. The temperature was 54 to 56 degrees and the air was "not too dry." If conditions were favorable, the mold would grow rapidly on the surfaces of the cheese, and blue tints would appear on the tips of the mold in two to three weeks, giving the cheese a gray-blue appearance.

The purposes of the drying room were to develop a relatively dry surface on the cheese and to make possible such mold development. (If the mold on your cheeses does not grow freely or if the cheeses shrink, the air is too dry. If the cheeses get greasy or if spots of dark green or black appear, the room is too cool or too damp. One suggestion from the old makers is that the cheeses be laid on the top shelves when first put in the room and then lowered as they ripen.)

Molds other than the desired one—such as green or black molds—were cut off the cheeses with a razor.

Once the blue tinge occurred and the cheeses felt soft and springy, usually at about three weeks of age, they were moved from the curing room to the cellar or a cave. Here it was damp and the air was still, with little ventilation. The temperature was about 50 degrees, and the humidity, I judge, was 85 percent or above. The shelves were covered with wheat straw, which was changed occasionally. At the lower temperature of the cellar, the mold's growth practically ceased. In two or three weeks the mold began to break down and to become reddish-brown, and the cheese became slightly sticky on its surfaces. The reddish colors and the sticky condition indicated that the cheeses were ripe; if kept too long, they would deteriorate and liquefy.

The total ripening process took about six weeks.

Decades ago the cheeses were packed in lots of six and were wrapped in straw. More recently they have been placed in wood-chip boxes and sent to market when about three-fourths ripe.

As you see, the making of Camembert is mostly a matter of curing. Conditions must be inviting to the mold, and to its friends.

When ripe, a Camembert should be soft to its center. A poorly made cheese is likely to have a layer of hard, sour curd in the center, even at the stage when the outside portions will be liquefying.

One can speed up the morning's work by renneting at 86 degrees and using twice as much rennet. This procedure will permit the curd to be ladled into the molds in one hour rather than in two hours or longer.

Factory-made Camembert

Factory Camembert usually is formed into 8-ounce wheels, 4 ½ inches by 1 inch high. If the finished cheese is more than an inch thick, the cheese is likely to ripen too fast on the outside, to become overripe before the inside of the cheese has ripened.

A hoop should be 4 ½ by 5 inches high. If you prefer, a square or rectangular hoop can be used, one about 4 by 4 by 5 inches high.

In factory-made Camembert as described here, the cheeses

ripen while their surfaces remain white; the surface does not turn blue-gray or reddish-brown at any stage.

Factories usually pasteurize milk that is to be used in Camembert and so at once limit the peaks of achievement, but I will report it as it is. They pasteurize the milk, then cool it to 90 degrees quickly. One way to cool it at home is to set the vat in cold running water.

Two percent active lactic starter (see Appendix 3 for suppliers) is added to the fresh milk and allowed to ripen it for twenty to thirty minutes.

Some factories color the milk, using as much as 14 drops of annatto cheese coloring for 17 gallons of milk.

The milk ripens until the titratable acidity is 0.22 percent, at which point ¼ ounce of rennet is added for 8 ½ American gallons of milk, the rennet being diluted with water (factories boil the water first, then cool it). After the rennet has been mixed into the milk for three minutes, the vat is covered and the milk is left to coagulate.

When firm curd has developed (in about forty-five minutes), either the curd is cut into ⅝-inch cubes, which are left for a few minutes to work in the whey, the temperature of the whey being kept at 90 degrees, or, better still, the curd is ladled uncut into the hoops. These open-ended, perforated cylinders rest on reed or nylon mats, which in turn rest on a draining board. The hoops are filled to capacity. No curd is added as the whey drains, nor is any pressure exerted. The room temperature should be 70 degrees.

Usually three hours will be required for the curd to drain enough to be turned; a worker sets a small metal plate on top of the hoop and quickly inverts the hoop. Two hours later the hoop is turned again. Thirty minutes later it is turned again. Thirty minutes later it is turned for the fourth and last time.

While resting in the mold, the cheese is sprayed on one side with a spray gun which releases a mist of *P. camemberti* culture, var. *Rogerii Thom,* in an aqueous spore suspension (see Appendix 3 for suppliers). The spray lightly passes over the cheese. In thirty minutes a worker turns the cheeses and sprays the other side lightly. He then leaves the cheese, still in its mold, for thirty minutes more.

The cheeses, ready now to be taken from the molds, are loosened around the edges with a knife and allowed to slip out and onto draining racks, where they are left at about 72 degrees for five or six hours without weights, or even cloth covers over them. At the end of that time they are salted, each cheese being dipped into a pail of coarse salt, usually one-half of the cheese at a time. Loose salt is shaken off and the cheese is put on a draining board and left overnight at about 70 degrees. The entire process to this point has been carried on at room temperature, 70 to 72 degrees.

Next morning the cheeses are put in the curing room, which in some factories is 50 degrees and has 95 to 98 percent relative humidity (in others, 55 degrees and 85 to 90 percent). The cheeses are laid on wooden racks which have narrow strips of cane latticed on them to permit air to circulate. After remaining undisturbed for about five days, or in any case as soon as the little white whiskers of mold appear on the surface, the cheeses are turned over for the first time in the curing room.

When they have a uniform mold, they are wrapped in tinfoil and stored at 50 degrees, 95 percent relative humidity, for seven days, then taken to a 40-degree room for re-wrapping and distribution. Since they cannot be stored for any length of time—*P. camemberti* continues ripening them even at low temperature—the chilled cheeses are distributed by factories as soon as they are packaged. They should be in the home of the consumer four or five weeks after packaging. By then they will, under most conditions, be soft and ripe.

Brie

Brie is made in the Department of Seine-et-Marne, southeast of Paris. It is certainly one of the most delicious, most highly honored cheeses in the world, and one of the most exasperating for the consumer, since there is only a fine line between underripe and overripe. When ripe, Brie is soft and quite creamy; when overripe, it has an offensive ammonia odor.

The cheese is harder to make than almost any other. Because of its flat shape, its low acidity, and its high moisture content, it seems to be much more susceptible even than a Camembert to irregularities in salting, handling, and curing, as well as to any impurities in the milk used. It is not a cheese to be approached by the amateur, or with a happy-go-lucky nonchalance by anybody. Even fifty years ago in France its manufacture was being transferred from the farmhouse to factories which could control its every stage of making and curing.

I will tell you how the cheese was made in farmhouses at that time, and you can try it if you want to.

The cheese is a flat disk. There are three sizes: 16 by 1 ⅔ inches, weighing about 6 pounds; 12 by 1 ⅓ inches, weighing 3 ½ pounds; and 5 ½ to 8 by 1 ¼ inches. The skin of some Bries is a mottled white, of others a reddish brown—and these are the better ones; the interior is a pale yellow and, when ripe, is almost a custard.

Brie is similar to Camembert and when fresh is identical to fresh Coulommiers. Its differences from both, the Brie distinctions, come in the curing and apparently are partially attributable to its flat shape. Some authorities suggest that bacteria, perhaps our reddish friend *Brevibacterium linens*, help in the curing of a farmhouse Brie. It is true that farmhouse cheeses are brownish red in color and differ markedly from the white factory product. In any event, the size itself, facilitating the exposure of so much of the cheese to the penicillin molds and to whatever bacteria naturally come to inhabit the curing room, is a controlling factor in the brown Brie's distinctive taste.

The curing room needs the same special attention given to the Camembert curing room. In fact, the two cheeses can share the same room.

The *petit* Brie is the easiest to make; it is less likely to break apart in the turnings and handlings. A cheese about 5 ½ inches by 1 ¼ inches is recommended for your first try. The mold should be four times as high—either that, or an extension, a metal sleeve, should be provided to hold the soft curd. There are no holes in the sides of Brie molds.

One pound of cheese can be made from 7 pounds of milk, which is about 3 ½ quarts. A cheese 5 ½ by 1 ¼ inches in size will weigh 1 ½ pounds. (A cheese 4 ½ by 1 ¼ weighs about 10 ounces.)

The milk must be absolutely clean. Any contamination in the milk will probably spoil the finished cheese. Perhaps for this reason milk used in France for Brie is not usually pasteurized—it is thought to be pure enough, and the process does affect detrimentally the curing and taste of the cheese. You do as you think best.

Contrary to what one might guess and some authors say, enriched milk is not used in a Brie. Actually the milk of Seine-et-Marne, which is not as rich as the milk of Normandy, is diluted by 10 percent of skim milk. The butterfat in the mixed milk was 3.25 to 3.50 percent. A higher butterfat was likely to lead to bacterial spoilage. In general the milk used fifty years ago was evening's milk kept overnight at about 65 degrees, mixed with morning's milk, or it was milk fresh— indeed warm—from the cows to which 10 percent of last night's skim milk was added. The acidity at renneting was low, about 0.18 percent.

The Brie is cured principally by penicillin spores, *P. camemberti* as a rule, since it has a high tolerance of salt and Brie is quite salty, and these spores were naturally dominant on the walls and shelves of the curing rooms. In making the cheese in your home, or trying to, you will perhaps want to encourage the spores by spraying them on the cheeses, which is what is done today in factories, and even initially on the curing room shelves and walls; or, instead of spraying them on the cheeses, you can add them to the milk before its coagulation or to the curds when they are ladled into the molds. The spores can be purchased (see Appendix 3). If you don't have the patience or time for that, you can introduce the spores to the cheese by making a culture from 1 ounce of ripe Brie; the flesh just under the rind is the best part for this.

Now to start.

The room in which you mix the milk should be 61 to 65 degrees.

The renneting temperature is 88 degrees, so milk fresh from the cow is probably near the proper temperature. To heat the milk practically any brass, copper, ceramic, steel, tin, or aluminum vat will do. Copper and ceramic are traditional.

The coagulation is to take 2 ½ to 3 hours. The usual amount of rennet needed is 4 to 4 ½ drams per 24 gallons of milk. The rennet should be mixed with about six times its own amount of tap water. If the measurement of rennet is too high, the coagulum forms too quickly and the cheese will therefore be too dry; if too little rennet is used, the coagulum will take too long to form and in consequence the cheese will take too long to dry and is likely "to run too much," to remain custardy and lack body.

The rennet should be stirred into the milk for five minutes. The surface of the milk should be rippled every five or ten minutes, intermittently, for another thirty minutes, but in no case after coagulation has begun. The temperature of the milk must be retained at 86 degrees throughout. One way to keep it constant is, as with other soft cheeses, to pour the milk before renneting into an insulated container, such as a picnic basket or ice bucket, and let the coagulation take place there. Another way is to set the vat in a bathtub and keep the temperature of the water in the tub at 86 degrees.

When the curd is ready, it will break clean over your finger, and the whey that fills the break will be limpid, not white. No coagulum will adhere to your finger. If the time required to reach this state is less than 2 or more than 3 ¼ hours, you might wisely decide to make cream cheese out of the curds and put aside your dreams of making a Brie just now. If the coagulation has taken proper time, carefully ladle the curd into the molds, using thin, horizontal slices. The room temperature should still be 61 to 65 degrees. The ladling should proceed gently but with reasonable swiftness.

Now cover the molds with a cloth and leave them.

At the end of twelve hours you can remove the extensions, if indeed you used them.

As the curd continues to sink even more in the molds, you are faced with yet a new problem. Since the cheese is broad and thin, turning it is a treacherous business, particularly now that the cheese is forming itself well below the top of the mold. To solve this problem, in France fifty or so years ago the farmer-makers used adjustable wooden bands, selecting for each Brie one not greater in height than the cheese's height. At the end of twenty-four hours a band was put around the hoop and the mold was rotated right, then left, so that the cheese came unstuck. The mold was lifted out of the band, and the band was tightened around the cheese. Thus the cheese was left, neatly bound in order to keep it from spreading, and could be turned over and handled easier than in the mold. Such wooden bands are not available today; metal bands could be used, but they are not available either. Efforts to use stiff plastic strips secured with thin rubber bands have been reasonably successful.

The Bries are now turned, as follows: The band is covered with a mat, then an individual-sized board. The cheese is sandwiched between mats, with a board under it and one over it, and a band around it. This cheese-filled sandwich is turned over, and the damp board and mat, which are now on top, are removed.

The cheeses can be stacked one on another, if you like. Otherwise each cheese should be covered with a clean mat or cloth.

The cheeses should be turned in about six hours, then again in another six hours.

Salting is the next obstacle, and the time for salting varies. If the coagulation took about 2 ½ hours to reach the proper breaking quality, the salting should be done twenty-four hours after the curd was ladled into the mold. If coagulation took longer, then the salting should be delayed up to twelve hours. If it took much less time, the salting should be done just before the board is put on. The amount of salt needed also varies. If the cheese has a dry body, too much salt adds to the breakability of the cheese; if the body is too wet, the salted crust will dry before the cheese is dry enough to sustain its shape and the crust will break. The moment to choose for salting is when the two sides show about the same amount of moisture. The salt should be dry and fine. A salt shaker is helpful. Hold the board which supports the cheese with one hand and salt the top of the cheese, starting at the outer edge and going in concentric circles toward the center. In about ten hours turn the cheese, remove the band, and salt the cheese on the edge as well as this remaining side. The amount of salt averages 1 ounce per gallon of milk.

When the cheeses are salted, the bands are put back on them. They are set on shelves in the room where they have been made and are turned twice, once each twelve hours. The bands are then removed for good, and the cheeses are taken to the drying room.

Here they are placed on shelves, on straw mats. The shelves are made of wooden slats, with spaces between the slats to assist in air circulation. The mats must be changed whenever they become even slightly damp. The temperature of the room must be kept between 54 and 69 degrees. If it is too high, the cheeses will run, losing moisture too fast; if too low, the ripening will be delayed and the risks, as a consequence, increased.

The development of the mold is rapid. The molds are the same as those that grow on the Camembert. They have to maintain their white aspect (or at the very least a pearl gray), or change colors as described in the old-fashioned Camembert section.

In about a week, when the cheeses are covered with the

mold, they are carried to the curing cellars. In France, even fifty years ago, these cellars were operated by distributors rather than by the farmers. The reason was that the temperature and humidity controls had to be so exact as to preclude most farmhouse operations, particularly since the land of Seine-et-Marne is not conducive to cellar making because of a high water table.

The commercial curing cellars are kept at about 54 degrees. The best ripening temperatures are 50 to 61 degrees. In the case of brown Bries, the mold is soon replaced by a glazed layer covering just about the entire surface of the cheese. The crust takes on a reddish-yellow tint, which gets darker and darker as the cheese ripens inside. The glazed layer is plastery at the beginning, but it softens; it becomes almost translucent and has an amber-yellow appearance when the characteristic Brie aroma develops. The Brie is now ready to be taken to your kitchen, and when it is ready to run, to exude its liquid goodness when cut, it is ready to be eaten and should be eaten soon.

Camembert and Brie are members of large families. The kin of Camembert include Chaource (which is 3 inches thick); Rallot from Flanders; Livarot (cured in a closed cellar that becomes strikingly pungent; it is wrapped in *laiche* leaves); Ervy from the Department of Aube, and Carré de l'Est (a square cheese with a white skin—in the making its curds are cut into small cubes before being transferred to the molds, and in this method, as well as in taste and the presence of a white mold, it is the prototype of factory Camembert).

Brie de Meaux and Brie de Meaux Fermier are two variations of Brie (the latter still made by farmers and considered the best Brie by many connoisseurs). Brie de Melun is a firm cheese, stronger and darker than most Bries, and Olivet is lightly pressed in the making. One Olivet is fresh summer cheese; another is sometimes cured while covered with ashes.

St. Benoit, similar to Olivet in taste, is made in the Department of Loiret; charcoal is added to the salt, which is rubbed into the surface of the cheese, and the cheese is cured for two weeks or so in summer and up to three weeks in winter.

The Wines

Boys should abstain from all use of wine until
their eighteenth year, for it is wrong to add fire
to fire.

—Plato, *Laws* II

Comments on a Lively Art

If you have wine and cheese, you won't starve and you can live a good life. Conceivably both were first discovered by the same person or family, no doubt ancestors of yours and mine, a tribesman and his wife who before the age of pottery and glass used stomachs of animals to carry liquids in. Once they made a journey in order to show their kin two juices they had come to favor, and found on their arrival that what they had was wine in one skin and cheese in the other.

An embarrassed and astonished couple.

Cheesemaking can be more complicated than carrying milk in a bag, as you have seen, and winemaking can be, too, but we need not be intimidated by either of them. The best wine-makers in the world work simply. Those in Burgundy do, with

199

few items of equipment or chemicals, standing as they do on the earthen floors of their cellars tasting the wine they make, swishing it through their mouth to aerate it and to enliven their taste buds, inhaling air through it to awaken it, letting it spray over their tongue before they swallow it, or, more likely with the new, raw wines, spew it over the floor. To taste wine as they do, and as professional buyers in their cellars do, take a large sip of wine into your mouth, prepare to whistle, and then breathe in, inhale through your mouth, filling the wine with air and your mouth with the wine.

I have occasionally wanted to use this tasting technique and to spew the wine over the floors of the home cellars of winemaking friends of mine. I fear they would drop to their knees at once with rags wet with disinfectant, so fearful are they, so fearful have some of the books on home winemaking made them, of bacteria, fruit flies, and other dangers. They should relax, as the Burgundians do, and even encourage the sweet souring of wines on earthen floors, to give their wines added flavor and aroma; wines do absorb aromas quite readily.

From a California college text on winemaking: "Wine spilled on the floor should be washed away immediately. If the spilled wine has stood on the floor for a considerable time, it is advisable to follow washing by applying lime or strong hypochlorite solution."

And again: "A separate room is needed for this [tasting]. It should be equipped with spittoons."

Of course, it is not absolutely necessary to spit on the floor to make wine or to have an earthen floor in one's cellar, but in home winemaking it is desirable to work with nature, not against her. Winemaking is a natural, self-fulfilling, self-purifying process. Wine is made and aged and stored in most

of the world's countries, some of them none too clean at anything, much less this; in many countries wine is drunk rather
than water, partly because wine purifies itself while water
cannot do so. Also, their wine is sent all over the world; their
water, if sent all over the world, would purge people's insides
out internationally. Wine is a staunch defender of itself. It
will cast off as sediment mud, dust, leaves, trash. It will even
try to cast off metal contaminants, within reason. It will try
to cast off any foul disease that afflicts it, given a chance, given
oxygen enough. It will not yield easily to illness or affliction,
the red wines being particularly staunch.

A winemaking book I bought recently says one rotten blackberry will ruin an entire batch of blackberry wine.

Not in my experience, not my blackberries.

One vinegar fly can turn a cask of wine to vinegar, we read
in another.

No, no. My flies are not that influential.

All utensils must be chemically disinfected and washed in
detergents, we read.

Well, sirs, I hope you'll rinse them well.

From an American text on winemaking I read that to ensure
protection of the grape, the factory, and the wine, the chemicals used include all of the following, and more: carbon
bisulfide, potassium metabisulfite, sodium metabisulfite, sodium sulfite, kerosene, chlordane, DDT, zinc phosphide,
ANTU, hypochlorite, strychnine, TEPP, parathion, FPN,
dieldrin, SG 77, Lethane 384, pyrethrin, rotenone, piperonyl
butoxide, DDVP, Vapora, sodium hydroxide, sodium metasili-
cate, ethylenediaminetetraacetic acid, trisodium phosphate,
Roccal, Emulsol, unslaked lime, chloride of lime, chlorine,
and Vel. I find the list frightening. However, since 1967,
when this text was published, TEPP, dieldrin, DDVT, para-

thion, DDT and trisodium phosphate have been widely out-lawed for use in vineyard or factory, a sign of progress and hopefully the start of a trend.

One group of California health inspectors has twelve rules. My favorite is number 10. "On using insecticide sprays in the plant, only those that are not toxic to humans are permitted. These are the pyrethrins, rotenone, and pipe-ronyl butoxide. Do not use the sprays in locations where the dead flies may drop into the must or wine, as dead flies in the wine are just as objectionable as living ones flying over the wine."

I showed that rule to the owner of a wine factory, and to my surprise he was not amused. Apparently when one makes 100,000 gallons of wine at a time, the flies breed by the billions, and something deadly must be done to them.

No doubt there are many other such disadvantages for factory producers, but the home winemaker with one to ten gallons need not adopt factory methods. The one chemical which you might ever need is potassium metabisulfite, or the similar tablet preparation named Campden tablets. This chemical does work itself free of a fruit juice in time if used sparingly. If the grapes or apples, or whatever fruit you want to use, are overripe or moldy, you can kill the spoil bacteria by mixing a tiny dose of meta, as it is often called, into the juice or crushed fruit. Thirty parts per million is enough to achieve this end. A larger dose, say ninety parts per million, will kill the wild yeasts, too, and make it possible two hours later, when most of the chemical has dissipated, to add a pure strain of wine yeast. Sometimes this is desirable. Finally, there are uses for meta in making sweet wine, as we will see.

Generally, meta is the winemaker's best friend, but it can be overused and often is; the chemical is a poison of sorts and it should be used properly, sparingly, if at all. I simply want to put this point in your mind here at the start, because my recommendations for its use, based on professional standards in France and England, will be more reserved than those of most other books, and of many merchants who sell meta and yeast cultures.

The first two chapters in the winemaking section deal with such simple-to-make wines that you need not be an expert. I have made most of these wines, and my friends have as well, and failure is unlikely. If you feel in need of comfort or advice, refer to Appendix 2, which discusses the different steps in more detail. I would not get inundated by details and advice, however, before actual experience has made them digestible.

Citizens in England, without government objection to trouble them, can make wines and beer all they please provided they don't sell them. In the United States we have a different situation. First of all, strictly speaking we cannot make ale or beer legally at all—there is a federal law, though not enforced: the Internal Revenue people say the law is needed to help them convict bootleggers of whiskey, and that it has not in their memory ever been used against makers of beer for home use. As for the wines, in the United States the head of a household can make wine, 200 gallons a year for his family's use. He or she is supposed to register and to keep a list of wines made, in case the premises are inspected. The premises aren't likely to be, and the whole matter is quite civilized in its current administration, but we ought to resent the intrusion anyway. Since no tax is involved, why the United States government needs to be informed who is making wine for his family's use, I don't know. And why a single person, unless he or she is head of a household, cannot make wine, I don't know. By law, one fills out each year two copies of a simple one-page form, obtainable in person or by mail from one of the addresses listed in Appendix 3, and sends the two copies in. One copy soon comes back stamped. There is no charge.

In addition there are state laws, presumably fifty sets of them. They generally are dormant laws. In some states they say one can make wine only if all ingredients have been grown on his or her own land. For all its crotchety aspects, this law comes to us out of sound tradition and one I respect. The best wines are made by men and women who use the fruits of their own land—rarely any other way.

As we will see.

11

Cider and Perry

One of the unique assets of England and France, one of hundreds, is the availability of cider in bottles and casks. A light cider is an especially refreshing drink, and if it is not made too strong with alcohol—and it isn't likely to be in these two countries, or in any other where its makers are conscious of its taste—a large swallow of it is worth a pause and lingering thought. I would rather have four glasses of 5 percent cider than two glasses of 10 percent, because it tastes better and can be drunk down in drafts, which is what one likes to do with cider, or what I like to do with it, and the evening is not drugged so soon.

Perry, which is pear cider, is not as readily available, but it shares with cider a long history, the two having been associated for centuries. They are distinctly different, but each when properly made can achieve excellence. They form a worthy team just below the better grape wines.

This chapter will tell you how they are made in England and France. I am starting this section with them because they are simple and inexpensive to make, and apples are one of nature's generously bestowed gifts. You can make a dry cider for drinking with your meals, or a slightly sweet cider for use on cold evenings before a fire, or a dessert cider, or all three, for a few cents a bottle.

Cider in England, *cidre* in France, is the fermented juice of apples. The alcohol content is 2 to 7 percent, perhaps— rarely more and rarely as much as 8. It is a popular drink in England, France, Germany, and Switzerland, as well as many other places, and seems to be gaining popularity in the United States, where unfortunately the word *cider* can also mean nonalcoholic apple juice, a source of confusion we expect will be corrected in time.

The largest producer of cider in the world is France, which makes five to ten times as much as any other country and uses most of it in the preparation of apple brandy, such as Calvados. Cider can be sparkling or draft, that is, still. It can be sweet or dry. The best ciders in the world are made in France and England, without, so far as I can find, any evidence of a dissenting vote, and one reason is that these countries have for many decades developed cider apple orchards. Germany, except for apples imported from France, uses what apples are at hand, and so do the United States and other places, but in France and England cider is made from cider apples, usually from three, four, five, or six different cider apples in a blend, the juices mixed before fermentation or the ciders blended after fermentation, or both.

The cider apple is, with only a few exceptions, not the best eating apple, and an eating apple, sometimes called a table or dessert apple, is with few exceptions not the best cider apple. The best cider apples are small and juicy, acidic and tannic—that is, they make your mouth pucker a bit.

Some of the cider apples are grown in the United States, so I will list a few of the more common names, past and present. If you can find these apples, you will be better served than if you must depend on table or cooking-apple fruit.

I wish I could list all the cider apples of England and France, but there are over three thousand of them, and the lists change often. I notice that the eleventh edition of the *Encyclopaedia Britannica,* which gives the best of them as of that time, retains only two of these in the current edition: the Kingston Black and the Improved Foxwhelp. Actually, I am stretching a point in including the Improved Foxwhelp, because the only mention of a Foxwhelp in the older list is Old Foxwhelp.

The old list was created, incidentally, by members of the Herefordshire Fruit-Growers' Association and the Herefordshire Fruit and Chrysanthemum Society, working together. I wish I could have attended that meeting. Among those they agreed to include were the Cherry Pearmain, Cowarne Red, Dymock Red, and Spreading Redstreak. Old apples others listed for Somerset and Devon included these wonderful names: Kingston Black, Jersey Chisel, Hangdowns, Fair Maid of Devon, Duck's Bill, Bottle Stopper, Golden Ball, Sugar Loaf, Red Cluster, and Slack-my-Girdle. Among still other old cider apples that I know about are the White Swan, the French Longtail, and the Moile.

Current lists usually divide the apples into three types: sharp, sweet, and bittersweet. The divisions are defined in

terms of sugar content, total acidity, and the tannic qualities—
the astringent, mouth-puckering qualities which in cidermaking are attributed to tannin whether caused by tannin or
not.

First of all, one class, the sharp class of apples, contains
a high percent of total acid, but almost no tannin. (Some of
these serve also as table apples.)

The second class, the sweet class of apple, normally has
less acid than the sharp apple, but more tannin.

Finally, the bittersweet apples contain a great deal of tannin, normally exceeding 0.2 percent.

A mixture of these apples can yield a cider balanced in
acid (about .6 percent), and tannin (.10 to .15).

Among the bittersweet apples of England today are the
Darlington Mill, the Kingston Bitter, the Hangdown, the Ellis
Bitter, the Dove, the Dabinett, the Red Jersey, Tremlett's
Bitter, the Brown Snout, the Ashtown Brown Jersey, and most
of the imported Normandy apples, which have French names
or include *Norman* as part of their name. Sweet apples in
England include the Sweet Alford, Sweet Coppin, and Court
Royal. Among the sharp apples of England are the Blackwell
Red, Colman's Seedling, the Climson King, the Kingston
Black, the Stoke Red, the Langworthy, and the Improved
Foxwhelp.

In Virginia a generation ago a few French cider apples
were available—the Omont (.20 percent tannin in France,
.21 in Virginia), St. Laurent (.27 in Virginia), Binet Blanc
(.13), Binet Rouge (.24), Maréchal (.50), Michelin (.29),
Rouge du Landel (.20). For comparison, Baldwin or Roxbury have about .06 percent tannin, McIntosh or Northern
Spy about .08.

If you are unlucky and cannot find cider apples in your
part of the United States, you can do fairly well by using

two or, preferably, three or four of these: Baldwin, Winesap, Northern Spy, Cortland, Russet, Rome Beauty, Gravenstein, Yellow Newtown, McIntosh, Spitzenberg, Jonathan, and Roxbury. You might use 50 percent Baldwin, 25 percent Northern Spy, 12 ½ percent Cortland, and 12 ½ percent Russet, as an example. Or you might use 50 percent Yellow Newtown, blended with the more flavorful and acidic Winesap. In either case, for these apples the addition of 5 to 10 percent crab apples will supply tannin; sweet cider needs less than dry.

In the old days in England, the ciders were made on farms, just as were cheeses. The fruit was crushed by hand labor and pressed by hand labor—and anybody who has ever pressed apples knows that this can be hard work. Sometimes a man with a crusher on his wagon would come along and help. The crushed pulp was shoveled into bags and the bags were put in a wooden press. The expressed juice was carried in buckets to oak fermenting casks or vats. If a cask was used it was filled up and the cider overflowed as it fermented; each day the cask was topped up. If a vat was used, it was filled two-thirds full and a cloth was thrown over it to keep flies out. Meanwhile children were out in the orchard shaking more apples out of the trees, that being the preferred method of harvesting, and women were sorting the apples to remove the rotten ones, being not as careful about this as visitors to cider mills in that day had expected they would be.

The fruit was not washed. The yeasts were on the peels, after all. And the juice was not sulfited. The natural yeasts and bacteria were left to do their work. The English makers thought to be the best of that time also prided themselves on not adding water or sugar. They simply crushed the fruit and let the yeast convert the sugar into alcohol. That was all.

Depending on the temperature, the tempestuous part of fermentation was over in four or five days in a vat, two weeks if a cask was used. The cider was then racked into kegs, which were filled to the bungholes. Usually they overflowed slightly as they continued to ferment, the juice being absorbed by the earthen floor. The bungholes were left open to the air until the fermentation had subsided to a mere bubbling; then the bung was wrapped in burlap and loosely put in place. In a few weeks the cask was topped up and the bung was put in place tightly.

Makers might filter the finished cider through a cloth bag. They might need to fine it—to clear it—in which case they were likely to use a bit of skimmed milk, whipped to a froth as it was mixed with dashes of cider; the mixture was then poured into the kegs, and a few days later the cider was racked off its lees. Filtering was often done, fining more rarely.

The cider was drunk most any time. If too young to have undergone its secondary fermentation, which is an acidic fermentation, it was left outdoors in freezing weather for a few nights, to precipitate out some of the acids.

Sometimes the trip to town reactivated the fermentation, so for a while the kegged cider had an effervescence to it.

Some makers preferred to hold their best cider until it was aged. The secondary, acidic fermentation was given a chance to complete itself in the spring, and the cider would probably clear without fining. Many would hold some cider for six months, a few for as long as two years.

These methods of manufacture on thousands of farms produced what we suppose were ciders of varying qualities. There were local distinctions, subtleties of taste and aroma, in the ciders of given places, largely due to the apples used, but also due to the talent and patience of the makers. Toward the end of the nineteenth century, however, factories began to take over cidermaking in England. The result, predictably, was a leveling off of quality; one can be sure now in an English pub of being served a cider that is quite good, but equally sure that it will not have local distinctiveness, nor will it hold any surprises.

A friend of mine in Blue Bell, Pennsylvania, makes an excellent effervescent cider for his family's use, using this old English method, except that he has changed from wood casks to glass carboys and glass bottles. He made this change about fourteen years ago. His name is Abby Wolf. His wife, Constance, is a balloonist and he is a pilot with his own plane, and when they are on the ground they are pruning their old apple trees or picking the apples off the ground or crushing them or drinking the most delicious cider I have had in this country. And eating some of the best food.

They use only windfalls; in other words, they do not pick the apples off the trees, only off the ground. They have several varieties, chief among them Old Stem, McIntosh, Gravenstein, Winesap, and York. They do not wash the apples. For two years in a row Connie washed the apples and took pains to remove the rotten ones, and Abby says they ended up with a less flavorful cider on both vintages. Now they simply crush what they find on the ground.

Abby does not sulfite. He does not add any yeast. He does not add any sugar. He pours the fresh juice into four 12 ½-gallon glass carboys (I would prefer to use smaller, lighter ones). He fills them to the top and sets an inverted finger-bowl on the mouth of each one. He tops them up every night, using juice from a spare jug kept for that purpose; he fills up the first carboy with juice from the second, the second with juice from the third, the third with juice from the fourth, and that one he fills up from the spare jug. After two weeks of fermenting, he siphons the cider into clean carboys, filling them to the top, and resets the flat-bottomed bowls. He keeps these topped up as needed but does nothing else to them. Sixty days after the first racking (seventy-four days after

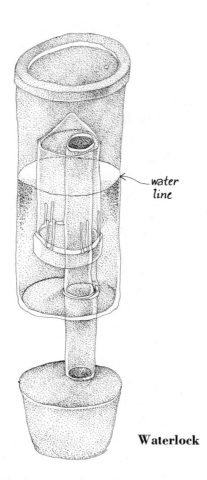

water
line

Waterlock

crushing the apples), he siphons the cider into Champagne bottles; he stoppers the bottles with plastic closures and attaches wire clamps, both of which he orders from a wine-makers' catalog (markets are in Appendix 3). In order to leave as little air as possible, he fills the Champagne bottles to the brim, then removes with a bulb baster an exact amount, which leaves room enough for the closure.

He sets the bottles upright in his cellar, which stays at 40 to 60 degrees. He does not move them or tamper with them. Some of the cider in his cellar when I visited him recently had been bottled six months, some had been bottled seven years. When he and Connie want some cider, one of them carries a bottle or two of it to their dining room, careful not to arouse the sediment which forms a coating on the bottom. They find that this is best done if the bottle is held at the neck, so that it dangles freely; the arm is able to cushion any shocks along the way. In the dining room Abby removes the wire clamp, then removes the plastic closure with a pair of pliers. He decants the cider. To do this he puts a white piece of paper on the table beside a decanter; this helps him see through the cider as he pours it; he pours cider into the decanter until he sees sediment move from the bottom of the bottle to the mouth of the bottle. He stops pouring at that point and dis-cards the last ounce of cider and all the sediment. The sedi-ment is harmless, as I said earlier, but he doesn't want it.

The cider in some bottles is sweeter than in others. He has no idea until a bottle is opened what subtle characteristics it has, but that only increases the anticipation. He tells me that the last apples of each harvest make the driest cider. All of his cider is effervescent, delicious and pure. He has been mak-ing cider for twenty-five years, the last fourteen by this method, and he hasn't in these fourteen years had a bottle spoil or turn to vinegar. He makes up to 450 bottles a year, and his cost is about three cents a bottle. That money goes to pay for new closures every five years, and for the wire clamps that hold the closures securely in place.

Abby does not use any equipment at all, except his bulb baster. He doesn't even have a hydrometer, which certainly would be a help in determining when to bottle. I wouldn't bottle a fermenting wine until a hydrometer gave a reading of about 1.005, for instance. But Abby tells me he has never had a bottle blow its stopper or blow apart since he changed from wood all those many years ago.

In any event, I take up the use of the hydrometer in Appendix 2, and I would use one, if I were you.

Modern factory cidermaking in England begins when the apples are brought in from the cider orchard. Some factories wash them, some do not. Most factories exclude the rotten and dried-out fruit. The apples are grated by a revolving drum which turns at two thousand revolutions a minute, cutting the apples with short knives. The pulp is pressed and a yield of 75 to 80 percent by weight is obtained.

Experiments have been carried out pasteurizing the juice before fermentation, but the taste is affected. Further, heating apple juice makes it difficult later to clarify it, so this isn't any longer done. Experiments with sulfiting the juice to stun or kill the wild yeasts and bacteria have afforded no advantage over the older way, and modern makers in the main do not sulfite at all. They ferment with the wild yeasts present on the skins of the apples.

The dry cider is allowed to ferment out and is then racked and filtered into clean casks for transfer to the pubs, or it is bottled.

Sweet cider is more difficult to make, on the whole, than dry. English makers halt the fermentation at the desired level of sweetness by forcing the cider under pressure through a thick layer of fibrous material. Usually a hydrometer, purchasable cheaply and as easy to use as a thermometer, will at the time of filtering show 1.025 to 1.030 on its scale. If after this treatment the cider resumes fermentation, its punishment is a second filtration.

Another way of making sweet cider in factories is to allow it to ferment out, then to filter out the yeast and add sugar. The sweetening used by factories is usually boiled cane or beet sugar syrup.

French Cider

The French cider apples aren't likely to be found in the United States. Among them are the Binet Rouge, Doux Amer, Ecarlatine, Frequin Audième, Frequin Rouge, Michelin, Reine des Pommes, Reinette Obrey, Tardive Forestier, St. Laurent, Bramlot, and Omont.

The cider orchards of France are chiefly located in Normandy and Brittany. The apples after harvesting are stored in bins for a few days, to develop their aroma. They are then washed, and the rotten fruit is removed. Then they are crushed. Some makers proceed to press the apples at once, but others leave them in their crushed state three to twenty-four hours longer, to develop color and more flavor. Juice escaping from the apples is put in the fermenting vats, and the juice from the expressed apples is added later.

Since the apples have lain around for several days, the juice is sulfited, as a rule, about fifty parts of sulfite per million parts of juice. This process is meant to kill spoil bacteria. It does not kill the wild yeasts; the French makers ferment with the natural yeasts that are on the apple peels. The juice is cooled after sulfiting, to 32 to 46 degrees, and is allowed to settle. This practice is called keeving.

The juice is siphoned off of the sediment and is fermented at 40 to 50 degrees, the makers believing that low temperatures are essential to attaining the best cider quality. They therefore hope for cool weather and usually, in Normandy and Brittany, they get it.

The cider is permitted slowly to ferment until the alcohol fermentation is almost over; however, before the brown cap disappears, the juice is racked into clean casks. A secondary, acidic fermentation continues for several months at 40 degrees. Before the secondary fermentation is completed, the cider is racked again and is bottled in order that it can develop slight carbonization in the bottle.

Disgorging is done, as with Champagne, by some makers. We will explain about that when we get to Champagne. Many allow the sediment to settle in the bottom of the bottles and decant the cider before serving it.

Notes for Home Cidermakers

As you see, the French process is more complicated than the English and requires cold weather during fermentation— either that or access at home to a refrigerator. The quality of the cider will be enhanced by the additional French requirement, but the chief determinant of quality will be the apples used in the first place.

One of the main problems is pressing the apples, unless you

have an old cider mill, which sometimes does appear for sale in a junk shop. The French device of leaving the crushed apples for three to twenty-four hours is helpful in the pressing, since it softens them. If you have no press, you can make a good cider by fermenting the juice on the skins for the first two days. To do this crush or cut up the apples, but do not cut the seeds; add a small amount of water in order to make the pomace more liquid, and cover the fermenting vat with a cloth to keep flies out. The fermenting process will soften the fruit, so that you can press the juice out through a bag or pillowcase by hand.

If you want to sulfite the juice, one Campden tablet will meta one gallon fifty parts per million. One level teaspoon of potassium metabisulfite, a powder, will sulfite 12 gallons about fifty parts per million. Stir the chemical into the cider.

Cider bottled six months after making reaches its peak two to six months after bottling. A slight effervescence can be obtained by bottling when the hydrometer reads 1.005, or by adding sugar to dry cider before bottling, 1 to 2 ounces of sugar for each gallon. Make a sugar syrup by boiling sugar and water, stir it into cider you have recently racked, then bottle and cap the sweetened cider in beer or cider bottles, provided the hydrometer reads no more than 1.007. Brown bottles are best for cider and green are better than clear ones.

If the cider has not cleared by the time of bottling—it will have done so in almost all cases—you can add a clarifying agent, such as Clairjus #3. At 60 degrees, 0.3 ounce will clarify 10 gallons in fifteen hours; half that amount will clarify it in thirty hours.

Cider should be stored in the dark and at low temperature—45 to 65 degrees preferably. Aging it beyond six months does not improve it.

The French often, and the English factories sometimes, add water to their apple juice. They then might add sugar to bring the alcoholic content up. English makers cannot legally add more water than half the apple juice. They add acid if necessary to bring the acidity to 0.5 to 0.6 percent as tartaric. We discuss acidity tests in Appendix 2.

Often in France and less frequently in England, another run of cider is made from the pomace—that is, the skins and pulp left after pressing. The cake of pomace is broken up and mixed with water, about the same amount of water as the juice that was pressed from it, and this pomace and water mixture is allowed to stand several hours before the juice is poured into a vat for fermenting. The pomace is once more pressed, and the expressed juice is put in the vat. Sugar is added to the liquid, about a pound for each gallon. Usually the liquid is sulfited fifty parts per million (see Appendix 2 for measurements), and the fermentation is allowed to proceed, yielding a low-quality cider called in France *cidre marchand*. As a tribute to French thrift, I am happy to report that the pomace left from this process is sometimes used yet again—once more watered, sugared, sulfited, fermented—and the result is called *petit cidre*.

In the United States commercial apple cider is made both in the East and the West. Like much else in the food industry in America, it tends to be overprocessed and overprotected. I understand that the United States federal law permits cider which is made naturally, with nothing done to alter or preserve it, to be sold tax free, yet this astonishing inducement to natural practice has found no producers in the country to take advantage of it. They would rather pay the tax than lose the use of their filtering, pasteurizing, and centrifuging equipment.

Briefly I will tell you how cider is made in the United States factories that I know of. The apples used are culls salvaged from table-apple orchards. They are sorted through, and the rotten and wormy ones discarded. The apples are then washed. The selected apples are crushed or grated. The pomace is pressed. The juice is sulfited 100 to 125 parts per million—although one American factory in the 1960s was adding metabisulfite at the rate of 2 pounds per 100 gallons of juice, a staggering excess. The juice is sometimes filtered before being fermented. Pectic enzyme is usually added. If natural fermentation starts overnight, another dose of meta stops it. Dextrose is added so that the cider will have 13 percent alcohol, about twice what a cider ought to have. A pure yeast strain is added, and the juice is fermented rapidly. When fermentation is complete, cane or beet sugar is added. The cider is clarified, usually with bentonite. It is passed through filters under pressure, and before this step high-speed centrifuging might be used to prevent the cider from clogging the filters. After filtration the apple juice might or might not be fortified with ascorbic acid (vitamin C) to enhance its nutritional value and help preserve it. It is then flash-pasteurized, its microorganisms being killed at 170 to 200 degrees in one to three minutes. It is packaged in sterile cans or bottles, and the higher-quality ciders are often frozen at 0 to −40 degrees and stored at 0 degrees, with the tin cans allowing 10 percent room for expansion during this process. If the juice is not frozen, it is likely to be preserved with a chemical such as sodium benzoate, 0.1 percent.

The cider is then sold.

I suppose we must try to keep a sense of humor about all this.

Perry

Perry is the cider of pears, a pale gold in color.

It is made best in England and France, and here again the quality is attributable to the growing of fruit specifically selected for winemaking, as well as to the method of making it. If anything, the best perry pears are even less suitable for table use than are the best cider apples. Among the pears grown in England for perry are the Taynton Squash, Barland, Oldfield, Malvern Hill (also called Morrcroft), Red-pear, Thurston's Red, Longland, and Pine Pear.

Normally, a single perry pear is used rather than a mixture, which is one chief difference between making perry and making cider. Those who do not have perry pears are instructed in old recipes to use a mixture of different types of pears, some sweet and some cooking pears, some comparatively dry and some juicy. It is not unknown in old recipes to find that crab apples are added, no doubt to contribute a tannin quality; this would be advisable when only table pears are available, 5 to 10 percent of crab apples by weight. Another way of adding tannin to table pears is to put some of the peels of the pears in with the juice. Perry pears contribute a high quantity of tannin on their own, and most of them afford enough acid. If not, as tested by an acidimeter, the difficulty can be corrected by adding up to $\frac{1}{4}$ ounce of tartaric acid, best U.S.P. grade, to a gallon of pear juice.

Yeast nutrient is recommended for pears, either the tablets available in winemaking shops, one for 2 gallons, or half a slice of old bread for a gallon.

When perry pears are brought in from the field, they are chopped and pressed. They should be ripe enough so that the stems can be pulled out of them easily. If they are not ripe, they can be set in the sun for a day or so, or even longer. The seeds should not be cut or broken in crushing. The stems are not used in the fermentation but can be left in during the pressing.

A hydrometer reading of the juice will show a potential of 4 to 7 and occasionally 8 percent alcohol, which is enough for perry.

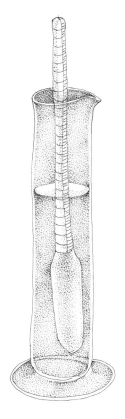

Hydrometer

Ferment the juice only, not on the skins. Use the yeasts that were present on the pears and are now present in the juice. The best fermentation temperature of the juice is about 78 degrees, although in cold weather a colder fermentation often is used, which of course takes longer, up to several weeks.

When the fermentation has relaxed its early surge, the juice should be racked into casks or jugs or other closed containers. These are topped up and loosely stoppered, often with wads of cotton. The jugs are topped up as needed. The juice is racked again in three months and is then more securely closed off from air.

Perry is made sparkling by the same ways used in making Champagne and cider. If you have a hydrometer, rack the perry at 1.025 or thereabouts, and bottle it when the hydrometer reads 1.005. This perry will have sediment in the bottom of the bottles, but that can be left behind when the perry is decanted—unless, of course, your hand shakes.

12   *Lords are lordliest in their wine.*
            —John Milton, *Samson Agonistes*

Mead

Mead is a wine made of honey. The honey helps flavor the wine, and most of the sugar in the honey is converted to alcohol.

The English bees make what the English believe to be the best honey in the world, and indeed they might be right. In most other countries the bees make honey in spring, summer, and fall, but the climate of England, about which we intend to say nothing more, does not provide much nectar in spring or fall, and the honey that is marketed in England is nearly all summer honey, strong and flavorful. I like to tell myself it comes from the rose hedges and beautiful gardens, that being fittingly romantic, and dribs and drabs of it do, but one acre of heather or clover is the equivalent of over 10

223

miles of rose hedges, and it happens that heather and clover honeys, each with a distinctive, lingering, full taste, make up the bulk of the honey to be found in England.

Mead is the product of such honey, and water, and yeast, and sometimes fruit flavoring.

I have one old recipe for mead which says "one part honey to one part water, let it ferment until it will ferment no more, then bottle it." I think the recipe is inferior to some others we will come to later, but it does indicate the basic process.

Mead, always a favorite wine of priests, was a wine of the gods of the Greeks, and was served at the people's, and presumably at the gods', orgies. The Romans also were fond of mead. So in fact were the Hindus, the Norsemen, and practically everybody else. All wines have been thought from time to time and in one place or another to hold aphrodisiac qualities, but mead from earliest writings and in every civilization in every country has been thought to hold aphrodisiac qualities, which means to me that it has aphrodisiac qualities.

A century ago mead, ale, and cider were the three drinks available in English inns and taverns. Since then mead has fallen from favor. One reason is the development of sugar plantations in Jamaica, with their slave labor; when sugar for the first time became available cheaply, it made possible the inexpensive making of sweet cider. Another possible explanation is lodged like a burr in the heather honey itself, which has a strong taste; a group of men sitting and drinking heather mead are likely to occupy themselves wondering how many years more it needs to lie in the cellar—eight to ten years is a minimum for that heavy brew. Still another reason is that ale and cider can be drunk copiously, while mead is usually too thick and sweet for that. So, as you see, there are many reasons, some better than others, though perhaps none of them quite adequate to explain why the aphrodisiac drink of the gods lost its storehouse position in English pubs.

The abiding truth remains that mead can be one of the best wines made. It can be as delicious as a fine white grape wine, it can be dry or sweet, and it can be made by home winemakers anywhere bees make honey, so we will deal with it in detail.

Some honeys are dark and heavy, some are light in color and taste. Interestingly enough, honey from a single flower is better for making mead than is a mixed honey. Fresh honey is better than store-bought, as you might expect, and pasteurized store-bought honey is the poorest of the lot. Also, we have seen pasteurized, homogenized, processed honey, which ought not to be used for mead, or anything else.

Florida orange honey is good for mead. Clover honey is good. Rose, wild rose, and rosemary honeys are good, and so are most all single-flower, pure honeys.

A hydrometer is not required but is helpful. I take up the use of this instrument in Appendix 2. With a hydrometer, you can tell quickly how powerful a wine you are going to make, 10 to 12 percent alcohol being ideal for mead.

The heavier meads made today require two years of aging, heather mead excepted; the lighter meads can be drunk in six to twelve months. In the case of mead, 4 gallons are as easy to make as 1. Once you have a mead recipe you like—I prefer a light mead which is dry enough to be used with meals—you can make 5 or 10 gallons of it simply by ordering enough honey from an apiarist.

Honey does not contain proper yeasts or yeast nutrients or tannin. The yeast to be added should be mead yeast, if you have any, or Madeira, Champagne, Montrachet, "all-purpose," or whatever, one packet for 5 gallons of mead. If you don't have any yeast at all, in an emergency use a handful or two of unwashed grape skins or apple peels; these will have wild wine yeasts on them. As for the nutrient, in the old days makers used old bread, one slice to 2 gallons of mead. You can use old bread, or yeast nutrient tablets. As for the tannin, some of the old makers added tea leaves. You can add, if you prefer, tartaric acid, best U.S.P. grade, as we will see.

Some makers added spices. The court mead used in Elizabethan England was so full of ginger and cloves that I enjoy imagining the expression of newly arrived ambassadors from France when first served it. I will put down one of these spicy recipes as a matter of record, but it seems to me that simplicity is a suitable rule here. I was about to say moderation is a suitable rule here, but if the mead is good, moderation is not a suitable rule at all.

After presenting the old people's recipe, with their tea leaves and slices of sour bread, I will give the way some of the modern home winemakers of England are making mead these days. There are hundreds of them busily at work, a good and happy lot, and anything we can learn which will return mead to its proper place near the top of the list of English wines will be worth such sacrifices as using their precautions.

A Nineteenth-century Mead, Hop Flavored

Bring 5 gallons of water to the boil and add to it 20 pounds of honey. Let them boil together, and remove the scum as it forms on the surface. Add an ounce of hops and let the hops cook with the mead for ten minutes to flavor it; then let the mead cool.

Pour it into a crock. When at blood temperature or cooler, float a slice of toast on the mead, having smeared the underside of the toast with a paste made of a tablespoonful of yeast and water or yeast and flour.

When fermentation subsides in five or six days, draw the mead into jugs and loosely stopper them, or fill a cask to the bunghole and loosely stopper it. When you are able, close the mead off securely from the air, but only when all fermentation stops. If a cask is used, you must continue to top it up until bottling, using other cider or, if none is on hand, water.

One of the flavorings sometimes, not often, used instead of hops was walnut leaves, twenty walnut leaves for one gallon of mead, the mead to be left on the leaves overnight.

Old Mead Recipe

Take 7 pounds of light, fresh honey, or for a sweet mead use 9 or 10 pounds. Boil the honey in 2 gallons of water, but only briefly. Siphon the mead into a fermenting vat and add half a pint of strong tea that you have just made and the juice of two lemons. When the mixture has cooled to 70 degrees, add yeast. (The old makers used whatever yeast was on hand, but you should use half a packet of dry wine yeast, or half a vial of liquid wine yeast.) Cover the fermenting vat and allow the mead to ferment undisturbed; in five or six days it can be transferred to jugs. If the mead does not quite fill the jugs, fill them with a little water that has been boiled and then cooled to room temperature; the mead should rise two-thirds of the way into the necks of the jugs. Do not close the corks tightly.

In a month, siphon the mead into clean bottles and cork the top loosely until you are certain fermentation has stopped.

The mead will be ready to drink in four months but is best in a year.

Cyser

A mead made of honey and a fruit juice is called a melomel; one melomel is Cyser, the name given to a mead flavored with apple juice.

The simplest recipe I have for Cyser calls for "one pint of apple juice to one pint of honey, the mixture being allowed to ferment." Another brief recipe suggests you mix apples as for apple cider and sweeten them with honey rather than sugar. The honey used need not be of as high quality as that for mead. The other aspects of the recipe are identical to those for making fruit wine or for making apple cider or for making mead.

Pyment

Pyment also is a melomel, made of honey and grape juice or grape juice concentrate. To 1 gallon of grape juice, as much as 3 pounds of honey can be added, the honey dissolved in the juice. This is intended to give a powerful, great wine, the quality of which depends more on the grape juice than on the quality of the honey used.

Orange juice melomels are sometimes made by this same recipe.

Red Currant Mead (or Black Mead If Black Currants Are Used)

This old recipe produces a traditional English drink.

Steep 7 pounds of light, fresh honey in 6 quarts of water

until the honey is dissolved. Into the hot sweet broth put 6 quarts of crushed red currants or 5 quarts of black currants. Let this mixture cool to under 85 degrees, preferably to 70. Add wine yeast and yeast food. Add raisins if you want to. Ferment the wine for about a week, then strain it and siphon it into jugs, which should have cotton stuffed into their mouths. In about a month, siphon the mead into bottles and cork them loosely. When you are sure fermentation has ceased, cork them tightly.

Spiced Mead

Boil 2 ½ pounds of honey in a gallon of water, skimming off any residue that rises to the surface. Into the boiling broth submerge a little bag containing 1 ½ tablespoons each of cloves, mace, and cassia buds. Let this steep in the broth five minutes.

Pour the mead, including the spice bag, into a fermenting vat and at once, while it is boiling hot, add 2 ounces of candied, chopped ginger.

When the mixture feels cool, add wine yeast and yeast nutrient. The fermentation will be rather slow, but in about ten days the mead can be siphoned into clean jugs. In another month or two the wine will be clear and can be siphoned into bottles. This wine can be served cold, or on cold evenings can be served warm, but do not heat it to steaming or the alcohol will escape.

A Modern Mead

The meads being made today by some of the home winemakers of England have excellent qualities. Here is a step-by-step procedure one of them, a friend near Woking, follows in making a dry mead.

First he gets a single-blossom honey, usually clover, buying it from an apiarist in 7-pound lots. The fresher the better. He prefers light honey.

He dissolves 6 pounds of the honey (he and his wife eat the other pound) in 1 gallon of lukewarm water. He does not bother to boil the water first to purify it or soften it. He does not boil the honey, either; he says boiling dissipates some of the flavor, and no doubt it does.

When the honey is dissolved, he adds enough water to yield 2 gallons of mead.

To this water and honey solution he then adds the following natural chemicals: 1 ounce of malic acid, ½ ounce of tartaric acid, and $\frac{1}{7}$ ounce of grape tannin (or, if he doesn't have it, $\frac{1}{7}$ ounce of tannic acid).

Now he adds four Campden tablets, which sulfites the bacteria and wild yeasts, if any, in the liquid at the rate of one hundred parts per million. In an hour or two, preferably two, he stirs the liquid and adds about half a packet of wine yeast. Having tried various ones, he claims there is a difference in the taste; he uses Champagne or Bordeaux. Any wine yeast will do.

He does add yeast nutrient tablets (purchased at a shop) or a yeast nutrient he makes up for himself, one currently being recommended by winemakers in England, composed of 9 grams of ammonium phosphate, 4 ½ grams of potassium phosphate, and 2 $\frac{1}{3}$ grams of magnesium sulfate. A chemist (druggist in the United States) weighs out packets of this mixture for him. When he feels particularly kind to his yeast, he will add a vitamin B_1 tablet, the 15-milligram size. He says the likelihood of a stuck fermentation is greater with mead than with fruit wines, and proper yeast food is needed.

This mixture is allowed to ferment for five to ten days in a fermenting vat—in his case a white plastic dustbin, as he calls it—a cloth covering the top. The vat is located in a room of approximately 65 degrees temperature. When no more foam or bubbles rise to the surface, the wine is carefully racked into a jug, without aeration—he uses a plastic siphon and does not let much air reach the mead during the transfer; that is, the wine is not allowed to splash with abandon into the receiving container.

The jug should be filled to within an inch or so of its lip. A fermentation lock is set on the jug (you can buy one or you can make your own, as we describe in Appendix 2). The mead is allowed to mature in the dark, being left quite still.

In three months the mead is racked again, by means of the siphon. Again in racking it is not aerated. Of course, in these rackings care is also taken not to transfer the residue, the deposit on the bottom of the old jug. Rackings proceed seasonally. Two Campden tablets are added for the 2 gallons just before the final bottling to secure the wine for its months or years of aging.

My friend's mead, he tells me, can be kept under a fermentation lock for as long as is desired and should not be bottled until a year old. It can be drunk before then. After one or two years in a bottle it will be at its best, but it will be excellent for six years or more.

To make a sweet mead using this recipe, he allows the mead to ferment out, so that he gets a reading of under 1.000 (gravity zero) on a hydrometer's density scale. Then he sweetens it with strained honey to taste, sulfites it one hundred parts per million to kill the yeast, and bottles it. If he did not kill the yeast, it would seek to ferment the new honey in the bottle, and the gas produced by fermentation would blow the corks.

A Bishop

In Queen Elizabeth's day the ambassador from France, after sampling the queen's mead, could order that evening at his inn a warm Bishop. He would see the porter roast a large lemon before the fire, into which a dozen cloves had been stuck, as meanwhile in a pot he heated a blob of honey, about ¼ pound, and a large glassful of water, now and then dropping into this pinches of cinnamon, allspice, and mace, simmering them until half the liquid had gone up in vapor. In another pan the porter was boiling a whole bottle of white wine.

Everything was mixed before the ambassador's astonished eyes, including the roasted lemon, and it was served up to him with a dash of nutmeg on top, alongside a glass of brandy.

O thou invisible spirit of wine!
If thou hast no name to be known by,
let us call thee devil!

—Cassio in *Othello*, II, iii

Come, come; good wine is a good
familiar creature if it be well used;
exclaim no more against it.

—Iago in *Othello*, II, iii

13

English Country Wines

English country wines and ales are a varied lot, the results of centuries of efforts by a creative, thirsty people who have lived on an island which provides them with all too few grapes.

They offer us an amazing spectrum of choices: berries, flowers, roots, grains. . . .

Some of the wines are sad and sorry, but a blackberry wine need not be, as most of us will agree, nor a ginger beer, nor a currant wine. In fact all of them are worthy of study by any of us.

For country wines there are two basic recipes.

In one, English makers crush the fruit and allow either natural or added wine yeast to ferment the peel and pulp and

233

juice together. Then they strain the juice into a cask or jug, filling it to the brim.

In the other, they crush the fruit and ferment the juice only, in a crock or cask or jug. This method yields a lighter wine, one which requires less aging.

Country wines are made with an alcoholic content of 6 to 12 percent.

Sweet fruit wines, even if but slightly sweet, are generally preferable to dry fruit wines, simply as a matter of taste. A dry fruit wine leaves the acidity unrelieved and unaccompanied and often has a chemical taste which sweetening overcomes.

The wines need to age six months or so; they will keep for years, but their taste and aroma will become less fruity.

The recipes for English country wines frequently contain admonitions to use only ripe fruit, and they suggest that fruit is sweeter when picked during dry rather than rainy seasons. Dried fruit, such as raisins and prunes, can be used, but today it is wise to boil them in water first to disperse any preservative on them, which might retard fermentation. Canned fruit can be used, with the same restriction. Frozen fruit can be used.

As you will notice, most of the recipes suggest the addition of water and sugar. Two pounds of sugar to a gallon of water and a pound of sugar additional for each gallon of fruit juice usually will yield a 10 to 12 percent dry wine. A sweet wine needs more. In either case, the sugar should be added in two or more stages.

Wild fruit will contain naturally too much acid, up to 1.5 percent, depending on the fruit, the season, the ripeness, and the location, and 0.7 to 0.8 percent is a working, ideal range for winemaking. Therefore, water is usually added.

Some recipes call for the addition of yeast, but most do not. If you add yeast, a vial or packet of wine yeast will suffice for 4 to 8 gallons. Some call for the addition of a yeast nutrient. Fruit and flowers do supply some yeast nutrients, but if diluted with water these might prove to be insufficient; therefore, experience long ago taught country winemakers to add to diluted juice half a slice of sour, dried bread for each gallon, or a small, sliced potato, or a widow's handful of grain or cereal. Too much yeast food for the yeasts to use might cloud the wine, so the amounts should not be exceeded.

Some of the old-time instructions go beyond the realm of practicality. One maker suggests that juices should be strained through straw and sticks of wood before fermenting. He used a flour barrel into which he first put wood and on top of that laid an armful of straw. He mashed the berries, poured them on the straw, and let the juice drain out of a hole near the bottom of the barrel. Next morning he proceeded to make wine from the strained juice. If he intended to add water to the juice, he poured the water through the straw to help retrieve the residue of the juice. I am sure he believed he was doing all this for a reason, and maybe he was wiser than I think. As I see it, all he attained by the process was yeast from the grain, actually brewer's yeast, which would work alongside the wine yeast of the fruit to produce a complex yeasty taste, but, assuming this to be desirable, it could be achieved by tossing a handful of rye or barley into the wine as it was left to ferment.

There are two basic stages in English winemaking. The first requires a vat of some sort—ceramic, wood, glass, white polyethylene or a plastic garbage can or wastebasket with a good-grade polyethylene liner. The vat can be covered with a cloth or loose-fitting top, but it must keep flies out and allow oxygen to enter.

When the initial fermentation, with its bubbles and often with its foam, has subsided, usually in about five days, the wine is siphoned or poured into jugs or casks, each being filled. These have cotton stuffed in their mouths, or waterlocks, if you prefer.

As a rule, the wine is bottled the middle of the spring after it is made.

If you make a few wines by this simple process, you will do very well. To do better you will want to refer to the more detailed notes in Appendix 2, which deals with the hydrometers to test sugar content, and practical means of testing acid, and with wine yeasts supplied in packages and vials, and with other matters which make it quite easy to produce excellent fruit wines consistently. You can devise your own recipe, as you will see.

One of my favorite writers of old English wine books is a gentleman named Frederick Accum, a chemist in Soho in the early part of the nineteenth century. In 1820 he wrote concerning English wine:

> The vine was introduced into Britain by the Romans, and appears to have very soon become common. Few ancient monasteries did not manufacture wine. In an early period of the history of Britain, the Isle of Ely was expressly denominated the Isle of Vines by the Normans. The Bishop of Ely, shortly after the conquest, received at least three or four tons of wine annually, as tithes from the vines in his diocese, and in his leases he made frequent reservations of a certain quantity of wine by way of rent. Many of them were little inferior to the wines of France in sweetness. . . .

Besides grapes, of which the most perfect wine is made . . . the following domestic fruits are well calculated for the fabrication of wine:—the gooseberry, elderberry, mulberry, raspberry, blackberry, strawberry, red currant, black currant, white currant, and cranberry. These ferment well, and afford good and wholesome wines. It is a vulgar prejudice to suppose, that the wines made from domestic fruits are unwholesome. They may disagree with the constitutions of some persons, but no fact can warrant the assertion that they are more injurious than wine made from the grape.

The pulpy indigenous fruits, such as the peach, nectarine, plum, cherry, damson, and apricot, may also be employed; but, upon the whole, they answer not so well for the fabrication of wine as the sub-acid esculent berries.

The gooseberry and currant are, of all other fruits, most commonly employed in the fabrication of home-made wines; and, upon the whole, they are best adapted for the purpose. When used in their green state, they may be made to form light brisk wines, falling little short of Champagne.

Ripe gooseberries are capable of making sweet or *dry* wine; but these are commonly ill flavoured, particularly if the husk has not been carefully excluded.

Ripe currants, if properly managed, make a much better wine than gooseberries. These fruits are much improved, according to Dr. Macculloch, by boiling the juice, for a few minutes, previously to fermentation. This is particularly the case with the black currant, which, when thus managed, is capable of making a wine closely resembling some of the best of the sweet Cape wines.

The strawberry and raspberry are capable of making both *dry* and sweet wines of an agreeable quality.

The elderberry is well calculated for making an excellent red wine. Its cheapness also recommends it. It does not, indeed, possess any great degree of flavour, but it possesses no bad one, which is a negative property often of great importance in artificial wine making.

The cherry produces a wine of no very peculiar character. If used, care should be taken not to bruise too many of the stones, otherwise a disagreeable bitter taste will be imparted to the wine.

The blackberry and mulberry are capable of making coloured wines, if managed with that view; they are deficient, however, in the astringent principle; nevertheless, they may be occasionally employed with advantage when a particular object is to be gained.

The sloe and damson are so associated in qualities, that nearly the same results are obtained from both. Their juice is acid and astringent; and hence they are qualified only for making *dry* wines. By a due admixture of currants or elderberries with sloes or damsons, wines not much unlike the inferior kinds of port are often produced.

Grapes, of British growth, are capable of making excellent sparkling and other wines, by the addition of sugar. I have made wine from immature grapes and sugar, which so closely resembles the wines called Grave, and Moselle, that the best judges could not distinguish them from foreign wines. The grapes may be used in any state, however immature; when even but half grown, and perfectly hard, they succeed completely.

Raisins are extensively used in this country for making domestic wines, therefore they deserve to be mentioned here. When properly managed, they are capable of making a pure and flavourless vinous fluid, well adapted for

receiving any flavour which may be required, and thus of imitating many wines of foreign growth.

The orange and lemon are likewise used for making domestic wines. Upon the whole, however, they are not very well adapted for the purpose, as they contain too much acid, and too little of the extractive and of the sweet or fermentative principle.

The apricot, peach, and quince, from its analogy to the apple and pear, is better qualified for making a species of cyder than wine.

I have books written about winemaking that go back to the mid-1700s. I will give a few museum-piece recipes that are still excellent.

Gooseberry Wine

When the weather is dry, gather your gooseberries about the time they are half ripe; pick them clean, and put the quantity of a peck in a convenient vessel, and bruise them with a piece of wood, taking as much care as possible to keep the seeds whole. When you have done this, put the pulp into a canvas or hair bag, and press out all the juice; and to every gallon [5 American quarts] of the gooseberries, add about three pounds of fine loaf sugar; mix it all together by stirring it with a stick.

Pour this into a convenient vat and allow it to ferment for a week or two, the vat being no more than three-quarters full. Cover it with a cloth or lid.

After standing the proper time, draw it off from the lees and put it into a sweet cask, filling the cask and stoppering it loosely. Let a cask of ten or twelve gallons stand about three months, and twenty gallons five months; after which it will be fit for bottling off.

[*Its Virtues.*] This is a curious cooling drink, taken with great success in all hot diseases, as fevers, small-pox, the hot fit of the ague; it stops laxation, is good in the bloody-flux, cools the heat of the liver and stomach, stops bleeding, and mitigates inflammations; it wonderfully abates slushings, and redness of the face, after hard drinking, or the like; provokes urine, and is good against the stone; but those that are of a very phlegmatic condition should not make use of it.

One old recipe calls for the fermentation to proceed in a filled cask, which will permit only a tiny bit of oxygen to reach the wine and thus will limit the rate of fermentation severely. Also the recipe specifies that the cask should be in a cool room, which will also serve to limit it. The author of the recipe, Mr. William C. Aham, writing in 1768, says the wine must ferment about two weeks if in a 9-gallon cask, forty days if in a 20-gallon cask. This is one of the methods now being experimented with by present-day home winemakers, and it's worth experimenting with by you, perhaps, when you tire of the more conventional way.

A few other recipes:

Mulberry Wine

Take mulberries when nearly ripe; bruise them in a tub, and to every quart of the bruised berries put a like quantity of water; let the mixture stand for twenty-four hours, strain it through a coarse sieve, and having added to every gallon [5 American quarts] of the diluted juice three or four pounds of sugar, suffer it to ferment, and when fine bottle it.

Raspberry Wine

To ten quarts of mashed raspberries add eight quarts of water [10 American quarts], let the mixture stand twenty-four hours, strain the mass through a coarse hair sieve, and to every gallon [5 American quarts] add from two to three pounds of lump sugar, and suffer it to ferment.

Cherry Wine

An excellent wine may be made from cherries in the following manner: Take Morello cherries, not over ripe, picked off from their stalks, mash them in a mortar or pan to detach the pulp without bruising the stones, and suffer the mass to stand twenty-four hours. Press the pulp through a coarse hair sieve, and to every three gallons

[3 ¾ American gallons] add from eight to nine pounds of loaf sugar. Put the mixture into a cask, suffer it to ferment, and rake the wine from its lees as soon as it becomes clear. Some manufacturers crack the stones, and hang them, with the bruised kernels, in a bag suspended from the bung hole, in the cask, during the fermentation of the wine, which thus acquires a nutty flavor.

Damson wine may be made in a similar manner.

Cowslip Wine

Dissolve 25 pounds of loaf sugar in nine and a half gallons of boiling water [11 ¾ American gallons]; fill with the solution a ten gallon cask [12 ½], and add to it, when no longer warm, half a pint of ale yeast and the juice and yellow rind of twelve lemons. Suffer the mixture to ferment, and when the fermentation has nearly ceased (not before) add to it eight or ten handfuls of the petals of cowslips, and suffer the fermentation to proceed in the usual manner. When the wine is clear, draw it off into bottles. If the flowers be added at the commencement of the fermentation, their flavouring substance is greatly dissipated: whereas, by adding flower petals at the end of the fermentative process, or suspending them for a few days in the cask, their flavour remains combined with the wine.

Apricot Wine

Take apricots, when nearly ripe, remove the stones, and bruise the pulp in a mortar. To 8 lbs. of the pulp add a quart of water; suffer the mixture to stand for twenty-four hours, and then squeeze out the juice; add to every gallon [5 American quarts] of it two pounds of loaf sugar;

put it into a cask and suffer it to ferment, and when perfectly clear, bottle it.

Peach wine may be made in a like manner.

English Grape Wine

Crush ten pounds of ripe grapes and add water equal to the lot, and let ferment in a covered tub. After three or four days remove the hulls and press the juice they contain into the tub. Add for each gallon [5 American quarts] of juice two to three pounds of sugar, first dissolved in some of the juice, the greater amount for a sweet wine. Cover and let ferment for three or four days.

Siphon the wine off its lees into glass or pottery jugs or into a cask, filling the containers and bunging up loosely. In the spring, once warm weather has well returned, siphon carefully off its lees and bottle.

Orange Wine

As the orange (and also the lemon), although not a native fruit, is familiar to us, we shall consider them in one view. They differ principally from other fruits in the quantity of their uncombined acid. Take the outer rind of 100 Seville oranges, so thinly pared that no white appears in it, pour upon it ten and a half gallons [13 American gallons] of boiling water; suffer it to stand for eight or ten hours, and having strained off the liquor, whilst slightly warm, add to it the juice of the pulp, and from 26 to 30 pounds of lump sugar, and a few tablespoonsful of yeast; suffer it to ferment in the cask for about five days, or till the fermentation has apparently ceased, and when the wine is perfectly transparent, draw it off from its lees, and bottle it.

Raisin Wine

Upon 24 lbs. of raisins, picked from the stalks, pour six gallons of boiling water [7 ½ American gallons] and add six pounds of sugar; let them macerate about 10 to 14 days, stirring it every day; then pour off the liquor, squeeze out the raisins, and add to it three-quarters of a pound of finely powdered super-tartrate of potash. Put the liquor into a cask, reserving a sufficient quantity for filling up the cask, and draw off the wine when the fermentation has ceased.

In the Museum Rusticum we have the following directions of making raisin wine: "put thirty gallons of soft water [37 ½ American gallons] into a vessel at least one-third bigger than sufficient to contain that quantity; and add to it one hundred and twenty pounds of raisins, picked from their stalks. Mix the whole well together, and cover the vessel with a cloth. When it has stood a little while in a warm place, it will begin to ferment, and must be well stirred about twice in twenty-four hours, for twelve or fourteen days. When the sweetness is nearly gone off, and the fermentation much abated, which will be perceived by the subsiding and rest of the raisins, strain off the fluid, pressing it out of the raisins, first by hand, and afterwards by a press. Let this liquor be put into a wine-cask, well dried and warmed, adding eight pounds of Lisbon sugar, and a little yeast, and reserving part of the liquor to be added from time to time, to fill up the casks whilst the fermentation is going on."

A raisin wine, possessing the flavour of Frontaignac, may be made in the following manner:—

Take six pounds of raisins, boil them in six gallons of

water [7 ½ American gallons], and when perfectly soft, rub them through a cullender, to separate the stones. Add the pulp to the water in which the raisins have been boiled, pour this mixture upon 12 lbs. of white sugar, and suffer it to ferment, with the addition of half a pint of yeast. When the fermentation has nearly ceased, add a quarter of a peck of elder flowers, contained in a bag, which should be suspended in the cask, and removed when the wine has acquired the desired flavour. When the wine has become clear, draw it off into bottles.

Mr. Accum favors fermenting his wines in casks, as you see. Others preferred to ferment them in a vat for the first four or five days, while the frothing of the fermentation was proceeding, then to siphon the juice into a cask or jug.

Mr. Aham in his 1768 book had a recipe for birch wine, which I particularly like to think about. I have never had birch wine and in a way never want to have it, but the recipe is a pleasant speculation.

To Make Birch Wine

As this is a liquor but little understood, I shall be as particular as possible in my directions concerning it. In the first place, as to the season for getting the liquor from Birch trees, which sometimes happens the latter end of February or beginning of March, before the leaves shoot out, as the sap begins to rise; and this is according to the mildness or rigour of the weather; and if the time is delayed, the juice will grow too thick to be drawn out, which should be as thin and clear as possible. The method of procuring the juice is by boring holes in the trunk of the tree, and fixing fossets made of elder; but care should be taken not to tap it in too many places at once, for fear of hurting the tree. If the tree is large, it may be bored in five or six places at once, and place bottles to let it drop in. When you have extracted a proper quantity, three, four, or five gallons from different trees, cork the bottle very close, and rosin or wax them till you begin to make your wine, which should be as soon as possible after you have got the juice.

As soon as you begin, boil the sap as long as you can take off any scum; and put four pounds of fine loaf-sugar to every gallon [5 American quarts] of the juice, and the peel of a lemon cut thin; then boil it again for near an hour, scumming it all the while, and pour it into a tub. As soon as it is almost cold, work it with a toast spread with yeast, and let it stand five or six days, stirring it twice or three times each day. Take a cask that will contain it, and put a lighted match dipped well in brimstone into the cask; stop it up till the match is burnt out, and then turn your wine into it, putting the bung lightly in till it has done working. Bung it very close for about three months, and bottle it off for use. It will be fit in a week after it is put in the bottles.

Flowers have been used for centuries to enhance the bouquet of English country wines. The pure-white elderflowers are the ones most often preferred. Rose petals, yellow for white wines and any color for red, are a close second, and a mixture of the two offers a whole world of varied possibilities. Of either flower, one-quarter to three-quarters pint per gallon is the approved range. The flowers are put in the must and are allowed to ferment with the fruit juice. Dried flowers, not as successful, are sometimes used; one-quarter ounce of dried petals is approximately equivalent to three-quarters pint of the fresh ones.

Here are other old recipes from other books, the gallons being American ones.

Blackberry Wine

Fill a crock with ripe blackberries. Add enough spring water, cooler than the temperature of your hand, to cover. Tie a cloth over the crock. In four days pour the juice through a coarse cloth and use the cloth to press out the juice remaining in the berries. For 1 gallon of juice add 2 pounds of brown sugar, or white if you prefer it. Let this ferment in the crock, cloth covered as before, stirring it once a day for a week. Then draw it off its lees into a jug. Cork it and set it in a cellar for two months.

Dandelion Wine

Pick a peck of dandelion blossoms and remove all stems. If you like, dry the blossoms in the sun until they smell like hay, but you need not. To 4 gallons of water add 8 pounds of sugar and boil the sugar and water and blossoms for a few minutes. Let it cool and add the juice and pulp of a fruit, in the amount of eighteen plums or six oranges or the equivalent of rhubarb stalks, currants, or whatever you like, or use a mixture of fruit. Add two chopped-up potatoes or two pieces of dried-out bread. Add yeast if the fermentation has not started by morning. Ten days after fermentation begins, you can strain and bottle the wine.

(This is a dry wine and might profit by further sweetening as fermentation nears its end.)

Clary Wine

The clary is a potherb grown in England, and other places.

Dissolve 3 pounds of sugar for every gallon of water used and let cool. Add 1 quart of the tops and flowers of the clary for every gallon. Add yeast if it is needed. Add the juice of a stalk of rhubarb or of one lemon. Put it in a wooden cask, three-fourths full. Stir it twice a day for one week or shake the cask. In the winter, siphon the juice off the lees, bottle, and cork it; add brandy if desired. Store in a cool, dark cellar for six months. If you do not add brandy, leave the bottles standing straight up so the corks can be blown if fermentation recommences the following spring.

Rose Hip Wine

In autumn when the rose hips are red or orange, crush or chop 1 gallon and add 1 gallon of water. Add 2 pounds of sugar for each gallon of water. Add yeast. Stir each day for one week. Strain and bottle but do not cap securely until fermentation has stopped, when no more bubbles are creeping up the inside of the bottle.

Ginger Wine

Ginger wine is also called ginger beer or ginger ale.

Crush an ounce of ginger root. Add the peel of a lemon,

only the yellow trimmings, not the white pulp. Add half a pound of sugar. If you can buy cream of tartar, add half an ounce of that. Put these in a pot and pour in a gallon of boiling water.

When it has cooled, put in the juice of a lemon and your yeast. Ferment it, like any other wine. Ferment it three days and drink it in three days more.

Ginger is sometimes used to flavor other wines; use either the root or candied ginger. Or to flavor ethyl alcohol to make a liqueur, one ounce to a quart, water and sugar subsequently added.

Currant Wine

To every gallon of juice pressed from one-third black currants and two-thirds red currants, add 2 gallons of soft water. If you have only hard water, boil it for one-half hour, but you must cool it to under 85 degrees before using it in the wine. Add 5 pounds of brown sugar. After fermentation rack into clean jugs and loosely stopper. Rack again in two or three months. If by the middle of spring the wine needs clearing, add 4 ounces of isinglass dissolved in a pint of the wine, which will fine and clear it. The wine must in a week be drawn into clean casks or can be bottled, whichever is preferable.

(This is a dry wine and when aged will resemble a dry French grape wine, an inexpensive Bordeaux.)

Rhubarb Wine

Use the stalks only. The roots and leaves are poisonous and have been used as a poison since ancient times.

To each gallon of juice add 1 gallon of soft water and 5 pounds of brown sugar. Fill a keg or barrel with this preparation, leaving the bung out, and keep it filled with sweet water, as it works off, until clear. Bung down or bottle as you please. The stalks will yield three-quarters their weight in juice. Fine and settle with isinglass if need be. "This wine will not lead to intemperance," the recipe says. Any other vegetable extract may be used if this is not liked, it says.

(This recipe will make a sweet rhubarb wine, and a sweet rhubarb wine makes the best use of the rhubarb taste; however, we suggest you add the sugar a bit at a time, until the yeast will convert no more, then if necessary add still more to taste.)

Peach Wine by a Modern Way

This contemporary recipe for sweet wine will also serve for plums or apricots, or for a mixture of fruit.

Destone 10 pounds of ripe fruit.

Add 5 pounds of sugar.

Add 4 gallons of water.

Add 6 teaspoons of tartaric acid.

Add 1 teaspoon of grape tannin.

Add wine yeast and ferment the wine in a fermenting vat or cask three-fourths full.

On the fourth day add 2 pounds of sugar. Dissolve it first in a quantity of the fermenting wine.

When the saccharometer reads zero gravity or thereabouts (1.000), add sugar slowly, grudgingly, each day until fermentation virtually ceases.

Sweeten to taste.

Rack into a clean cask or carboy and attach a waterlock, or bung the container reasonably tight at first, quite tight in a week or two.

Keep topped up.

Rack in three months. If it needs more sugar, add it. Re-attach waterlock or bung tightly.

In three months rack again as before.

In the spring, after warm weather returns, rack and bottle and cork. Store in a dark, fairly cool place. Before bottling, if you want to, sulfite it with one Campden tablet for each gallon, to help maintain its color.

Root Beer

The roots used are burdock roots; this is a big-leafed plant that volunteers to grow in old farms and sometimes in city fields, and it will take digging to get the roots out. Dig out 2 pounds of them if you can, wash the dirt off them, cut them up, and put them in a pot.

Also put in the pot ¼ pound of hops, ½ pint of corn which you have roasted until brown, and add some sassafras, either dried or the roots of the sassafras bush, using only a little of it. Boil this all together in 3 gallons of tap water for twenty minutes or so, using a cover on the pot, then strain the liquid into a fermenting vat. Fill the vat up to the 5-gallon mark with water. You want only a 3-percent-alcohol brew. You can sweeten with molasses, syrup, or sugar, either brown or white sugar or a mixture of them; of sugar you would add ½ pound for each gallon.

At about 70 degrees, add a packet or vial of yeast, and yeast nutrients; it helps in getting quick fermentation to have started the yeast a day or two earlier in fruit juice, or in sugar water and nutrients.

Let this mixture ferment. In two days' time—that is, if you start it all at noon on Thursday, then on Saturday noon—you will be able to drink it. It will not be clear, but root beer need not be, and it will be effervescent. It ought to be chilled before use.

Persimmon Beer

I tried to make persimmon beer once before I knew much about winemaking, and had a fearful mess because the instructions were to put straw in the bottom of a fermenting vat and alternate layers of persimmons and of locust pods. To say the least, there are simpler ways. Get a gallon of persimmons which are dead ripe, mix them with an equal quantity of bran, and mash them together. Add a few gallons of warm water, and when the temperature is lukewarm, add yeast and yeast nutrient. Let this mixture ferment. When the persimmons rise to the top, siphon off the beer and drink it.

Rice Wine

In England brown rice is used, as I suspect it is in Japan, where rice wine is called sake. In England the intent usually is to ferment as strong a wine as possible, and this usually means, by wine yeast fermentation standards, 14 to 16 percent. Some yeasts will reach higher, but you might more reasonably expect 14 and add sugar at the end, if the yeast responds to it a bit at a time.

This is a modern recipe.

Soak 2 pounds of brown rice in 2 gallons of water for eight hours or longer, then boil the rice in this same water until it is soft. Any scum which forms on the surface should be removed.

Pour the rice and its water into a fermenting vat. Add ½ teaspoon of green tea leaves.

Add 2 pounds of sugar, white or brown.

Add half a packet of dry wine yeast and yeast nutrient tablets.

In two or three days, add 2 more pounds of sugar.

A day or two after that, add 1 pound of sugar, and at that time, or on the next day, rack the wine into a jug, or jugs, filling each, and put cotton in its mouth, or a fermentation lock. Let the wine ferment at 65 to 75 degrees, adding sugar a bit at a time, until the yeasts are exhausted.

The wine will in time clear, even if it is not siphoned off its lees again. It might take a long while. If it does not clear, fine it before you bottle it, as described in Appendix 2.

Some makers add raisins, as much as a pound or so for 2 pounds of rice.

Sake should be served at room temperature, or warmer.

Potato wine can be made the same way.

14

French Red Wines

Burgundy is a region of small holdings and of small holders who grow their own grapes on their own land and make their own wine in their own homes. Which is the way winemaking should be everywhere.

The part of Burgundy most famous for wines lies just south of Dijon, a narrow strip perhaps 30 miles long which has been named the Côte d'Or, either for the golden color the vine-covered land assumes in autumn or for the high quality of its wines, or both—nobody really knows. Its hillsides yield many of the great wines of the world: Clos-Vougeot, Chambertin, Eschezeaux, Romanée-Conti, Musigny, Richebourg, Corton-Charlemagne, Montrachet. . . . Vintners work the acres of vineyards and tend to the making of their wines.

For our purposes in this chapter on red wines we will deal with the northern half of the Côte, the Côte de Nuits, named after its largest town, Nuits-St.-Georges. Each time I have traveled through the Côte d'Or, I have been surprised by how unimpressive it appears to be, which sets me at odds with the travel books. The fields are routinely laid out. The towns themselves are pretty but are seen at a glance; Nuits-St.-Georges alone, with three thousand people, is large enough to turn around in. There is a small hotel there, which sometimes locks its door and shuts off the lights at 9 P.M., and a charming, tiny inn, the Cultivators. I like that place best, but by all means insist on a room on the back, should you go there for the night. The front two or three rooms are on the highway that goes from Lyon to Dijon, and the trucks snort along it, one after another, all night long. The food is good here, as it is most everywhere in France, and the wine list is a dear marvel.

There is no commercialization of wine tasting in the Côte, the sport which attracts us in California from one winery to another—attracts me, anyway. The Côte d'Or is nothing in the world but an agricultural district of gentle hillsides and wide valleys, its vineyards crowded side by side, the best ones on the hillsides rather than on the flatlands, their vines exposed to the sun on the lower slopes of the hills, facing east or southeast by south. Its earth has a limestone base, and the soil is mixed with fuller's marl and crumbled rock. The soil is rich in potassium and phosphorus and rather lean in nitrogen.

Burgundies are assertive, big-shouldered wines, with a delicious aroma derived in part I suspect from their moldy cellars. All the red wines on the Côte de Nuits which bear the name of their own vineyard are made from Pinot noir grapes, low-yield dark-blue, almost black grapes, tightly packed in small bunches. When they ripen, the fields are populated with anxious growers and their families and neighbors, and thousands of students who come to Burgundy to work for sixty cents an hour, room and board, yes and wine—or so the salary was when I was last there. The grapes grow on three wires strung post to post, the middle line of doubled wire, the top line about 3 feet from the ground. On the valley floors the Gamay grows and produces three or four times as much juice, but its juice when harvested in Burgundy makes an inferior wine.

The selection of pickers involves a vintner with time-honored considerations, some of them unlikely to pass scientific review. He might ponder whether a picker is an old woman, or is a mother, or is a virgin, for it used to be generally believed and still is believed by many that a picker's personality and personal attributes make a difference in the finished wine. One vintner explained to me perfectly seriously that one picker who was menstruating would taint all the wine she helped to pick. I asked him how in selecting pickers he determined such a matter, and the best I could tell from his answer, which was admittedly evasive, he determined it as best he could. This restriction goes alongside another infrequently encountered, the one barring women from wine cellars, particularly pregnant women.

When the vintner gives the word, the pickers he has assembled move into his rows, hauling bunches of Pinot noir in baskets to the clay service roads, where they are loaded into big baskets and into trucks.

The grapes at harvest should reach about 23 percent sugar in their juice. The acidity of the juice ideally should be about 0.8 percent as tartaric. Too much rain will dilute the juice,

and a clouded sun will fail to increase the sugar. The problem always is to mature the grape with sugar enough, at the
time the acidity is reduced enough. Nearly every year is a
compromise with the ideal, each grower deciding when to
compromise, some unleashing their bevy of pickers on their
small holdings during one week, only to see their friends
waiting day by day, even week after week, in the next vineyard. Meanwhile the sun is either shining or not shining, the
rain is falling or not falling, and the workers have to be paid.

The *cuverie* to which the grapes are taken is in the vintner's
house or barn, or is in one of the towns. In the latter case it is
shared by a number of vintners, a cooperative venture which
saves them individually from the expense of buying crushers,
de-stemmers, presses, fermentation vats. It also encourages
the further celebration of the harvest.

The grapes are not washed. They are crushed by machine.
The machine does its work more efficiently than did humans using their feet long ago, and it is quicker and drinks
less new wine. The machines are constructed so that they do
not crush the pips, which would impart bitterness to the juice.

Overripe and green grapes are removed, insofar as practical. The grapes are de-stemmed, since the stems and husks
contain more green acid than is wanted in the juice; some
makers de-stem completely, others only partially, the decision
resting on their judgment as vintners and the amount of acid
in the year's crop of grapes.

The crushed grapes, their juice and skins and pulp and
pips and some of their husks and stems, are put in big oak
vats, the juice from a given vineyard and of a given vintner
being kept separate from all others.

When brought from the field the grapes have on their hulls
a misty coating of wine yeasts and of bacteria, a complex

assortment, some highly desirable and some of the bacteria, particularly if the grapes are overripe, undesirable. The vintners mildly sulfite the juice to kill these spoil bacteria. A few vintners go farther and seek to kill the yeast as well, and they then introduce new yeast. Most, however, make wine the way their fathers and grandfathers made it and entrust the juice to the two or three types of wild yeast which naturally grow on the grapes, some simply because their fathers did, which after all is a satisfying reason since their fathers made good wine, and others because they believe that the replacement of the many yeasts and bacteria with a single strain of pure yeast results in a less complex, less distinctive taste and is undesirable.

The oak fermenting vats are left open to the air for a while, or merely have a cloth drawn over them to keep flies out. Quite soon the wild yeasts that were on the grapes, now that they have access to the sugar inside the pulp, begin converting it into ethyl alcohol and carbon dioxide, the carbon dioxide gas escaping out of the top of the vat.

If the weather turns cold, a cold-fermenting yeast is likely to be added to the must. This bad weather happens one year in twelve, an acquaintance, a vintner in Nuits-St.-Georges named Marcel Bouquinet, tells me, but as he says, "The twelfth year could come almost any time, even twice in two."

If in waiting for the grapes to mature the vintners find that the acidity has fallen below the desired level, they might go into their fields for a supply of the hard little green grapes which did not ripen and crush and add those. Or they will leave in more of the stems and stalks. Or they will decide to leave the juice and hulls together an extra day, so the juice can extract more of the tannin and acids contained there. They could do as many home winemakers do and add tartaric or other acids, but they do not, contending that such artificial changes alter the taste of the wine. Actually, too little acidity is a rare occurrence in Burgundy anyway. Too much acidity is more common, but this is not as serious a problem when it occurs, for the grapes can be more thoroughly de-stemmed and if necessary the skins can be removed sooner than usual.

More frequently, perhaps two years in five, the vintners have too little sugar. Two percent sugar in the juice will yield about 1 percent of alcohol in the finished wine. If the grapes do not have 23 percent of sugar in them, the finished wine will not have 11 ½ percent of alcohol, the minimum required by the *Appellation Contrôlée*, the control agency under which the best vineyards in Burgundy are listed. Therefore, in such a year, supposedly under officials' supervision, sugar is added to the must. A hydrometer is used to test the amount of sugar in the grape juice, as most home winemakers soon discover, and it is then possible to determine how much sugar is needed for the wine to reach its minimum strength. Occasionally, though infrequently, a wine has too much sugar, as in 1947. In that year the grapes had up to 32 percent sugar, and the yeasts in some vats drugged themselves before their work was done. The result was a sweet red wine, a novelty in France. The 1947s, in the main, were shipped out of the country, I understand.

Any sugar to be added is put in on the third or fourth day of fermentation, not during the first few days, because there is enough natural sugar in the must to start a burst of activity, even overactivity, and yeasts do better in a lean rather than a rich environment. Also, it is in the best interest of the wine that the fermentation, which generates heat, not go beyond bounds. The more sugar, the more danger of excess.

In the fermentation vat, foam and skins and froth rise in a protective cap and will overflow if the vats have been filled beyond, say, three-quarters full. Once or twice a day the vintners remove the cloth cover and push down this yeasty head, which protects the wine, break it up, and even aerate the wine, encouraging the yeast, but they aerate it less each day as the fermentation proceeds. The Burgundy vintners permit high fermentation temperatures, higher than those of most other vintners in France, in spite of the advice given them by scientists, who contend that fermentation beyond 80 degrees is undesirable. Most Burgundy vintners ferment in the 90s as a matter of course and tradition and do not become alarmed if the temperature rises as high as 103 degrees. Even at 95 the heat will have a caramelizing effect noticeable in the finished wine—sometimes too noticeable, perhaps. Some of the larger vats are likely to have refrigeration devices, used to keep the juice from exceeding 99 degrees.

Modern researchers also point out that the lower temperatures, about 75, retard the development of spoil bacteria, and they suggest further that a closed vat, after the initial stage of aerating the ferment to get it started, will handicap these bacteria and will improve the performance of the yeast. Burgundy vintners ignore this advice, too, and usually cover the vat thickly only if the temperature goes too low to suit them. In arguments of this sort—and arguments of this sort go on in Burgundy all the time—one is prompted to remember that the Burgundy makers produce the best red wines made anywhere in the world—or one of the two best, if you prefer claret.

The color of the wine is another consideration. If it isn't dark enough, the vintner might well heat a pot of skins and juice to 140 to 170 degrees, which extracts more color from the skins, and pour this into the vat, repeating the process as he finds advisable.

When the yeasts have gorged themselves—they are in fact plants, but I think of them as tiny germs—and have begun to work more lazily in a solution they have made alcoholic, the froth becomes less heavy. On the fifth or sixth day the wine is racked off the skins into another vat, and a press is used to crush out the juice remaining in the skins. This new juice is usually added; the juice from a second pressing is sometimes added, though it often is kept separate to be made into an inferior wine. The pressed juice constitutes 10 to 20 percent of the whole.

After about a day in the new vat, the wine is put into casks, usually about 60 gallons in size, and taken to the vintner's cellar. These are oak casks, properly cured, and some of them are old, some new.

The wine cellar is under the vintner's house as a rule. It probably has casks of last year's wine along one wall, casks of year before last's wine along another—unless they have been bottled or shipped to a merchant. The barrels for this year's wine find a place, and the bungs are left out of the bungholes entirely. If a few fruit flies lay their eggs in the open bunghole, the vintner will now and then flip them out with his finger, if he bothers. "They are not enough to matter," I have been told by one. I understand that many Burgundy makers tolerate a slight amount of vinegar in their wine anyway, about one part in fifty thousand; they like the taste when added with the whole.

One of the duties of the vintner and his family is to keep the casks topped up. The wine evaporates out of the bunghole and through the staves, and some is absorbed by the wood. Another task is to keep the cellar, which normally is about

56 degrees, at a warmer temperature, about 68 degrees. This is done in my friend Marcel Bouquinet's case with an electric heater, which he operates only at night since electricity is cheaper at night in France. He heats the cellar to a rousing 70 degrees each night and allows it to cool somewhat during the daytime.

In a week or so the bung, wrapped with one thickness of burlap, is loosely fitted in the bunghole. The duty of topping up the wine continues, a small cask full of the same wine being kept for that purpose.

In about a month from birth, the wine is racked off its lees; the juice is siphoned or pumped into a clean cask, leaving behind the bits of pulp, pasty masses of yeast, and the other residue of the alcohol and acid fermentations. The bung is more securely fitted now. The wine will be racked again in March, then seasonally three more times its first year and once or twice its second.

None of the vintners that I have ever seen use the water-locks, a device described in Appendix 2; they simply keep clean burlap around the bung and tap the bung into the barrels, more tightly as time passes. (Am I right in thinking there is the faint, sweet aroma of burlap in the bouquet of some of the best bottles of Burgundy?) The gases formed by the continuing slow fermentation can find their way out through the burlap, once they develop sufficient pressure, and this will require the formation of a protective layer of carbon dioxide in any air space remaining in the cask.

The wine tastes abominable. There is nothing in the world of foods more unpromising when young than a red Burgundy, unless it is a white Burgundy. Six months after it is made it is fit, in the judgment of strangers who taste it, only to be poured down the drain. It is muddy, yeasty, acetic, and has no saving graces. But even at the *cuverie,* and with more assurance as each month passes, a Burgundy vintner can evaluate its properties and estimate its finish. He decides that this is as bad a year as he thought it was, or this is going to be as good a year as three years ago, or whatever. Some years yield high quantity but disappointing quality, and some the reverse. Only now and then do quality and quantity arrive together. Always the vintners hope that a wine will be as good as in 1959 or 1966, which were outstanding years for red Burgundies. They hope it will not be as bad a vintage as 1968. If it is, many of the vintners will do something not required by the law or rules: They will take the wine to the vinegar factory in Dijon.

The oak used in the casks is French oak, as a rule. Old vintners would sometimes take their cooper to the forest to select the trees they wanted used, even the side of the trunk they wanted used. Vintners are particular about their casks, which impart more tannin to the wine, and tannin not only contributes to the taste and finish but, they believe, helps preserve it in its old age. Some vintners sell their wine in the casks, as early as the March racking. Recently, within the last thirty years, they have begun to bottle their own wine, or some of it. The best red Burgundy is today bottled at the end of the second or third year; it needs to be breathing at least two years in oak wood before being bottled. It should age in the bottle for two to six years longer. The slant-shouldered, hefty green bottles are likely to be stacked in the wine cellars where the newer wines are casked. They are sometimes stacked according to the cask from which they were taken, since even from the same field, even if made by the same vintner, wines from two different casks are sometimes not quite the same—although the likelihood of significant differences is easily exaggerated.

Marcel Bouquinet prefers a relatively young wine to an

over-aged one. "Young women are prettier," he told me. I
wondered at the time whether his opinion had been governed
at all by his limited storage space. I have bought wine from
him on two occasions. He charges considerably less than
half what the wine would cost in Paris, but in Paris, he tells
me, "You cannot buy a good bottle of wine. Last year in Paris
for three days I looked everywhere and did not find but one
good bottle." The adulteration of Burgundy wine and the
mislabeling of cheaper wines as Burgundy apparently remain
problems for the Frenchman, as well as for the Englishman
and American.

Marcel's wine is a typical, full-bodied, dark-colored Burgundy, enhanced by the aroma which the best Burgundy wines
have. Some people claim they can taste raspberries in the
wine of a given Burgundy vineyard, or blackberries or currants. The bouquet and taste do have differing subtle qualities,
but I insist on no such specific, subtle qualities in a bottle of
Burgundy. I do want the complex, long-lived Burgundy bouquet and taste, and the wine Marcel makes has them.

The corks used are Spanish or Portuguese and permit the
wine to breathe through them. Just before use they are put
in hot water for fifteen to thirty minutes to sterilize them and
to soften them, so they will be easier for the little corking
machine to insert. Before insertion they are dipped briefly
in a bowl of the wine, to keep them from sticking to the neck
of the bottle, in which case they might have to be dug out.

Marcel's wife pastes the label on a bottle only after it is
purchased. The label is applied with glue, by hand. She sits
in the outer room of the cellar and one by one pastes on each
bottle a label which carries the name of the vineyard, then
under that the words *Appellation Contrôlée*, and under that
her husband's name, followed by the word *Propriétaire*. Then

she fixes on each bottle a label giving the wine's year, its vintage, which is a critical consideration in Burgundy.

Foil is put on over the cork with a small hand-operated machine. This further decreases the amount of oxygen the wine can obtain from the air. Over the four years of its life, the breathing of the wine has been more and more limited, from the bursts of aeration at the start, to the casks with open bungs, to casks with closed bungs, to the trickle of oxygen coming into the bottle through the cork, and now to the partial seal set over the cork. This whole operation is in accordance with historic practices, all having been endorsed by the French chemist Pasteur, who first discovered that yeasts were the fermenting agent in wine and who decided that oxygen in controlled and decreasing amounts was necessary for their best performance in making the best wine.

There are hundreds of red wines in France, and most of them are made in the same way as Burgundy, with a few differences we can mention here. The vast differences in the character of the wines come from the grapes used, rather than from the techniques.

The long-lived wines of Bordeaux, which take fifteen to twenty years to mature and will last up to eighty, have for centuries been called clarets by the English, from the old French word *clairet*. They are blended wines made 60 to 95 percent of Cabernet Sauvignon grapes. These grapes give the wine body and finish and longevity. Less frequently than in Burgundy is sugar added, Bordeaux being just enough farther south for the grapes to ripen with enough sugar. The fermenting temperature is lower, in the 80s. Bordeaux vintners sometimes refer to the Burgundy wines as "cooked wines."

Unfortunately, an effort is being made today to make Bordeaux wines which will mature younger than those of past generations. The trend is to shorten the maturing, which also shortens the life-span. These practices include the following: Stems and husks are removed entirely—sometimes by hand, incidentally. The vintner uses less of the pressed juice than before, the free-run juice having less acid and tannin in it. Some makers use less Cabernet Sauvignon in the blend. Some rack the wine more often, so that it develops quicker. Some use smaller casks, which permit more breathing through the staves and therefore allows it to age quicker.

Some of the makers sulfite the juice—many do not—and most makers ferment with the natural yeasts that come on the skins of the grapes.

The wine made today is bottled near the end of its second or third year and ages in the bottle for four to ten years.

There are hundreds of châteaux in Bordeaux, and they make larger quantities of excellent wine than do any other makers in the world. St. Emilion, a robust, fleshy, friendly wine also made in Bordeaux, is the equal of much of the château wine.

The Beaujolais vineyards lie just south of the Côte d'Or. The vintners there, in order to help keep a fruity flavor and aroma, do not crush the grapes. They are de-stemmed, which process tears them, and then the juice is allowed to ferment on the skins. The grapes used are Gamay, black with white juice. The Gamay does far better here than on the Côte d'Or. The wines are not left in the cask long; sometimes they are bottled as early as six months—sometimes they are served out of the casks themselves when under six months of age, again to take advantage of their fruity taste. Within two years they begin to lose their charm and by two years have lost much of it. The demand is so great in France for this light, happy wine that in Paris alone each year more bottles labeled Beaujolais are used than the total output of Beaujolais, which gives you some idea what chance you and I have of getting a genuine bottle of it in most places.

In the Rhône Valley, Côte Rotie, Hermitage, and Châteauneuf-du-Pape are three varieties. They are blends of various grapes but in other respects are made by the same process as is used in Burgundy. They need as much aging as a Burgundy, too, and rarely receive it.

15

White Table Wines of France

White wines require more precautions in their making than do red. They are lighter and more fruity in taste and aroma and have by nature precious little coloring matter or tannin, so any defects in taste or appearance are more noticeable.

Most of them have a touch of sweetness, even the so-called dry ones, and some, of course, are quite sweet indeed.

They are made from white, green, red, purple, dark-blue, or even black grapes. They don't ferment on their skins, and the skins are where, in almost all grapes, the color resides. So the color of the grape is not necessarily the color of a wine made from it.

White Dry Wines

One of the best wines of France is Montrachet, a resident of the southern half of the Côte d'Or. Its vineyard is located just north of Beaune. By reputation, Montrachet is the best of the white Burgundies, the wine Alexandre Dumas said should be drunk kneeling, with head bowed.

The hillside vineyard is divided by old walls into three sections across the slope, the center part being Le Montrachet, the lower part Bâtard-Montrachet, and the upper Chevalier-Montrachet, meaning servants of Montrachet. I suppose Bâtard-Montrachet has to do with near-relatives of Montrachet. The nineteen acres in the center contain the certain soil where the wine is made that Dumas and thousands of others have praised. The rows, identical in all respects, above and below it yield lesser wines which have not quite the same finesse and dignity, the same grandeur, or so we are assured.

The vineyard faces the east and southeast, but the sun falls on it even at suppertime, a trick of topography which might contribute something to its quality. The soil of the Montrachet is 34 percent silica, about 28 percent clay, about 32 percent limestone, and has no appreciable amounts of ironstone. In comparison, the soil of Clos-de-Vougeot is almost 46 percent silica, about 39 percent clay, has 12 percent limestone and about 3 percent ironstone.

The nineteen acres of Le Montrachet have sixteen owners. Some of them own only a bit of it, merely as a prestigious consideration. In fact, all except three of the sixteen have so little that each one's wine will not fill a single cask.

South of Beaune is another outstanding vineyard for white

wines, that of Corton-Charlemagne, once owned by Charlemagne. It lies on the south side of a round little hill, near the
town of Aloxe-Corton. Charlemagne left it to the Church, and
in the sixteenth century, because of the plague and labor
shortage and who knows what else, the Church let it fall into
neglect, and an innkeeper leased it and served its wine at
his inn. Sometime later, a generation or so, perhaps, the vine-

yard was broken up into three parts, and these have come to be owned by seven growers, one of them M. Louis Chapuis, who has from time to time shown me his vineyards and his cellars and has told me how he makes wines.

Corton-Charlemagne often is the equal of Montrachet. Fortunately, it is not in quite the demand and can be purchased more reasonably. It is not as soft as Montrachet or its other famous Burgundy white-wine neighbor, Meursault. It is assertive in taste and aroma—there is nothing elusive about it. I love it dearly, but I understand that the wine is decreasing in quantity because the vineyard is treacherously difficult to work. It is so steep that it must be worked by men without even teams to help, and after every severe storm topsoil must be gathered at the bottom of the hill and carried up the slope. Finding men to do such work is difficult in France, as it is almost anywhere else. We can only hope that as great a wine as this will not be allowed to die away.

Both these wines, Corton-Charlemagne and Montrachet, are made exclusively of the Pinot Chardonnay grape, a white grape which turns from green to yellow as it ripens. From the time the grapes start turning until they are harvested is about fifty days—a slow process, indeed. For the last ten of those fifty days the increase in sugar and decrease in acidity is quite slow.

Only sound, ripe grapes are used. Moldy bunches, which sometimes occur after a rain, are not picked. The grapes are often picked early in the morning, before the sun warms them. The crushing is more thorough than that given red grapes, to make the pressing easier. Although the wine will in the ensuing processes reject most iron or copper that contaminates it, an effort is made to keep the juice away from all metal parts, except stainless steel or those which have been enameled or painted with a plastic paint, in order to diminish the risk of moldiness in the taste and cloudiness in the finished wine, no matter how many years it has aged in the bottle.

The stems are left on; they help in the pressing to form channels for the juice.

Pressing white grapes can be a demanding task, even with wine equipment. The grapes become slippery and do not give up their juice easily. Time and again the press must be opened so the workers can stir and mix the skins and stems.

The first pressing is called a *cuvée,* the second pressing is called the *première taille,* and the third pressing is the *seconde taille.* The juices from these three pressings are mixed, but the juice from the fourth pressing is kept separate and is made into a separate wine, which is inferior to the rest.

The makers mildly sulfite the juice to eliminate unwanted bacteria. However, natural yeasts, those on the grapes, are usually used to ferment the wine.

The fermentation for these white wines is not as dramatic as for the red; the skins and stems cannot rise to form a hat over the wine, simply because there are no skins left in the juice. The vats, which are the same type as those used for red wines, are filled about four-fifths full. Some winemakers elsewhere prefer to ferment white wines in casks, four-fifths full for the first week or so, then full, to the bunghole, but this is not the method used in making white wines in Burgundy.

At the start there is occasional stirring to be done to aerate the must, encouraging the yeast. The vintners try to get the wine from the bottom of the cask to change places with that on top. One other problem is to watch the heat of the fermentation. Initially white wines are fermented in Burgundy at temperatures as high as 95 degrees, but after a few days, when the burst of fermentation lessens, an effort is made to keep the fermenting wine at a constant 65 degrees. In three weeks, for the average vintage, the wine is put in casks filled to the bunghole. The bung is left out for a week or two, then is inserted loosely, then later more tightly, usually with a single thickness of burlap around it. The casks are oak and are used for about ten years each. Since they are not new each year, tannin is added to the wine in old casks, to supply it with more bite, more tartness.

In about a month the wine is racked again into clean casks, and still again in about six months and a year. It is not racked more than two or three times. In rackings, often the Burgundy maker will avoid aerating the wine, for much fragrance can be lost.

Bottling is in eighteen to twenty-four months.

Fining and filtering are more often done with white wines than with reds. Casein is the fining agent used, and number 3 or 5 plates are the filtering papers used.

A newly fermented Montrachet or Corton-Charlemagne is a bad-tasting commodity, and like its heavier-bodied red cousins of Burgundy it is not promising when a year old, either. I mention this in case sometime you make a wine you need to wait for and decide unwisely to dispose of it.

The method described here for making dry white wine is used for most of the dry wines of France, except that some vintners ferment in casks, not vats, from the start. Also some vintners do not use oak cooperage, finding it not as important for white as for red wines. Further, most whites are bottled sooner.

Pouilly-Fumé and Pouilly-Fuissé are two delicate, fruity wines, both bottled in their first year, usually during their

first spring, and are drinkable early, though they improve in
the bottle for up to five years. The first is made from Sauvignon grapes, the latter from the white Pinot.

Chablis is made from Pinot Chardonnay grapes, except for
petit Chablis, which is inferior. The grapes are slow to ripen
this far north and usually do not ripen fully; when they do
the wine has a Burgundy, rather than a Chablis, taste. The
wine is dry, acidic, tart. The French call it a "fish wine" because its acidity helps to enhance the taste of fish dishes. It
is so much in demand that mislabeling is quite common, a
worry to the vintners of Chablis. They say only 10 to 25
percent of the wine labeled Chablis in France has any right
to that label at all.

The Sweet Wines

The Frenchman is less interested in sweet wines than in dry
ones, and wine connoisseurs generally are, too. But most
wines made in California and New York State are sweet, so
apparently Americans prefer sweet wines, and the English
have a liking for sherry and port, and their country wines are
usually sweet. I suppose people ordinarily start out liking
sweet wine better, but many find the dry wines more useful
at mealtime and less cloying. One can't drink a bottle of sweet
wine at a sitting, or I can't, or won't, but one can drink a
bottle of dry. Also, tainting the judgment of the connoisseurs
is the knowledge that a dry wine has not been tampered with,
whereas a bit of sugar is often used to mask the taste of a poor
wine.

In France sweet wines are either white or *rosé*. I know of
no red sweet wines in France.

To understand the process by which sweet wines are made, it is perhaps helpful to recall the basic principle of making wine, that sugar in grape juice is converted to alcohol by wine yeasts. The process continues until either the yeasts have used all the sugar or the alcohol has drugged them to sleep. At 13 to 14 percent, the yeasts will become quite drowsy. Some of them reach 15 or even 16 percent, and special yeasts aspire to 18, but anything beyond 15 is usually intolerable. Unless the alcohol has put the yeasts to rest, any sugar in a sweet wine is likely to arouse them to further labor and will reduce the sweetness of the wine.

One way to negotiate that problem was developed in the eighteenth century by the English. Most of their wines came from Portugal, because Portugal offered a more favorable market for their products than France. The English people, however, didn't like the Portuguese wines as well as the French, and the wine merchants began to experiment with them, trying to improve them. One experiment was this: At a point in the wine's fermentation when it was still sweet, they added brandy, enough to increase the alcohol concentration beyond the yeasts' powers to continue working. The wine was thus stabilized and made safe to ship, and it was, they decided, delicious to drink. They named it Port.

Sherry is another fortified wine, a Spanish wine, but it is not fortified until the yeasts have converted all the sugar in the grape juice. At that time brandy is added, making the resumption of fermentation impossible, and sweetening can then be added, and often is, along with flavorings.

So fortifying, which is not a French process, except that it is used by a few small vintners in the south of France, is one way to make a secure sweet wine.

A second way is to kill the yeast once a desirable alcohol content is reached but before all the sugar is converted. The

French use this method, for the most part. It involves refrigerating the wine, or putting it under compression, or, more likely in France, sulfiting it heavily. Sulfiting is the oldest of the three, but it is not easy to stop the thrust of a thriving fermentation, and the dose used is sometimes so heavy that the nose-tickling aroma of sulfur lingers in the wine itself. Particularly has this been the case in the cheaper wines of Graves.

To make a sweet wine by this method, the vintner seeks grapes with high sugar content. Usually they are grapes grown in warm, sunny valleys, and they are not picked until they are dead ripe. The grapes are crushed and pressed, and the juice is fermented just as for any white wine, except that once the yeasts have produced at least 11 ½ percent alcohol content the wine is racked, then sulfited heavily, then filtered. It is subsequently racked seasonally, with a small dose of sulfite at each or every other racking.

Should the juice not be sweet enough for both minimum alcohol content and sweetness in a certain year, the vintner can add a small amount of sugar, or he can settle for a dry white wine, which vintners sometimes do, particularly in making Sauternes. Normally a Sauternes in France is sweet, but not always; a California Sauterne (as it is named and spelled) is dry, a long-ago misinterpretation of the French wine.

There is a third way to make sweet wine, and that is to use so sweet a juice that the yeasts cannot convert it all, so they go to sleep in their own brew. This feat is accomplished artificially by adding sugar, as in English country wines, or naturally in France by growing an excruciatingly sweet grape in order to attain the desired high degree of sweetness.

Château Yquem, the most famous château in Sauternes, in

Bordeaux, and other châteaux of Sauternes permit the grapes to be partially devoured by a fungus, which saps them of much of their water and uses up some of their acid and in this way, in effect, concentrates their sugar. The fungus is called the *pourriture noble*, the noble rot. To attract it, the grapes are left on the vine until the rot cracks their skins and feeds on them. The result is not a pretty sight, but the grapes become sweet as honey. The wine yield per acre is reduced, and the costs of the wine are for that reason alone increased. The labor is increased, too, another expense, for the field workers must gather the grapes only as they are ready, which requires repeated visits down the same rows to the same vines, even to the same bunches. The more dedicated the grower, the more insistent he is on perfection in the picking. His pickers will gather the grapes from the bunches. (The German wine Trockenberrenauslese and the Hungarian Tokay are made from grapes similarly afflicted and picked, and the German Berrenauslese is made from grapes similarly afflicted but picked off the vines in bunches rather than individually.)

The grapes are crushed in the usual way for white wines, and fermentation is allowed to proceed naturally until the alcohol in the wine kills the yeasts—hopefully, as in good years, before the sugar is exhausted. The result is a high alcohol content and a delicious, balanced wine once it is matured, with the advantages of an entirely natural process. In years when the rot does not appear, the best makers do not release their wine, except as a regular Sauternes.

The best of the château Sauternes, year after year, is made at the Château Yquem, which labels its wine Château d'Yquem. Its wines are twice as expensive as those of most of the other châteaux, because of its reputation and consistency of excellence. The château itself is impressive, even for Bordeaux;

it is a castle left from the Middle Ages and perches atop a hill. Rows of vines lead up to it, a fabled, fabulous procession. Most of the winemaking machinery used here is of wood; the only metal to come in contact with the wine is bronze.

The 230 acres of the vineyards at Yquem grow on the left bank of the Garonne, where the soil is siliceous and consists

of quartzy pebbles and gravel. Two grapes are planted, the Sauvignon and the Semillon. The Sauvignon contributes most of the aroma, and the Semillon, which constitutes three-fourths of the wine, contributes much of the finesse and elegance. The juices are blended at the time of crushing.

The initial fermentation, which is quite active, requires a few days in oak fermentation vats; then the wine is put into oak casks. Not until the end of the third month does the first racking take place. The second racking occurs in three more months, the third in three more months still, and the fourth when the wine is a year old. At the time of the fourth racking the wine is fined. It is fined again at the end of its second year. After three years in oak casks it is filtered and bottled.

The wine is by now crystal clear. It has an amber quality which will become golden as it gets older and brown as it gets very old. The taste is mellow and holds beautiful bouquet and finesse, but these will improve with age.

Because of its high alcohol content and the care with which it is made, a château-bottled Sauternes is virtually indestructible. It can last a hundred years. The ideal age for drinking it, however, falls between the fourth and twentieth years. The wine should be drunk cool but not cold; it should be served at cellar temperature, about 55 degrees.

Rosé

There are three ways to make a *rosé*, the sweet, fruity, rose-colored wine.

One is to use rose-colored grapes and to ferment the juice on the skins, as in making a red wine.

A second is to blend a mild red and a fruity white wine.

The third, and the only one which is used to any extent in France, is to use a dark grape and to allow the juice to ferment on the skins for twelve hours to three days, depending on how much color the skins provide and how much is wanted. The wine is then treated like any other dry or semisweet wine.

Rosé wines are made in most wine districts of France, but they seldom travel well and consequently do not build reputations or markets away from home. Four do travel well, all from the Côtes-du-Rhône: Tavel, Chusclan, Orsan, and Lirac. The main grape used in all four is the Grenache, with Carignane or Syrah or some other grape added. Lirac has a brilliant rose color; the other three have a ruby color with an onionskin quality. They have no orange tint, as do many cheaper, more quickly made *rosés*. Tavel's taste once was described as being "a little like a rock warmed in the sun."

A *rosé* usually is bottled when young, in its first year, sometimes after its first spring, and is drunk when young—although the four from the Côtes-du-Rhône improve with age. A *rosé* can be served with any food—meat, fish or fowl, soup, cheese, salad, dessert—but in France is almost never served except to accompany a light lunch. These wines are best when served at cellar temperature, about 55 degrees.

16

In the United States . . .

Every time you have the chance, you should travel along the Sonoma and Napa valleys in California. Go out of San Francisco across the San Francisco bridge, and pass Sausalito with its beautiful waterfront. Drive into the hills and in good time, though none too soon, taste the wines that are produced there, the best made in this country thus far and comparable to the best St. Emilion in France.

Most of the vineyards welcome visitors. They have certain times of day for tours and for the use of their tasting rooms; thirty-six wineries by my count now have tastings. Considering their great number and tiny glasses, it takes several days to do halfway well with them. Beaulieu, Martini, and Inglenook are within four miles of each other along one road,

Highway 29—my favorite stretch of highway in California. If one seeks them out, he can find a few bottles of well-aged Cabernet and Zinfandel; at ten to fifteen years of age, a Cabernet comes into its own in California, I am told, but no vintner can keep appreciable quantities that long, and no distributor that I know of worries to do so in this country. The shops and stores selling California wines do not age them, and even retain the depreciating habit of setting the best California wines, even the Cabernets, on their bottoms, with their corks drying out each day more and more, while the most common European wines lie nearby on their bellies. A pity. This little sign of an ingrained attitude comes from a concept that a California wine is merely a "commercial product." The concept was valid before prohibition and just after it, but giant steps have been taken since then. Even the *vins ordinaires* of California, for instance, the dry reds and whites of Italian Swiss Colony and Gallo Brothers, are better than most *vins ordinaires* of France, and the best wines of the vineyards I mentioned above, as well as those of a number of others, are of high quality, not as high as my California friends claim, but admirable.

My favorite California winery is up in the hills east of Highway 29. I would not have gone up there one evening— it is way off the beaten track—except for two reasons: I wondered whether the hills might produce a better wine even than the Napa Valley itself, might give the grapes a more lingering ripening. And all the other wineries had closed their tasting rooms for the day and I had not had enough wine as yet. Some close at four-thirty, some at five, and only one vineyard, up in the hills, maintained tasting until five-thirty.

There were four of us, and we set our car that way—my wife, Ted McIlvenna from San Francisco, his wife Vinney, and I. He is a minister by ordination, and if we had been stopped by the Highway Patrol, they would have discovered a rarity even for California, a half-drunk Methodist preacher driving a rental car. We were not stopped. In fact, there was almost no traffic along the mountain road.

It's beautiful country. These aren't mountains, not in the sense that the high California peaks are mountains, or even that the North Carolina mountains are mountains; they are made up of useful, usable land with only occasional roughness.

When at last we got to a small sign which said Nichelini, we walked down the path, down a hill, alongside an old house. There was much excellent stonework about, and a huge press, a Roman wooden contraption, no longer used. At the very back of the house, at the door to a cellar, was a small table, and behind the table was a middle-aged, kindly lady who had no doubt been sniffing wine all day, whether she had been drinking it or not, and I suppose she had. She was Mrs. Nichelini.

All of us liked the wine better than any other we had tasted that day. It wanted more aging, particularly the Cabernet and the Zinfandel, but it had body and bouquet and finesse. Remarkably good wines, as we all agreed.

And the price was less than anybody else's, which further enhanced it to our taste.

Mrs. Nichelini was sleepy, she said. It seems she was the one who had to awaken on the coldest night to go turn on the sprinklers in the fields where her husband had planted new vines; the sprinklers kept the vines from freezing. The last three nights had been cold ones, she told us, and the warning bell had rung every night.

"Is the Zinfandel this good every year?" I asked.

"It is different. Sometimes it is better than in other years," she said.

"What shop sells your wine in Beverly Hills?" we asked her.

"None."

"In San Francisco?" Ted wanted to know.

"None."

Little shops here and there sold Nichelini, she said, but 80 percent of their wines were sold to customers who came to the table, there at the cellar door.

"How many generations of Nichelinis have made wine up here?" I asked her.

"My husband is the third generation," she said. And she told us about the family, which made simple wines in the old days.

"And who works the vineyards?" I asked.

"My husband, and I help him," she said.

"Who makes the wine?" I said.

"My husband and I," she said.

At which moment I felt as close to Burgundy as I have ever felt in the United States.

There are between thirty and forty small operations like this in California, where the family grows the grapes, crushes and ferments them, racks and protects and bottles and labels and sells the wines. They make about 10,000 gallons of wine, about 50,000 bottles a year each, more by far than the average vintner in Burgundy, about half the production of Château Margaux or Château Lafite-Rothschild in Bordeaux—so they are not small except by California standards. In California the large wineries, such as Italian Swiss Colony and Gallo, can store as much as 90,000,000 gallons each.

The small vintners get many offers every year to sell out, or to merge with companies trying to form conglomerates, but they resist that temptation, and the other equally pressing temptation to expand. The whiskey companies are moving into the wine field, a particularly crippling development, in my estimation, for they are alcohol men primarily, packagers, distributors, advertisers. We have begun to see big expenditures for advertising, with increased prices of the wines, the ads even appealing to our sense of quality by emphasizing that their wine is the most expensive in America. I understand that we will have wine in flip-top aluminum cans before long, no doubt flash-pasteurized, then carbonated by a machine just before another machine stamps the can shut. The ads will doubtless show healthy handsome people swilling this concoction, loving it, and so the nation will inherit yet another abomination, another adornment to our canned culture.

Well, I make it worse than it might be, but I don't want to underestimate the power of Madison Avenue.

Some of the small wineries are operated by young executives who have chosen this way of life over that of being a marketing executive in San Francisco, as did Jack Davies, who runs Schramsberg winery and now makes Champagne, or being an investment analyst, as did Bob Travers of Mayacamas vineyard. In the winter they do their pruning and planting. In the spring they cultivate the vineyards. In the summer they bottle wines of previous vintages. In the fall they pick and crush the grapes. They store the wine until bottling time, and they store the bottles for a while. Some of their time is spent entering wine contests. Nichelini, a year after I visited with his wife, won a major contest for two of his wines, the Zinfandel and the Rosé.

The brightest future of the wine country of California might be in the hills, I don't know; nobody knows where the secret pockets of land are which hold the most beauty in their soil and light, the Clos-Vougeot, the Romanée-Conti places. Maybe alongside Highway 29. But I do think the vintner who does his own growing and makes his own wine is the type to seek. Hundreds of such craftsmen with their own operations are needed if the wine is ever to rise to its highest achievement, which we all want very much for some part of our own country.

In eastern America the French-American hybrids are flourishing, and their wines are friendly and zestful. The whites and the reds are good, useful wines, and better of late than they were five years ago. So we are making progress. We need several thousand people to plant their own vineyards of these grapes and make their own wine, and to give their wine time to develop before judging it, for on the whole the eastern factories clear out their stock each year. These hybrid grapes now represent fully 20 percent of the wines produced in France.

The sweet wines of the older eastern grapes are still flowing from the tanks of New York State. Their Champagne is the best of it. Wine from our native grapes is ineptly made in the South. The muscadine and its relative, the scuppernong, were here when the first English settlers landed in what is now North Carolina, and they marveled at this grape. Many of us in the South have made scuppernong wine, or have made a *rosé* out of the muscadine hybrid, the James grape. These are moderately sweet wines, if properly made, with a fruity, complex flavor. Once I even made a dry scuppernong that was delicious. It happened by mistake. I had siphoned 3 gallons of wine off its lees and had poured the lees and other sediment into a canning jar, merely cleaning up, and I forgot the jar. A month later the yeasty, muddy leftover had cleared, had thrown its own sediment to the bottom of the jar, and the clear wine on top of the sediment had no foxy taste, no taste of the wild land from which it came. It was dry and delicious.

I hadn't even topped up the bottle or laid a lid on it, and by all odds it should have been spoiled. So this accident was a tribute to the scuppernong's durability.

An acquaintance of mine started making a pretty good scuppernong wine commercially. One of the worst winemakers in eastern America came around and asked him to sell out. This maker takes grapes from field to grocer's shelf in two or three months; he had built an empire on this sort of processing. My acquaintance said no, he didn't want to sell. So next harvest season the big company's buyers came into the district at picking time and bid the price of scuppernongs so high my acquaintance decided he must sell after all, and in his contract to sell went the stipulation that he would not make wine again for anybody.

So we don't always make progress in this business. The knaves are involved. And the whiskey companies. The total picture is murky, maybe depressing. However, there are two factors which offer hope. One is that more and more Americans are visiting Europe, and there they come to appreciate and know about wines; they want for daily use *vins ordinaires* and for occasional use exceptionally good wines. Of equal importance is the existence of tens of thousands of home winemakers in the United States. Not only are they making good wines inexpensively, but they are poking about in new corners and crevices, planting vineyards and making all manner of tests, and they are becoming particular about what they do and what they drink.

Meanwhile, the demand for quality European and American wines exceeds the supply. Prices increase. So do mislabeling and dilution. In London recently, my purchases of French wines led to more surprises than satisfactions, and the situation in New York City is not secure either, even at the best wineshops and restaurants. One can buy a Corton, a Vosne-Romanée, a Nuits-St.-Georges, a Puligny-Montrachet, or almost any other, only with fingers crossed and a prayer that it will indeed after its dilution have some resemblance to the wine of that name.

I am sometimes asked if one can import his own wine from France. I have done so and am trying to do so again, but the experience is contaminated by laws and hoaxes. The tax is not itself the deterrent. The federal tax and duty on a bottle of foreign wine is eleven cents a bottle, and the state tax usually is about the same. But in order to get its few cents, a state is likely to license distributors, whose services cost many times as much, in effect requiring its citizens to pay a dollar or so a bottle to the distributor, which is unfair and absurd.

If one goes to New York or New Jersey, which have no requirement of a licensed distributor, he gets involved with the rigmarole of the Port of New York, which is a box of broken crackers watched over by thieves, so far as I can tell. (Baltimore, Norfolk, Wilmington, and Charleston are less theft ridden, but there I suspect one must negotiate varying state restrictions, as I have said.) I have imported wine through New York and New Jersey, and after months of excuses, after considerable expense, after finally asking the shipping company for my money if not my wine, after twenty-two letters, I got it—120 precious Corton and Corton-Charlemagne bottles which had not, as it turned out, been stolen after all but had spent the winter unprotected in an unheated warehouse. It survived even that and was great to its last bottle.

In this transaction, I must admit the French were not gentlemen, either. The French vintner was, but not the firm we had authorized on our own to package the wine and ship it to Le Havre, to the vessel. That firm charged a dollar a bottle to package it, and in addition charged more to send it by truck to Le Havre than the vessel charged to bring it across the Atlantic Ocean. So the charges went like this:

For the wine, a reasonable price, about $2.00 a bottle, one-third what it sold for at that time in New York.

For packaging, half as much as the wine cost.

For trucking to the French dock, a tidy sum.

For shipping across the ocean, a reasonable fee.

For services of a New York City company to accept the wine and transport it to New York City, several exorbitant fees, one after another, the final one of which was $81.91. I never did find out what it was for.

For duty and federal taxes, $13.08.

For state tax, $2.04.

So we got no bargain.

All expenses had to be paid, those incurred in France and this country, fair or not, before the wine could be got.

Our mistakes were numerous. We should have asked the vintner to crate the bottles and transport them, or send them by a carrier he trusted to the dock. We should not have shipped to the Port of New York. I don't know where else, mind you, but that port is hopeless. We should have arranged to collect the wine ourselves, or arranged for a reasonable company to do so. We should have imported more bottles at a time; three hundred bottles need cost but little more to ship and handle than one hundred.

Many of our state and federal laws are left over from prohibition. They ought to be removed, but whenever a state considers its wine-distributing laws, it turns for advice to its wine distributors, who don't want you and me importing wine from out of state or from Europe; they want to do everything for us and take their healthy percentage.

Do they import for us a wide selection of wines? In most states, no.

Do they keep their wines in cellars or rooms suitably cooled? In most cases, no.

Do they know wines? Not usually, no, and they are often cheated, and pass their ignorant choices on to us.

I used to drive to Washington, D.C., to Central Liquor or Burka's or one of the other wineshops, where a wide selection of American and European wines is available at prices far cheaper than those in my state, and I took my wine home. I found out even this was against North Carolina law. If caught, I could lose not only the wine but also my automobile.

So I started transporting the wines on the train. I might lose the wine, but I figured Southern would not lose the railroad. Once my wife and I wrestled six cases of wine, disguised in brown wrapping paper, into our little pullman bedroom and stood on it while we undressed for bed. And drank some of it, I admit. A Musigny was wonderful, I recall, one of the best bottles of wine in my life thus far, and on another trip we had a bottle or two of *Vougeot, premier cru,* not a great wine by label but happy by chance. Last year the federal government took over train passenger service and did away with the whole train.

I mention these experiences to give you a flavor of the wine user's experience in most parts of our country. You must make your own arrangements and your own peace with your conscience.

So I buy California wines and age them for myself.

I import grapes from California and make my wine.

I have planted a vineyard of French-American hybrids. And I am now seeking—for eighteen months have sought—permission of my state to import wine from vintners I know in Burgundy. I still have hope of obtaining that permission in cooperation with an importer who has taken pity on me. I hope he will be able within another year to work this out with a state board which will consider requests only twice a year, and which must have a bottle of the wine to test for alcohol content before it will consider the request, which does give one cause for thought: I must, in order to import wine from Burgundy, deliver a bottle of the wine I want to import before I can import it.

Well, enough. You see the point of it, or the pointlessness of it. I recommend no action, I mean to join no citizens' groups, I am weary even of discussing it.

17

Champagne and English Ale

I have put Champagne and English ale together because of my own perversity—I don't think Champagne is as noble as its reputation maintains—and because the two are brothers. Or sisters. Or maybe the ale is the brother and Champagne the sister. She is the flavored effervescent wine of certain mediocre grapes, and he is the effervescent wine of certain exalted malted grains. She can be expensive to make and usually is; he most often is made by the inexpensive method. She has been presented to us as a sophisticated lady, he as an unsophisticated commoner. She can be replaced with a chilled Pouilly Fuissé or a German wine or a California Chablis, but there are no substitutes for him, for he is distinctive, as well as friendly. Both are most endearing because of past use and associations.

292

The best beers in the world are made in England and Germany, and I will deal here with England. France makes a poor beer, but it makes Champagne, and we will get to that in good time.

English Ales and Beer

There is no agreed-on distinction between a beer and an ale, except locally, in one place or country or another; an ale might be considered heavier or lighter in flavor or color. The dictionaries are at odds about the matter. My authority for using the two words interchangeably is a lady bartender in a pub in the Midlands who told me, "It's all the one. They're two names for the same." I agree with her.

First, a bit of history. The Saxons, when they were the occupiers of England, commonly drank mead and *aelle* (*oelle*). Dr. Johnson in his dictionary derived from that the word *ale*, which was then pronounced *yell* or *yal*, and still is in the northern counties. Ina, the king of Wessex from 689 called the beverage *oelle* in his laws. King Edgar the Pacific about two hundred years later decreed that only half a pint of ale could be drunk at each draft. A tankard held 2 quarts and had seven pegs, dividing it into eight portions.

The Danes, who took possession of the country, were sots, inordinately fond of ale. When a Saxon and a Dane drank out of the same bowl, they were by that custom pledged not to stab each other while drinking. The ale back then was flavored with herbs. The Danes enjoyed entertainment with their ale and mead, and jugglers, tumblers, gleemen, and harpers frequented the guesthouses and the ale shops, in which women usually were the brewers. The Danes particularly approved the ale made in Chester and decreed that anybody brewing bad ale there should be placed in a ducking-chair and plunged into a pool of muddy water, or should forfeit four shillings.

In 1066 the Normans arrived and their register, or inventory, of what they found does not list a single brewhouse or malthouse, so presumably ale was made in home kitchens. The Normans were in control until 1208, when the Magna Charta was signed, and among their changes was a schedule of two abstemious meals a day, replacing the Danes' and Saxons' four heavy ones. However, it is recorded that some of the Normans ate and drank heartily, including the Bishop of Ely in the reign of Henry I who daily served "all sorts of beasts that roam in the land, of fishes that swim in the water, and of birds that fly in the air," along with French wines, spiced mead, mulberry hypocras, pigmait, cider, perry, and ale. (Hypocras, more recently spelled Hippocras, is a cordial, a wine flavored with spices. Pigmait is probably an early or erroneous spelling of pyment.)

During Henry III's reign, women continued making ale, selling it for a penny a gallon in the cities, and as cheaply as 4 gallons for a penny elsewhere.

The old British word *beer* was revived about this time, or soon thereafter. In 1289 among charges paid by a nobleman traveling from Oxford to Canterbury were sixpence for beer and a halfpenny for apples.

Edward III, who passed a severe law seeking to restrain eating and drinking, once gave a thirty-course meal at nine in the morning, the fragments of which fed a thousand poor people. In 1389 Richard II gave a little housewarming at Westminster and for breakfast brought on boiled beef, sprats, herrings, brawn, bread, butter, mustard, malmsey, wine, and beer. I think this is the King Richard who had two thousand

cooks. During his reign monasteries became known for superior brewing, and men began to take over from women.

King Edward IV gave breakfasts of bread, salt fish, and
ale to his noblemen, who had to rise at seven in the morning
for it and at ten sat down once more, this time for three hours,
for a daily feast enhanced by a side table for wine and ale,
"which were handed to the guests in goblets of pewter, wood
or horn," or so W. L. Tizard tells us in his 1850 book, *The
Theory and Practice of Brewing*. Supper was at nine and the
lords and ladies were given a gallon of beer and a quart of
wine each. There probably was a difference between the breakfast ale and the supper beer, but nobody knows what it
was.

The Earl of Northumberland, who in the time of Henry
VII and Henry VIII had a family of two hundred persons,
allowed each a quart of beer and a quart of wine at six o'clock
breakfast, and did as well by them at dinner at ten, and he
figured it cost him for food and drink 2 ½ pence per day
per head.

It was during the reign of Henry VIII that an ex-mayor of
London offered to give a brewhouse to the city, one which
adjoined London Bridge. We assume there were many brew-
houses in England by that time, and about 1524 hops became
the standard bitter for beer. Ale was by then a strong-tasting
drink fermented without hops, and beer was fermented with
hops.

In 1578 a book by Reynolde Scott said:

> You cannot make above VIII or IX gallons of indiffer-
> ent ale out of one bushel of mault, yet you may, with the
> assistance of hoppe, draw XVIII or XX gallons of very
> good beere . . . if your ale may endure a fortnight, your

beere, through the benefit of the hoppe, shall continue a moneth; and what grace it yieldeth to the taste, all men may judge that have sense in their mouthes.

In 1586 when the Queen of Scots was confined in Tutbury Castle, the conspirator Babington, of Dethick, managed to get a letter to her, using as messenger the brewer who supplied the castle with ale. The brewer probably was from Derby, which was known as an excellent place for ale as well as Derby cheese.

Over the years hops won a place in ale as well as beer, and the two have grown side by side. In London beer is likely to mean porter and ale a paler, lighter drink. In the south and west of England, beer is a strong old drink, and ale is a weaker, milder, fresher drink. In Manchester the stronger drinks, except porter, are called beer. In some parts of the north and east, ale used to be thought a malt distillation and beer a treacle distillation. In the United States, in some cities ale is considered to be a lighter drink, in others a heavier drink than beer. In all places today they are made of much the same grains, and both use hops and brewer's yeast.

Beer or ale is made from malt, and you first must "malt" the grain, that is, must convert the starch of the grain to malt, which yeast can convert to alcohol. You can buy malted barley, or you can if you insist malt your own provided you have access to a suitable barley strain. Most barley is grown for feed, not malting, and doesn't malt well. At the end of this chapter are suggestions about how proper barley can be grown and how it can be malted. For the moment let's assume that at a winemaking shop you have purchased 5 pounds, or whatever, of barley that has been properly grown and malted.

You should buy a light barley for light beers, such as lagers, which are preferred by the French and the Americans, and dark barley for stronger beers, preferred by most of the English—and by many others in all countries, of course.

Crack a pound of the barley for each gallon of ale that you plan to make, using a rolling pin or a coffee grinder. Just barely crack it. Then steep the cracked barley in hot water for two hours in the case of a light ale and as much as eight hours in the case of a heavy one; the water's temperature should be 145 to 148 degrees for a light ale and 152 to 155 for a dark brew. You can use a fish-tank submersible heater to keep the temperature constant; another way is to start out with less water than you plan ultimately to use and to add hot or cold water as needed. This process is called mashing, and the product of it is the wort, pronounced *wurt*.

Once the wort is ready, boil it for half an hour and add hops to flavor it. Generally ¾ ounce of hops for each gallon will be about the proper amount, but this is a matter of taste and a matter of the strength of the hops. Since the flavor of the hops is dissipated to some extent by boiling, ideally you should add a small cloth bag of "finishing hops" the last five minutes—these can be purchased at winemakers' shops—and you can leave them in during early fermentation.

(If malted barley is not available, mix 3 pounds of dried malt extract, 3 of hopped malt syrup in 4 gallons of water.)

With the wort at about 75 degrees, take a hydrometer reading and add corn sugar if you want to increase the alcohol potential. I hope you will decide not to add sugar, which can give a home brew taste. Actually, I prefer a 4 percent ale to a 6 percent ale , prefer the taste and would rather drink three 4 percent ales than two 6 percent ones. One-quarter to one-half pound of corn sugar for each gallon will be about right for a light ale, in the case of nearly all malts. Should the initial hydrometer reading show more alcohol potential than you want, add water. (Beermakers' hydrometers are more accurate at the lower readings than wine hydrometers and should be used, if possible.)

When the wort is cool enough, about 70 degrees, add a packet of brewer's yeast for 4 to 6 gallons. You can use a top- or bottom-fermenting yeast. A light ale, such as a lager, uses a bottom-fermenting yeast; a heavier ale, such as a stout, a top-fermenting one. Add a level teaspoonful of citric acid to feed the yeast; either that or the juice of two or three lemons for 4 gallons, or use yeast nutrient tablets.

English home brewers often ferment initially in a plastic dustbin (garbage can) with a polyethylene liner. They put the lid on the vat, or a towel. In about two days, when the foam begins to abate, they carefully skim the foam off. At three or four days from the start, or when the hydrometer shows a reading of 1.015 to 1.020, they carefully siphon the ale off its lees into glass carboys, filling them up to their neck, and attach waterlocks. They let these ferment in a 55- to 60-degree room for seven to fourteen days, or as long as needed. When the hydrometer reads 1.005, they put the ale in brown or green bottles, brown being somewhat preferred—I wouldn't worry about the color—and cap the bottles, and store them in a cool, dark place. (A high-quality lager beer is enhanced if the closed fermentation takes place at 40 degrees, but fermentation at such a low temperature takes longer, two or three months.) Age the ale for 5 or 6 weeks.

An alternate way to bottling at 1.005 is to allow the ale to ferment out, so that it reads under 1.000 on the hydrometer, then rack the ale carefully into a clean carboy, add 2 ounces of sugar for each gallon, and, when fermentation resumes, bottle and cap the ale. Or put the sugar, one level teaspoonful, into each pint bottle before filling it with the ale.

Light ale should be served chilled to about 50 degrees. Heavy ale should be served at about 60 degrees.

If you prefer more carbonation, bottle at 1.006 to 1.010, or in the alternate method add 2 ½ ounces of sugar per gallon rather than 2.

Brewer's yeast can be saved from one making to another, as follows: From the residue at the bottom of the vat remove the middle layer, which is yeast, put it in a bottle, cap it, and refrigerate it. Do not allow it to return to normal temperature while capped—this is important. A packaged yeast should be used every third or fourth time, to be sure alien forces do not get in control.

The yeasts used, as we say, are brewer's yeasts. Wine yeast will ferment the malt, but it contributes a winey taste to the brew. Baker's yeast ought not to be used, because it imparts a strong, distinctly inferior baker's yeast flavor. Vierka and Grey Owl are two excellent brands of brewer's yeast.

The top-fermenting yeasts don't like to be cut off entirely from oxygen for the first few days; they might sour and cause odors. The lager type can be fermented in a carboy from the start, and just such closed fermentation is favored by the Germans.

If you are bothered by the sediment in your bottles of ale, you can do as a friend of mine does. He uses a 5-gallon compression tank purchased from a cola bottler. After the beer completes its fermentation in the tank, building up carbon dioxide inside, he puts the tank in a deepfreeze and freezes it to 22 degrees, or as close to that as he can. At 22 degrees the carbon dioxide is inactive but the ale is not yet frozen. He siphons it into bottles, leaving the sediment behind, caps them, lets them return to cellar temperature, and so captures the carbonation inside the bottles.

You can use polyethylene jugs with airtight screw caps to achieve the same result. The beer at 1.005 is siphoned into such a plastic jug up to the neck and a screw top is attached. In three or four days the jug is put in a freezer. When well chilled, the ale is bottled and capped.

One ought to know the names of beers and ales.

A *lager* is a light beer.

Bitter is a light beer.

Pilsener is a type of lager, the type we use in the United States predominantly.

Bock is a lager with a strong hops taste and a dark-brown color.

Stout is a brown ale with a medium hops flavor.

Guinness is the trade name of the most famous Irish-English stout. Some books say grape juice is added to the wort, but on a recent visit to a Guinness brewery I was assured that this is not the case. This is a wonderful drink in England and even better in Dublin and Connaughmara.

Porter is a stout with a reddish tinge. Some say it has a few blue grapes fermented in it to provide the color and give it a tinge of sweetness, but I doubt it.

Brown sugar is sometimes used. Invert sugar is sometimes used; it speeds the start of fermentation, but offers no significant advantages.

Coloring is sometimes added. One teaspoon of caramel will color 3 or 4 gallons of wort. The English prefer dark ales. Given two identical ales, one light in color, one dark, they will prefer the dark, or so their studies indicate.

Sometimes fermentation will "stick"—more often at 1.016 to 1.020 on the hydrometer than at other points. To "unstick" it, you can add new yeast, or you can aerate it, or, if the ale has stuck because the temperature is too low, you can slowly increase the temperature, or, if the ale has stuck because the ale's temperature is too high, you can reduce the temperature slowly. If it sticks at 1.011 or 1.012, you can add ale from another batch or add water to bring the reading down to a safe level, 1.010 or under, then bottle it.

Some English beermakers use a floating siphon. This consists of a wooden platter that will float and has a hole through which the siphon hose can be pushed. Some of these contraptions have a screen-guard as well. Short legs (about 1 ½ inches high) are attached to keep the platter from settling into the bottom residue.

You can disgorge a bottle of beer, as you do Champagne, but it is much work for slight advantage. The brewer's yeast forms a paste at the bottom of the bottle and will not get into the brew when you pour it, if you are at all careful.

Factories use adjuncts, maize and other grains, in addition to the more expensive barley. This practice is followed extensively in America, but it is not customary in home alemaking here or elsewhere and is illegal in some countries, Germany among them, for factories.

Old-fashioned Stout, an Old Recipe

For 4 gallons, you will need 2 pounds of black malt, a pound of dark and a pound of light. You will need a pound of black treacle, 4 to 6 ounces of hops, as you prefer, and 3 or 4 pounds of sugar—any household sugar, white or brown. Put the malt in a pot and the hops in a bag and boil them together in about 2 gallons of water. Let them boil fifteen to thirty minutes, then add the sugar and stir it in until it dissolves.

Cool the beer. Pour it into a fermenting vat with a cover. When it is at the proper temperature for yeast, 70 to 75 degrees, add yeast and two pieces of old, sour bread, and let the fermentation begin. Once the fermentation has about stopped, bottle it, and store it in a cool place until it clears. A few months' aging will improve it, but the stout can be drunk a week after bottling.

Champagne

Champagne has nothing like the history of ale. The method of removing the sediment from Champagne bottles is comparatively new, from the nineteenth century, and that made Champagne acceptable. Before that Champagne was clouded with lees, which is the reason the early Champagne glasses— not many are left today—were made of clouded glass, and the drink was not popular as a consequence.

Since the Champagne vineyards were as far north as grapes can consistently be ripened in France, the fermentation was almost always interrupted by the advent of cold weather. In the spring the alcohol fermentation began again and was completed. The winemakers of the Reims Epernay area became aware that if they stoppered bottles of the wine before this spring fermentation began, or while it was under way, the gases formed in the bottle became part of the wine itself; so they would stopper the bottles with wads of cloth. Dom Perignon, a blind monk, a cellar manager, began stoppering them with corks and tying the corks to the bottles with strong cord. This was his contribution, one for which he has received more fame than he probably expected. His wine had more carbonation, but it still had lees. Others found a way to get the lees out of the bottle without losing the carbonation.

There are two main types of Champagne, vintage and non-vintage. The vintage usually is made exclusively from Pinot noir grapes of one or more years; the others are made by blending juices of Pinot noir and other grapes. In either case, the Champagne can be more or less sweet—there are in all six different degrees or categories of sweetness. There are no dry Champagnes; some are simply less sweet than others.

The Pinot noir grapes are the same grapes used in making Burgundy red wines. Their skins are dark blue outside and red inside, but their juice is white, so the Champagne is white, for the skins are not used. The grapes are carefully picked and at the vineyard are examined at the roadside by a group of women, grapepickers in their youth, who remove with scissors the defective berries, those that are overripe or mildewy or broken and might color the juice. The remaining berries are put into osier baskets, loaded on trucks, and quickly taken to be pressed.

The grapes are put directly into the press without crushing or de-stemming, partly to help keep the coloring of the skins from coloring the juice. Four tons of grapes are pressed at once, as a rule, and until recently this heavy labor was done by manpower, but now it is usually done by hydraulic power. The press bursts the grapes, and the juice is put into large vats, the juice from the first pressing being kept separate from the juice of the second, which is not likely to be as "white" or as sweet, or, as a finished wine, as good.

The fermentation is done in open oak vats, though some firms now use concrete or glass vats. After fermenting for twenty-four to thirty-six hours, during which time the wine throws off as sediment any dust or leaves, the wine is racked into oak casks which hold about 50 American gallons each, and these are transported to a chalk cellar in one of the three main manufacturing cities for Champagne, Ay, Epernay, and Reims. The cellars of Reims were once Roman stone quarries and descend three and four stories under the city. The casks are kept topped up, a loose bung in the cask's mouth.

When the wine is about ten weeks old, it is racked into new casks, the sediment being left behind. A vineyard's wines are often mixed during the racking simply for convenience' sake; the wine of a given grape from a given vineyard might be mixed with the wines from different pressings from that same vineyard. The cellars become colder as winter settles in, and fermentation is quite slow.

In four or five weeks the wine is racked again, chiefly in order to give it a breath of oxygen and help the fermentation along.

In the spring, fermentation is completed and decisions are made as to the blends. The blends can be mixtures of these new wines or can be made of new wines and old wines. Economy as well as taste is a factor, since some of the grapes cost almost twice what others cost. A traditional blend might be one-third the wine of the black grapes of Dizy, one-third the wine of the black grapes of Pierry, one-third the wine of the white grapes of Cramant. There are over a hundred such places, so the combinations are virtually limitless.

Once a blend is decided on, the wines are mixed accordingly in vats and are tested for sugar content. They are then sweetened with sugar or crushed sugar candy melted in wine. This sweetening is called *liqueur de tirage,* and the amount added is enough, when combined with the amount of sugar left in the wine, to produce the right sparkling effect in the bottle. The sparkling effect is caused by the gas, and that, of course, comes from the fermentation that goes on within the bottle. About 3 ½ ounces of sugar per American gallon, or about ¾ ounce to a bottle, will produce as high a pressure as the maximum desired.

Yeast is sometimes added. Then the wine is bottled in heavy-glass bottles, designed to withstand pressure, which will develop slowly, day by day, and each bottle is corked. The cork is secured to the bottle by a metal clamp. The corked bottle is kept on its side in the cellar, actually in the chalk caves, and is left for one, two, or even three years. It can be moved if there is need to move it during that time, but in general practice it is left still.

Each bottle of wine not only develops 5 ½ to 6 atmospheres of carbonation, which dissolves in the wine, but casts off lees, mineral and vegetable sediment, and this sediment has to be removed. One way to do this is to place the bottles cork down in a special wine rack, at a slight incline at first, and to turn each bottle, gently shaking it, every second day, giving it a one-eighth turning each time. The bottle gets twenty-four of these little turnings, and by the twenty-fourth, the end of its third complete revolution, the bottle stands vertically in the rack, cork down, and all the deposit rests on the cork. An experienced worker using both hands can turn three thousand bottles an hour.

The bottle is removed from the rack. The metal clamp is released, and the gas pressure is allowed to eject the cork and the deposit. The bottle is quickly righted, and a rubber stopper is stuck into its mouth temporarily. This disgorging is done with almost no loss of wine and but little loss of the gases, which, as I said, are dissolved in the wine itself.

Now the bottles are filled with wine, leaving enough room for a *dose*, as it is called, a flavoring added to the wine by a *doseur*. It is a sticky, sugary substance made of wine, sugar, and sometimes a drop or two of brandy. The *dose* varies in amount, depending on the sweetness desired in the bottle of Champagne. Sweet champagne might receive as much as a 5 percent *dose;* other types—semisweet, *Goût Américain,* dry, extra-dry, and *brut*—receive less, the last using the best wines. The *dose* for *brut* might be as little as ½ percent. All Champagnes have some flavoring added to them.

The bottles are then passed to a worker who corks them, using a cork that is about twice the diameter of the mouth of the bottle. He drives the cork approximately halfway in, leaving a cork ball outside the bottle. A wire netting is fixed over the ball, and a foil, either metal or paper, is attached to enhance its festive appearance. Formerly the foil, which was pewter, was put on to keep mice from nibbling the corks.

The wine is now ready to be offered for sale. If the blending has been successful, the bottle of Champagne will taste similar to others previously offered by its maker. Uniformity of product is sought, and generally is attained.

Another way of disgorging the sediment from the bottles, also used in France and somewhat less explosive, is to freeze the necks of the bottles in shallow, refrigerated pans. Later each bottle's clamp is removed, and the ball of frozen sediment is expelled, but the gas, less than half as active when reduced to a low temperature, does not expel it so forcefully.

Blended Champagne does not improve in the bottle. A vintage Champagne will improve modestly in the bottle, not much. The vintage bottle costs more and is produced in relatively small quantity. One reason for its scarcity is that some years the vintage is not really any good, and a producer does not like to establish a market for a product which he cannot consistently deliver. Another reason is that the best wines, which are the only ones used in vintage Champagnes, are needed in the blends, not only for the year of their vintage but for other, less successful growing seasons as well. In a poor year the wines of the Champagne area would scarcely be salable, which is another reason for Champagne.

Some non-sparkling wines are made, called *vin nature de la champagne*, and they develop their best qualities when five to ten years of age. They taste good in Reims but do not travel well, and this peculiarity is one reason Champagne was developed in the first place, to make use of the wine. After maturing, these still wines rather quickly become rude in taste, even foxy, a quality found in dry wines made of native grapes in eastern America, as you know.

In opening a bottle of Champagne at home, you will find that less carbonation is lost if the cork is loosened slowly, so gradually that it is left in the opener's hand. I admit preferring the older way and letting the corks pop; that adds festivity to a party, and a small loss of carbonation is small cost for it. Swizzle sticks are not recommended, the twirls of the stick doing away in a few moments with most of the carbonation instilled in the wine during several years, all for no gain. The best glass to use is not the shallow sherbet type, but a tulip-shaped glass, which helps to conserve the carbonation. The best temperature for Champagne is 55 degrees. The dry Champagnes can be served before, during or after meals, the sweet ones after meals.

The total vineyard area for Champagne is 25,000 acres, somewhat less than 1 percent of the total vineyard area in France. The best Champagne wine comes from grapes grown on chalky ground, earth poor by customary viticultural standards. Chalky soil gives a clean, dry wine taste.

The vineyards are roughly divided into two, the black

grape vineyards and the white. Some 80 percent of the best grapes grown are Pinot noir. The white grape considered to be best is the Chardonnay. Among other varieties planted are the Pinot gris and the Pinot blanc.

Blanc de Blancs is a white wine produced exclusively from the white grapes and entitled to be called Champagne when carbonated. It is lighter than the traditional Champagne, which is not necessarily an advantage, since no Champagne is heavy.

Whereas Burgundy is populated by farmers who make wine, and Bordeaux by landowners who grow grapes on their estates and make wine from them, Champagne is made by farmers who grow grapes and sell them to factories. Of the eleven thousand growers, over four thousand have less than half an acre, and nine thousand less than two acres and a half; only twenty-three own more than fifty acres. The French here, as elsewhere, have been more successful in protecting their small holders than has England or the United States.

Sparkling Vouvray is perhaps the best of the other sparkling wines of France, and in fact its flavor is more complex than that of most Champagnes. It is slightly richer, and the wine is never as dry as *brut*. The grapes are grown on chalk hills, much like those of Champagne, located in the Loire Valley.

Golden Guinea has been popular in England for over fifty years. A sparkling wine from Saumur, also in the Loire Valley, it has a slight muscat flavor and is never as dry as *brut*.

Sparkling Burgundy is sometimes red, sometimes white, sometimes pink. The white and pink are generally considered better than the red. All are made from average Burgundy wines, the best ones being too valuable to be used in this way.

Sparkling wines are made in other centers in France, often by means of pumping gas into inexpensive wines, or by having inexpensive wines undergo a second fermentation in a pressurized vat, then filtering the wine as it is bottled in order to remove the sediment. If the wine is made by the first method, the bubbles won't stay in it long after it is poured; if made by the second, the sparkle will be retained for a reasonable period of time, and this inexpensive process has gained favor in making the inexpensive sparkling wines.

To make Champagne at home, you will need bottles that will withstand pressure. Champagne bottles are the best, but quart-sized beer or ginger ale bottles can be used with caps. Also you will need a supply of crisp, dry, light wine, preferably white or *rosé*.

When the wine is ready to be bottled, test it with a hydrometer to be sure it has no sugar left in it. To every 5 gallons, add 10 ounces of sugar that has been dissolved in some of the wine. Also add a packet of Champagne or Montrachet yeast, and a yeast nutrient tablet.

When the wine is fermenting, and when it registers 1.005 on the hydrometer, bottle the wine and cap or cork it. In the latter case you must secure the cork with a clamp, available at winemakers' shops. Also at shops are plastic closures which are easier to use than the champagne corks. Keep the bottles in a room at 55 to 65 degrees.

After two weeks, move the bottles to a rack where they can be stood mouth down. Gently shake them now and again over a period of weeks, until the sediment settles in the neck, or inside the cork if you use hollow plastic stoppers. When they are all so situated, remove the sediment just as in France, and at once top up the bottle with a *dose* and cork and secure it with a wire net; the *dose* is wine flavored with a bit of syrup made from rock candy or sugar that has been boiled in water.

If next round you want more carbonation, use a trace more sugar at the first bottling. Never bottle a champagne which reads over 1.010 on the standard hydrometer; 1.005 is safer and will give as much effervescence as beer.

You will not want to store the Champagne where heat might stimulate it.

Aging does not improve it much, although this depends on the wine you used.

Growing Barley

Some of you perhaps live now in the country, either on farms or near farms or on communes or whatever, and you might want to grow your own barley, or have it grown, and make your own ale for a few pennies a gallon.

Having the right barley is as important in making ale as is having the right grapes in making wine, or the right apples in making cider, or the right honey in making mead, or the right milk in making cheese. And just as the best eating or best yield fruit is not best for wine or cider, or the richest milk is not best for cheese, so the richest barley is not suitable for malting. The variety used should produce a small yield of low-nitrogen grains.

In Ireland, Scotland, and England, two-rowed barley is usually used for malting, and among the varieties preferred before World War II were Spratt Archer and Plumage Archer. Both have been partially replaced since by Proctor, and at present Proctor is giving way to a number of varieties, among them Zephyr and Miris Badger. Others used now and again include Carlsberg, Earl, Freja, Maythorpe, Provost, Irish Archer, and Cambrinus.

In the United States and Canada, six-rowed barley is most often grown for malting, and among the varieties used are Olli and Kindred.

Before World War II most of the barley in Britain was cultivated to produce grain of the low-nitrogen type preferred for malting; farmers now find that they can make more profit from feed barley, which they grow with copious applications of nitrogenous fertilizers, so maltsters there, as in the United States, in spite of a premium paid for malting types of barley, often have to compromise with quality.

The barley should be of a proper variety, the seed certified to be of a pure strain. The earlier in the spring the seed is sown, the higher the yield of grain and malt got from it; an early planting gives a longer growing season for the starch to be formed. The seed should not be sown thickly, and the proper depth is 1 ½ inches. The soil should be moist but not waterlogged. The soil ideally should have a neutral or slightly alkaline quality. The lighter soils, often with chalky subsoils, are better than clay or rich soils. Nitrogenous fertilizer can be used at planting and a small quantity can be applied as a topdressing early in the plant's life, at or before the three-leaf stage, but not later.

Dry weather at harvest ripens the grain best and fullest, and results in less moisture content, but, of course, the grower doesn't always have ideal weather.

Barley in the old days was cut just above the ground before it was fully ripe and the plants were bound in sheaves which were arranged in stooks. When these had dried in the field they were made into stacks. Then when the grain had dried and matured, the barley was threshed. Today's factory farmers are likely to use machines to cut and thresh in one operation, and the barley is not harvested until it is ripe and the weather dry. The barley grains are then dried out enough to store.

Malting barley ideally should have even-sized grains, unstained and unweathered, with few seeds of weeds or of other grains among them. The grain should not have started germinating; in other words, the coleoptile should not have begun growing under the husk. If cut in two, most of the grains will have an opaque or mealy appearance; "steely" grains are likely to be high in nitrogen and will not malt as well.

Grains containing considerable moisture must be dried either by ventilation or some other way—and slowly, not in a furnace. Slight moisture is essential to the life of the seed.

Barley should, of course, be stored away from rodents and, insofar as possible, away from insects; storing it in a cool place will help with the latter problem.

Conversation with a Dublin taxi driver:

"What time does the tour start at the Guinness Brewery? Do you know?"

"10:30. Or 10:00. Or 11:00. I don't know actually. Take my advice and don't take it."

"Why?"

"It's the most boring thing in the world, going through a brewery."

"What about the whiskey factory?"

"I've never been, to be honest with you. Going through a factory's not the sort of occasion that would interest me. The end product might."

18 *Freedom and whiskey gang thegither.*

—Robert Burns, "The Author's
Earnest Cry and Prayer"

Notes on Irish Whiskey

It is interesting to speculate about the hundreds of thousands of people in Ireland, Scotland, England, the United States, Australia, New Zealand, and the other subcontinents, islands, nooks, and crannies where English is spoken who have crept into the woods to make whiskey. Some are confined at this moment in federal penitentiaries in this country, and tens of thousands of others also have suffered the stings of outraged governments.

The first President to send armed militia against them in our own country was George Washington.

No other nonviolent crime has so consistently attracted government police forces—I suppose because this one provides a hide-and-seek game for the police, and an opportunity "to

313

take the air," and the promise if successful of a plentiful supply of whiskey for themselves and their friends.

Essentially the crime is that taxes due on the whiskey are not being paid, but no other evasion of taxes—for instance evasion on income tax or import duty—brings such harsh terms in penitentiaries.

We even have states in the Union actually selling whiskey in their own state-operated stores which they will imprison a citizen for making. Some of them will not even permit a factory to locate within their borders; they will only sell stuff made by other, less righteous places.

In France, families make brandy and Cognac, marc, liqueurs, and the like, and many, many individuals—over five thousand of them—make Cognac alone. And in France the distiller's art has stayed at a high standard, higher than anywhere else.

We will not change our own situation tomorrow, though I am pleased to see that some federal judges have begun to fine illegal distillers for taxes due, and to refuse to imprison them, which is at least one step toward sanity. We are bound by emotional bonds that do not respond to intellectual argument, old ones arising out of religious fervor and the distress of families who see their members and friends destroyed by alcoholism, and of governmental leaders who see society contaminated by the overuse of alcohol. We must find ways to deal with the problems of consumption, I know, but we need not limit the quality of what is consumed, or relegate its manufacture to those least willing to do well by it, the fugitive in the woods and the factory.

I will now set down the method by which great whiskey once was made. I do so not to encourage you or your neighbor to become part of the treacherous game which whiskeymaking represents in our country. By federal law, and by the laws of some states, you can as a citizen apply for a permit to make whiskey legally, but if such permits were administered by the factory distillers they would not be more grudgingly granted. In effect, you cannot get a license at this time. It is, therefore, for historic record and for a happier time that I write; indeed, historic record is about all that is left of this ancient recipe.

The barley was the first grain to ripen each year. Maybe centuries ago, when the Romans introduced distilling to the British Isles, this early ripening was why the Irish first chose barley, but after trying all the other grains, they decided barley was the best. Oats they liked too, or barley and oats mixed.

They malted the grains. Malting required them first of all to encourage the grains to germinate. For this purpose they immersed the grains in water and let them soak. Or they might fill sacks about half full and steep them in a marsh or creek. Two or three days were needed for the grain to swell. The water was quite cool, about 50 degrees, as an average. If the water was still, it was changed three or four times with fresh, cool water.

The grains then were heaped—that is, spread out thickly to dry on a clean floor where they would not be contaminated by unwelcome odors—and the bed of grain was disrupted from time to time, gently turned by the hands two or three times each day, so that it would dry evenly. This process went on for eight to twelve days. The place chosen for heaping was between 50 and 60 degrees, and was damp. The barley started to put out roots and to push its blade or acrospire along the inside of the grain. We know today that the starch of the grain was being converted into maltose, a type of sugar, to feed the shoots, and it is this maltose which later on yeasts convert to alcohol.

The acrospire grows within the grain, on the dorsal side, toward the apex of the grain. When it almost reached the end of the grain, it was said to be ready. The maltster could see the acrospire through the husks of most varieties. When ready, the grains were crunchy and hopefully there were no hard tips remaining.

The grains were then dried in a kiln, an oven which stopped the germination or growth process of the grains. A peat fire was used traditionally, though the fuel had no special effect on Irish whiskey. In Ireland the smoke was closed off from the oven, so as not to impregnate the grains with its odor, whereas in the highlands of Scotland the ovens were perforated, so that the smoke could give the grains a flavored, burnt taste, which was the chief difference between making Irish and making Scotch whiskey.

The ovens at first were about 125 degrees. The temperature was increased gradually to 175 degrees in order to kill the shoots, thus protecting the storehouse of maltose which each grain held.

The grains were then cracked, either by a miller with his stones, or in a farm handmill, or with a rolling pin, or however. Boiling soft water was poured over them to make a mixture with the consistency of porridge. The water absorbed most of the maltose in an hour or two and was drained off; this liquid was called the wort (pronounced *wurt*, just as in beermaking). Hot water was poured over the grain again, and perhaps yet again, to absorb still more of the maltose. It was spring or creek water, as a rule, pure, soft, and made even more pure and soft by boiling.

Hops were sometimes used to flavor the ale, up to 1 pound for 30 gallons being steeped in the hot water.

The spent grain was fed to cattle, who came quite soon to appreciate it and grow fat on it.

When it was cool, the wort was put in a vat, often a barrel with the top removed. Brewer's yeast was added, ½ pound for 30 gallons, or more. Some makers used yeast from a previous fermentation. Others, believe it or not, used a sod of turf which was saved from one fermentation to another and was hung in the chimney when not in use. Some makers threw in a double handful of rye, which naturally had yeast on it and which also formed a mass on top of the wort and helped keep oxygen from too freely reaching the wort. Fermentation lasted from two days to three weeks, depending on the temperature of the wort and the amount of oxygen admitted to it; the cooler and the less oxygen, the slower.

The barley wine, called the wash or pot ale, was then left to settle for a week, either in a full cask or in a vat from which air was pretty well excluded.

The pot ale was next distilled in a pot still. The still was set on a firebox, sometimes on a stone ledge that permitted the fire's heat only to sweep upward against the sides of the still. Sometimes the still was set on the ground with the firebox on one side of it and the flue on the other, so that the heat would swirl around the sides but would not burn the residue which settled to the bottom of the still.

There were four parts to the still: (1) the large vessel in which the pot ale was heated; (2) the head of the still, actually a tight-fitting cap for the vessel; (3) an arm, the pipe which led from one side of the head to (4) the worm, a coiled pipe which could be submerged in cold water, to serve as a condenser. As the pot ale was heated by a small fire, a worker stirred the ale until steam arose. He then attached the head. The steam filled the head, found its way into the arm and then into the worm, and was cooled there and returned, therefore, to the liquid state. The liquid dribbled from the end of the worm into a container. Since alcohol has a lower boiling point than water, the first dribblings were almost entirely alcohol. As the process continued, more nonalcoholic steam was condensed, and when the dribblings had so little alcohol that they would no longer ignite (the men would splash a bit of the whiskey onto the hot still, to see whether the steam burned when a burning stick was held to it), the distillation was stopped. The remaining pot ale, called barn (or burn) beer, was fed to the cattle, who got mildly high on it and came to like it even more than the spent grain.

The liquid captured in the receiving container, called singlings or first-shot, was harsh and was not drunk. Rather, once the still was cleaned out, the singlings were again distilled. This time the first little bit was set aside for the fairies —left on a wall for them or sprinkled on the ground. This appeared to be a heavenly sacrifice, but the distillers had learned long before that the first gushing from the worm was not suitable for good whiskey. After this first gush would come a brief period of dribblings, then the next gush would start the good run. This run was kept until such point as the maker decided the distillate was no longer as good tasting as he wanted, and at that time he stopped distilling. What was left in the still he set aside to mix at a later date with a new lot of pot ale. Some makers distilled a third time to make a whiskey called double-refine, but this was rare.

Care was taken during the process to keep the distilled whiskey well away from the fire, since it and its vapors would burn fiercely.

Whiskey was aged in wooden casks for three to fifteen years. Whiskey to be aged ten years was made 25 percent stronger than ultimately it was expected to be. The whiskey that was to be aged three years had correspondingly less excess alcohol in it.

To judge the amount of alcohol in whiskey, the home makers often had to rely on taste and estimates. If they figured they had 4 percent in their pot ale, and if they had put 50 gallons of such ale in the still and had taken 4 gallons from that of doublings (more, of course, from singlings), they would have about 50 percent alcohol in the 4 gallons, which after three years' aging would result in almost 4 gallons of whiskey of eighty-five to ninety American proof.

They also knew that a liquid which begins to boil at 157 degrees had 91 percent alcohol in it by weight, while one boiling at 181 had only 6 percent in the liquid (though 49 percent in the steam). Given a thermometer that was accurate, the distiller could make responsible estimates, along these lines:

BOILING POINT		PERCENT ALCOHOL (by Weight)		PERCENT ALCOHOL (by Volume)
In Fahrenheit	*In Centigrade*	*In the Liquid*	*In the Vapor*	*In the Liquid*
157°	78.2°	91	92	over 100.00
160°	80.2°	64	83	80.00
163°	82.0°	41	79	51.00–50.00
165°	83.0°	33	78	41.00–40.00
171°	87.0°	17	70	21.00
176°	90.0°	10	61	12.50
181°	93.0°	6	49	7.50
185½°	96.0°	3	33	3.75
189°	98.0°	1	19	1.25

In the United States proof usually is given for beer in terms of alcohol-by-weight, and for whiskey in terms of alcohol-by-volume. In England proof is given for whiskey in

terms of alcohol-by-weight. In either country 1 percent alcohol
is equal to 2 proof. For example, a whiskey containing 40
percent alcohol is 80 proof.

The stills used in homes were 10 to 80 gallons in size, and
the best ones were solid copper. To make their joints tight
enough to keep steam from escaping, the makers plastered
the joints with dough or porridge, or with a cement made of
clay and straw or even horse dung.

The whiskey was aged in uncharred oak casks. In Dublin,
used casks, ones that had contained sherry were used, as they
were in the counties, too, whenever available. Casks allowed
the whiskey to breathe through the wood, and in two or three
years it lost its sharpness and accepted a mellow taste. It
would improve for another twelve years, slowly but significantly, some little bit evaporating each year. There was no
danger of spoilage.

This was the old process for making malt whiskey. As you
see, there was a good deal of time and labor to it, but not
much expense for the maker. The amount of barley needed to
make a gallon of whiskey, about 2 ½ pounds, was cheaply
obtained. Usually it was grown by the whiskeymaker. No
sugar was used; nothing was needed except soft, pure water
and barley and fuel for the fire. This whiskey was assertive
in taste and aroma, was a sipping whiskey, the richest and
most distinctive and distinguished whiskey made, matched
only by highland whiskey from Scotland, which, as I mentioned, also was made from barley or oats by an almost
identical process.

In 1661, however, the government, in this case the British
government, entered the picture by levying an excise tax on
Irish whiskey; actually the tax was reimposed for there had

been a slight tax long before. The tax was four pence a gallon. By 1785 it was twelve pence a gallon. By 1815 it was 61 ½ pence a gallon. Factory whiskey was then retailing for 108 pence (nine shillings), so we see that the tax was over half of the price. The Irish were a tragically poor people, were governed by outsiders, were in bondage to English landlords, and had little respect for what government represented. Also, their social life was dependent on whiskey, at least the men's was—women were not encouraged to drink. So there developed a hide-and-seek game of bootlegging, treacherous to the Irish although often amusing to outsiders.

Early in the 1800s, the standards of the distillers began to fall, as a consequence. For a generation or two many makers refused to compromise with expediency. They paid off the revenue officers and continued operation (the revenue officers would check by often and charge them according to the amount of whiskey on hand). But the poorer people couldn't afford such protection, and even those who could found it impossible to maintain standards, one generation after another, one revenue officer after another.

One of the first refinements to go was the aging of the whiskey. Few could take the risk of having much whiskey on hand at a time. The whiskey that was made was quickly sold, and its fiery, raw taste came to be tolerated. Only the best makers continued to age their whiskey.

Another change had to do with the grain used. Most makers preferred barley to any other, some preferred oats, but unaged whiskey made of either was heavy and strong tasting. Also, the malting took time and space and increased the vulnerability of the maker. So raw grains of various kinds were ground and boiled and used, and since they had no maltose available, sugar was added. In the last half of the nineteenth century, beet roots, maize, even potatoes were sometimes used. When sugar was unavailable, fruits were used, apples, rhubarb stalks, blackberries, currants, almost anything. Another substitute for sugar was molasses.

A further deterioration had to do with equipment. The stills were destroyed whenever they were found, so cheaper stills were introduced, and lighter ones (usually tin) that could more easily be carried into the woods. Only the worm, the condenser, was of copper, that being the part of the still most likely to taint the whiskey, but finally that was sometimes made of tin, or even lead piping, which held a risk of poisoning. Empty tar barrels, milk churns, potato pots were used. In County Longford a kitchen kettle was "commonly used" to make a small amount, a nip or two. The kettle was partly filled with pot ale and a pint mug was stood inside it on a rock. The spout of the kettle was sealed, and its lid was turned upside down, "with the nipple descending into the mug" or hovering over the mug. The lid was filled with cold water. When the kettle was heated, the vapor condensed on the under side of the lid, ran in rivulets to the nipple, and dripped into the mug.

Another deterioration had to do with the locations and facilities. Grain, if malted at all, was malted under the bed or in a hiding place near home, but as the risk increased, the grain was malted far from home, in a cave or abandoned shed, where rats shared in its use and where the workers dared not go for fear of discovery, or were too weary or lazy to go three times a day to turn the piles. Some makers built outhouses with secret chambers and false partitions, the entrances known to but a few people. Others had malt-steeps sunk in hidden recesses and hollow gables so they could steep their barley and later turn and air it, but the poor people had no such facilities.

Smoke was a giveaway in this day before pressure stoves. Whenever there was a riot in Ireland, which would call away the police and army, thousands of furnaces were fired up throughout the countryside for malting, as well as for the stills.

Water was a giveaway too, since the worm had to have cold, running water to cool it. Government agents were likely to investigate along the creeks and the lake banks, so makers dug out places in bogs, or located in caves where water collected.

The island makers were better protected. On the Inishkea Islands, as one example, the makers waited for high winds and rough seas before starting their fires. Then, if police cast off from the Mayo coast, the islanders loaded both stills and whiskey on their curraghs and took to sea, going in every possible direction. The police would need to single out one or two to chase, and these would lead them as far off as they could. Then the men would pour their whiskey into the ocean and dump their tin stills as well, before they cast out fishing lines. In 1834 a happy drinker wrote in a letter that on these islands, where the proper processes were still followed, the whiskey was of such "superior excellence" that the "gifted islanders are worthy of being canonized."

Lake islands were used, too. A visitor to an island in Donegal in the late 1800s said, "The whole area of the island was one dunghill composed of fermenting grains; there were about twenty immense hogs either feeding or snoring on the food that lay beneath them; and so alive with rats was the whole concern, that one of the boatmen compared them, in number and intrusiveness, to flocks of sparrows on the side of a shelling-hill adjoining a corn-mill."

On the mainland the whiskeymakers stored their stills in the lakes. (When an animal died, they buried it in the lake, as well, and ran a rope to the bank, so the police would find it and pull it in.) They placed sentinels on roads to transmit warning, sometimes using children for this purpose whom they had taught to whistle shrilly or to blow horns. Some placed rows of torches along a hillside, which could be quickly lighted should police appear. Some made pits in pathways leading to their stills and filled them with manure. Some distillers armed themselves; gangs of as many as eighty men would make whiskey in a glen, their guns at hand, prepared for an attack. Only the army dared investigate such a gathering, and the army was sometimes beaten if it did. If they retreated, the makers would leave enough raw whiskey for the English militia to drink, which ploy delayed pursuit. One report of 1813 says the exhausted English soldiers "tumbled down senseless to the heath," to be taken to "the poor people's cabins, where they lay until they had slept themselves sober."

To assist the revenuers was a crime against the Irish. Suspected informers were forced to leave a county, and perhaps leave behind their possessions too. Sometimes they were whipped or beaten, or more rarely, scarred on the face for life with knives.

The poteen was sold in Dublin, occasionally openly on the streets. To some towns around 1800 it was brought in tubs. More often men transported their whiskey on their backs, in casks or tin cases, or put two kegs in a bag and slung the bag across a horse's back. Some makers in Donegal had pockets of tin made for their women, exactly in the shape of a woman's pockets, and a tin breast made for them as well, and a tin half-moon that fastened on their abdomen, "and with a cloak round them they will walk with six gallons, and it shall not be perceived." One maker in Joyce country had a tin vessel made with head and body like a woman's, and he would fill it with whiskey and dress it in women's clothing and ride it to market. In some places men would gang together, arm themselves with whips and loaded cudgels and sometimes with guns, and bring their whiskey to market.

Revenue officers were often bribed, of course, and chaotic was the condition of Ireland when the famine came. After that tragedy, whiskeymaking, an integral part of the Irish economy, faltered, just as did everything else, and the aftermath of the famine left a milder social order. Many of the landlords were replaced by peasants who owned their own land and who no longer needed to turn to illegal distilling to make a living for their families and to pay rent on their fields and houses.

By then poteen was foul, anyway. The makers were even adding soap to it to please the customers who thought that a bubble at the top was the mark of a strong whiskey.

The Irish legal distillers were left to carry on. At that time they made their excellent product in Dublin and several other places.

In 1878 the four big Dublin whiskey manufacturers, J. Jameson and Son, Wm. Jameson and Company, John Power and Son, and George Roe and Company, released a book. It says that they and "perhaps fourteen other distilleries in Ireland" were then making only pot-still malt whiskey.

They wrote:

The pot-still, as already stated, does not yield a product containing merely alcohol and water, but one which also contains, in intimate mixture or in solution, many other matters which are yielded by the grain. . . .

The grain constituents of perfectly new Whisky [their

spelling] are not palatable in the estimation of people in general. But after about a year, the Whisky may be said to be drinkable, after about two years to be good, and, after about three years, to be as good as anything with which the average consumer is likely to become acquainted. Those, however, who have only drank three year old Whisky, can scarcely form an idea of the effect of longer keeping, always in the wood. . . .

When a bottle of such Whisky is opened, it literally, like fine old Burgundy, fills the room with its fragrance, and that fragrance is more delicate than anyone who is unacquainted with it, or who is acquainted only with the smell of common so-called Whisky, could by any possibility conceive. The fragrance is an evidence that all the grain products additional to the alcohol have undergone decomposition, and that their elements have been re-arranged into fresh combinations, of a kind analogous to the vinous ethers, and which, like these, are among the most exhilarating of all stimulants.

Later the authors take up their lack of esteem for the Coffy patent still, a column still which in Ulster and the lowlands of Scotland was being used more and more by factories. They said this process sent over alcohol and water alone and "by arresting or destroying all the flavoring matters which are derived from the mash" resulted in a tasteless product which was remote from the ancient craft of distilling whiskey and ought not to be called whiskey at all.

Such spirits do not improve with age, the Dublin distillers point out. Also, they must be flavored with pot-stilled malt whiskey to have any quality or taste at all. The four big whiskey manufacturers of Dublin decried such blending, the dilution of a great whiskey by the addition of alcohol and water. Or to be more accurate, the addition to alcohol and water of a small percentage of good whiskey for purposes of flavoring. This particularly galled them because some of the English and lowland Scots were shipping Coffy distilled whiskey to Dublin, mixing a bit of aged Irish whiskey with it, then exporting it from Dublin as Irish whiskey. They would not lower their own standards, they declared.

Yet last year, while in Ireland, I found only one bottle labeled pot-stilled Irish whiskey, and that bottle had been diluted, it seemed to me. I am told only about 25 percent of the stills of these same companies are pot stills; the other 75 percent are column stills of the very type another generation of Irishmen decried, turning out flavorless alcohol which is then flavored with what the small pot stills make.

Twenty-five percent is a better percentage than we have in the whiskey factories of the United States, admittedly. We have none. All our whiskey is flavored, usually by the barrel it is stored in. However, our deficiency cannot excuse others for theirs. Irish whiskey, good as it is, is not today the wonderful drink of a generation or two ago and is only a reminder of it and the time when Irish whiskey was the standard of the world.

In Dublin, which is by any comparison a wonderful and friendly city, I went into one of the best bookstores I have ever seen, and there were two displays of books by Irish writers. They included the works of Yeats, Synge, Shaw, Joyce, and others of the older writers, and whole shelves of writers who were new, astonishing in quality and quantity to me. This display was fantastic for a country of four or five million people. I think no country of similar size can do better in quantity, and I am persuaded that no country can do better in quality. I mention this here, at the close of this chapter, should anybody decide the men and women who worked their crafts in Ireland were only moderately able. The arts of Ireland are not to be dismissed, and the Irish are a highly creative people.

Incidentally, the Irish have a new law which permits writers and other artists of any nation to live there tax free. That is all the more surprising, considering the number of writers Ireland already has, and commends their sense of values, as I see taxes and other things. Particularly as I see taxes.

19

Of No Special Topic

One of the pleasures of making wines and cheeses is that we
come to appreciate those who succeed even if we do less
than well, and we begin to seek out the best products and
makers.

One morning I recall my wife and I drove with Marcel
Bouquinet and his wife and daughter over the narrow roads,
old beyond measure, which lead from Nuits-St.-Georges to the
vineyard of the Romanée-Conti. That mighty vineyard lies on
a gentle hillside, bordered at the valley edge by an old stone
wall. Its vines are only 2 ½ feet high, its wall is even lower,
and it is decorated with a 10-foot cross, a long-stemmed, awk-
ward, inept cross which could have been made by any village
stonemason, a few years or a few centuries ago. Sometimes

in books the cross is shown in a painting, rather than by photograph, and artists are able to enhance it, and do.

The size of the vineyard is 4 ½ acres. The exposure is toward the morning sun. The history of the vineyard goes back to the thirteenth century, and I suspect anything as historic, anything of such established value whether historic or not, in most places would have high fences and impressive gates and admission fees. That morning, as every morning, the Romanée-Conti lay open to anyone who wanted to walk its rows and taste its grapes for himself.

Pinot noir is an acidy, sweet grape. It falls severely short of being good for eating, just as most table grapes fall short of being suitable for wine. It offers a small yield—the best wine grapes do—about 300 imperial gallons of wine to an acre, on average.

These Pinot noirs of La Romanée-Conti were grafted onto American roots, starting in the mid-1940s. Until then, for over fifty years, the domain had resisted *Phylloxera,* a genus of root-destroying plant lice that had infested France. The vines were given constant care in an effort to preserve them. But World War II, with its accompanying disruptions of chemical supplies and labor, forced the domain to plant new vines on American root stock. Also, the domain used to mulch its vines with cuttings from the vines, but diseases in the cuttings became a problem, so this old-time practice was ended, too. The growers now use manure, and even fertilizers, like almost everybody else. Manure is preferred, but it isn't always available in sufficient supply.

Old vines make better wine than young ones. The average Pinot noir vine in Burgundy is about thirty-five years old, and I understand fifty years is now the expected life-span for a vine on grafted roots. One hundred years is the life expectancy for those not grafted. Today the vines are planted in rows, so that they are easier to cultivate and harvest, but before the root grafting, they were planted at random. Each vine had its own small territory.

We went to the house of the whole domain, a rather modest one with a walled court. We were introduced by Marcel to the lady who is a manager there, a gracious, hefty, middle-aged woman, who asked us to come on into the room where she and the workers were celebrating the harvest. They were in a room with high rock walls, furnished with several old wooden tables, but with chairs that had folding legs—frivolous chairs which seemed out of place or out of time here. The workers were drinking marc, an 18 percent brandy, sweet and rather raw, which is distilled from fermented grape hulls and pips once the pressing is done. Also, they were eating cookies. We drank marc, too, a previous year's distillation, and ate cookies with them, and listened to Marcel and the lady discuss the harvest.

Later we walked down into the cellars, their earthen, graveled floor by my estimate 14 feet below ground, their vaulted ceilings, stone and concrete, about 11 feet above the floor. A worker said the cellars keep an even temperature the year round of 57 degrees. From time to time in wet seasons, particularly following a snow, the cellars flood a foot or two, of course burying the bottom rows of Romanée-Conti, La Tâche, and Richebourg bottles, the three types of wine which were stored there. The private cellar of the owners, a cellar which we ventured into with obeisance, was there, too, with its several hundred bottles of wines from many vintages, many vineyards.

A bottle of four-year-old La Tâche was opened for us, and we drank it at cellar temperature. It had a ruby color, was somewhat lighter than most Burgundies. It had only a modest aroma at this low temperature, but it had a sound body and was striving for the distinctive Burgundy character.

The La Tâche vineyard, which is but 3 ½ acres in size, is located a mile or so from the Romanée-Conti. Its wine is considered elegant, but not quite as elegant. Perhaps its soil has less marl in it, or more; maybe the morning sun does not rest on it quite as long, or rests on it longer; maybe in fact not much difference exists except in the minds of a few Frenchmen who have an advantage in maintaining high real estate value for certain identifiable properties, and the lighter, balanced wine is a product of less time on the skins and fewer husks left on. I don't know, though I suspect there are differences in the soils and the lay of the land which contribute distinctiveness.

The Richebourg is a vineyard of twelve acres and is a next-door neighbor of Romanée-Conti. Its wine tastes similar to the best of Clos Vougeot. I understand the Romanée-Conti owner helps regulate the demand for Romanée-Conti by asking that distributors buy his Richebourg and La Tâche as well. Romanée-Conti is the most expensive and difficult-to-procure wine of Burgundy.

Marigolds were in bloom, I recall, as we left the courtyard, and the raspberries and apples were ripe. A big ripe pear hung heavily on the pear tree. A pile of manure had been uncarted at the center of the courtyard.

Before noon we were at the château of Clos de Vougeot, the only château in Burgundy, a monstrous, impressive but unappealing, solid, square fortress set in the middle of over a hundred acres of vineyard, all surrounded by a wall which, for some reason, took a hundred years to build. I suppose the monks had other things to do. The vineyard is now divided

among about seventy owners. I have often read that the château isn't used any longer for winemaking, but that morning
workmen were pressing grapes and seemed to be pleased to
have us as an audience. One of them was an English university student who had worked here through the harvest, learning about winemaking. His ambition was to be a wine merchant in London someday. I hope he learns to label wines
honestly.

The grapes were Pinot noir, of course. In an outer room
they were being de-stemmed, or partially de-stemmed—
mostly de-stemmed as it turned out. In another room a hydraulic press had been installed in the center of the floor.
Tall wooden fermenting vats were lined along one wall. They
were 9 feet high, about 5 feet in diameter. A vat containing
juice of grapes that had been picked seven days ago, their
initial fermentations completed, was being emptied. The juice
had been pumped into another vat, and now the skins and
soft pulp were to be pressed. The skins were unloaded by
two barefooted men working inside the vat with shovels, filling hampers, which were pushed up to a third man, who
dumped the contents into the press, which had a door along its
cylindrical top.

When the vat was empty, the press was locked shut with
noisy clanking, and its electric motor sent two massive plates,
one at either end of the cylinder, slowly moving toward the
center, forcing juice out. The exuded juice was pumped by
electric pump in with the other. The Englishman told us seven
or eight flour sacks of household sugar were to be added
under government control, because the grapes this year lacked
enough sweetness. The wine would stay in this vat only one or
two days, enjoying a fresh, rapid burst of fermenting, while
the workers would try to keep the temperature as low as 95

degrees. When fermentation became calm and steady, the wine would be drained through a rubber hose into casks in the cellar. The bungs would be left off the casks or loose in the casks for one week and then, wrapped in burlap, would be inserted more tightly. The barrels would be kept at about 55 degrees and would be topped up every week, later every two weeks.

We were told all this by our English acquaintance while the big press groaned and squeezed and whined and squirted red juice. The pressing took an hour. The pressure was then released, and the mash was stirred and tumbled; a second pressing began, a shorter one. After that the mash was poured out upon the floor, and workers wearing rubber boots shoveled it into sacks to be taken to the distillery, so marc could be made of it. Only a few stems were in the mash, I noticed, and millions of seeds. According to the English student, for one batch of wine the grapes had been used stems and all one day earlier in the week, simply because the de-stemming machine broke down.

We noticed that a plastic sheet was being pulled over the top of one of the fermenting vats in an effort to keep the temperature high. It seems that sometimes the effort was to heat, sometimes to cool the wine. Cooling here meant running the juice through plastic pipes immersed in ice water.

If the wine in a vat stopped fermenting, the workers usually had a hard time starting it again. Along with temperature change, they generally had to prepare a yeast culture and inoculate it, being careful not to allow the juices to cool too rapidly.

We toured the vast, dim, damp cellars downstairs, which we were assured did not flood even after a snow. The English student told us the entire cellar, ceiling and walls, had been scrubbed recently and sprayed.

Outdoors we watched an old man in the yard pouring boiling water into kegs, rolling them around on the ground, making them ready for the wine that soon would be entrusted to them. Behind him lay acres of low-trained vines, inheritors of a tradition of growing and winemaking initiated here by monks centuries ago.

On the way back to Marcel's home we stopped at one of his vineyards and tasted the grapes that had been left on the vines for the poor to use in making their wines. Just off the road Marcel had dumped a load of hulls and seeds, which he had got back from the distillery and would use to nourish his vines. There were more stems in the residue of his wine, I noticed, than in the residue at Clos-Vougeot.

I remember that he told me he had had fourteen helpers in his harvest this year. The helpers used by one of the major makers at Clos de Vougeot had numbered seventy.

We went on to Marcel's house and had lunch with him and his family. His son, eighteen, was home, and the six of us ate in his comfortable, pleasantly furnished dining room. Their dog, a mongrel, and their cat, a tabby, both of which had been rescued from the Animal Protective Society, joined us. The food and wine began to flow—it was like a farmer's kitchen in America except that we had wine and paté. We began with the paté and a white wine that Marcel had traded for; vintners rarely buy from each other, they trade. We had *entrecote* and wild mushrooms, the mushrooms having been gathered from a place Marcel and his wife had discovered on a mountain years ago; they appeared each year in a fairy ring. The sauce was mild and dark. Mrs. Bouquinet opened a can of green beans she had done some sort of miracle with. The bread was French, the wine was Marcel's. Everything was fantastically good, and the meal had been prepared without preknowledge of our coming to see them, so it was not for us that it was made. The quality of French cooking is phenomenal. It isn't a restaurant specialty—restaurants in France came into being only two generations ago; it is from the home that great cooking emanates in France.

Their cat was named Bébé and would, if invited to do so, sit on Marcel's shoulder and eat whatever his right hand raised toward his mouth; its paw would dart out to deflect the fork to its own mouth, but it would not bother what Marcel raised with his left hand. Meanwhile the dog would stand on her hind feet and eat anything offered to her, but she didn't beg for it. "She's a gourmet," Marcel said. The family had affection for both animals, quite obviously, and we were, people and animals, a friendly lot indeed, and happy and successful on this particular afternoon.

"This is better than George V," Marcel told us, referring to one of Paris's great hotel restaurants. He said he didn't like George V's stiffness or the smallness of its tables.

We had cheese and a crust of bread. Then Marcel and my wife and I went downstairs into his cellar and tasted his new wine, muddy, yeasty, unpromising, and the wine from the year before, also unpromising as yet. Then he opened a bottle of wine of an earlier vintage, and we drank it at cellar temperature, sitting on stones and waiting for the day to end.

These are good days, rich, pleasant ones to be recalled gently, and to be lived and appreciated most by those who themselves have a body of experience in the crafts of wines and cheeses and foods. Just as those who most love music are likely to be those who have played it, or have tried, even if they have failed.

Appendix 1

Cheesemakers' Notes

These general notes might be of interest to you, and some will be of help in making cheeses. They are here more or less in the chronology of cheesemaking, and make sense only in terms of the preceding chapters and your own experiences. Most people would probably have put them at the beginning of the book, but I believe a great many details at the start of an experience are a handicap rather than a help.

1. In England, on average, a Jersey dairy herd will give milk of 5 percent butterfat and a Guernsey herd 4.6 percent; both milks are too rich for most cheeses. An Ayrshire herd gives 3.8, a Lincoln Red 3.6, a Red Poll 3.6, a Shorthorn 3.6, a Holstein-Friesian 3.3, and all these are suitable for all

cheeses; 3.2 to 3.5 is the fat content most often desired. The fat globules of the Jersey and Guernsey also are larger, which is a disadvantage. Except for butterfat, the milks are similar and have similar properties.

The milk of a cow which has just weaned her calf is not suitable for cheesemaking. Milk from cows which are being fed chiefly on hay does not make the best cheese. Milk from cows which are being treated with penicillin will not coagulate.

Milk in the spring will produce about 80 percent as much cheese as will milk in the fall.

Milk for soft cheeses is not ripened before use; milk from a farmer's cooler is almost always fresh enough, since the temperature is kept at about 40 degrees and the cooler is emptied two or three times a week. Milk for hard cheeses needs to be ripened. Let it stand at room temperature for about five hours, less time if it is not absolutely fresh.

You can make tests of the milk's ripeness, its acidity, as described in the acidity section, number 6 below.

For hard cheeses the old cheesemakers found that evening's milk kept overnight at 60 to 70 degrees to ripen, mixed with fresh morning's milk in equal proportions, was properly matured. For soft cheeses they kept the evening's milk cooler or used only fresh morning's milk. Next morning some makers would skim the cream off the night's milk, heat it up to 120 degrees, and stir it into the vat with the morning's milk, which would reduce the risk of fat losses in the whey.

2. It is not necessary to put all the milk for a large cheese on the stove, in order to heat it. For instance, suppose you are using 20 gallons of milk. Heat a small quantity, say 2 gallons, to any temperature up to 109 degrees, never over.

Add the 2 gallons of heated milk to the larger amount in order to raise the temperature of the whole. Then continue, proceeding in stages. You should not increase the overall temperature more than 3 degrees at a time. There is a mathematical formula for this. Multiply the amount of milk reserved by 3 (in this case, 18 gallons would be multiplied by 3). Divide that figure by the number of gallons on the warmer (in this case, 2). To the resulting figure, add the temperature desired at this mixing (that is, if the milk reserved is 75 degrees, and you want to raise it to 78 degrees, then add 78). In our example this gives you a total of 105 degrees, the temperature to which the 2 gallons of milk in the warmer should be heated in order to raise the temperature of the 20 gallons of milk to 78 degrees.

3. Factories using professional equipment pasteurize milk by heating it while stirring to 163 degrees for sixteen seconds, then they cool it to renneting temperature quickly. The old people felt milk should never be heated beyond 150 degrees, but then the old people felt that cheese milk should never be pasteurized at all. The lowest temperature at which milk can be safely pasteurized is 145 degrees; you will need to hold the milk at this temperature for thirty minutes to meet United States standards.

If the cheese is to be cured for over sixty days, authorities feel, and United States law concurs, that the milk need not be pasteurized. Most cheeses produced in Europe, aged or unaged, are from unpasteurized milk. Interestingly enough, studies indicate that many cheeses sold in the United States that are labeled pasteurized are not, and that just as many that are not so labeled have in fact been pasteurized.

The pasteurization of milk will delay the time needed for

the ripening of the cheese by up to 50 percent, indicating that the microorganisms in cheese play a leading role in protein degradation and flavor development, about which scientists know less than enough as yet. One reason factories often pasteurize milk is that the diverse bacterial population in their milk, which comes to them from many different dairies, leads to variability in making, to less adaptability to time schedules. The taste of raw-milk cheese is better, as they know. The bitter aftertaste which afflicts many American cheeses is due to the pasteurization of the milk; no bitterness should ever be found in a cheese, mild or sharp, fresh or aged.

If you pasteurize the milk, you will want, once it cools to 86 degrees or thereabouts, to add starter. The amount of starter varies, depending on cheese type and the milk used. As a working average for pasteurized milk, add 1 cup of starter to 5 gallons of milk in summer and fall, up to 2 cups in spring. Mix well, wait fifteen to thirty minutes, and proceed.

4. If you want to color your cheese, red and yellow annatto cheese colorings, both liquid and tablets, are available (see Appendix 3). Cheese coloring has an alkaline water base; butter coloring has a vegetable oil base and should not be used for cheesemaking.

The coloring should be added well before renneting. Otherwise coagulation might set in before the coloring is adequately dispersed, causing streaking.

Dissolve the tablet in a cup of water, or dilute the liquid with about twenty times its volume of water, and pour it in while stirring, or, if you prefer, immerse the cup under the milk, emptying the cup under the surface of the milk while stirring. One-half teaspoon of liquid coloring will color 5 gallons of milk adequately, on average.

You will, I hope, decide not to color your cheeses except where, as with Leicester, the bright coloring is part of the mystique and tradition of the cheese. There is much folly to the whole business.

5. A starter is milk with a high concentration of helpful bacteria: cultured buttermilk, or a commercially prepared lactic acid starter are usually recommended. Yogurt and sour cream are sometimes recommended. The starter assists in ripening the milk from which the cheese is to be made and, later, the cheese itself. It contributes some flavor to the cheese and helps to crowd out various species of bacteria which are not desirable. Lactic acid starters can be ordered through the mail (see Appendix 3), and cultured buttermilk can be bought in most grocery stores. A starter can be made to propagate itself from one day to another, but Mr. Mossholder's experience of using a single strain for many years, as described at the close of Chapter 1, is unusual; also, it is likely that during those years new viruses and bacteria have come to dominate the culture and that the starter does not contribute the same effective taste as it used to.

Special lactic acid cultures for hard cheeses, for cottage cheese, for Gruyère, and for certain other cheeses are available from cheesemakers' shops and manufacturers, and for those sources you will want to refer to Appendix 3.

The old people often used yesterday's whey as a starter, but this practice tended to transfer from one day to the next any taint which developed in the manufacturing operation, and in the course of several days often resulted in poor cheese and distressed dairymaids. Many of them never could understand about starters anyway. One dear dairymaid I read about was seen to dump into the milk a whole bucket of yesterday's whey, and when told that she had used far too much, replied, "Well, what's the good of keeping it?"

6. Mrs. Kirby used no acidity tests, but these tests do take some of the guesswork out of cheesemaking. The old people would squeeze a piece of curd dry, then rub it against metal heated to a "black heat," perhaps the door of a stove or an iron frying pan. They would slowly draw the curd away in a continuous motion. The length of threads drawn was an indication of acidity: the longer the thread, the more acidity.

Acidity	Hot Iron Test
0.17–0.19%	¼ inch thread
0.24%	½ inch thread
0.45%	¾ inch thread
0.65%	1 inch
0.85%	1½ inches
0.95%	2 inches

Later, some cheesemakers began to use litmus paper graded to a color chart, and in the 1890s to use chemical tests, those still in use today. The makers would neutralize the milk or whey to be tested with an N/10 NaOH solution. The equipment needed can be purchased as a set, complete with chemicals (see Appendix 3), or you can put a set together yourself if you buy a 25-ml. burette graduated to measure ⅒-cc. gradations, and a stand and clamp for it. You will also need a glass or plastic stirring rod and a cup. Finally, you must buy a pipette for measuring up to 10 cc., or get a disposable 10-cc. hypodermic syringe from a surgeon. As for supplies, buy a small bottle of phenolphthalein indicator and a pint of N/10 NaOH solution, which a druggist can prepare for you or a chemical supply house or cheesemakers' shop will sell you.

Now, to use them:

Measure out with the pipette 9 cc. of the milk or whey you want to test. Put this in the cup. Add three drops of the phenolphthalein solution.

Fill the burette with the N/10 NaOH solution up to the point marked 0.

While stirring the solution in the cup, let the N/10 solution drip into it. When the solution in the cup permanently turns pink, stop. If the pink disappears while you continue stirring, start again, continuing until the pink does remain permanently.

Now read the number indicated on the scale of the burette. This will tell you how much of the neutralizing N/10 solution you used. If you used 2 cc., the acidity of the milk is 0.20 percent. If you used 2.6 cc., the acidity is 0.26 percent, and so forth.

If you have fresh rennet extract, you can make an acidity test of the milk in yet another way: Measure 1 dram of rennet (56 drops) into a lukewarm cup. Put one or two small pieces of straw in the cup. Add 4 ounces of milk at 84 degrees, noticing the time exactly, and stir for a few seconds. When the milk begins to coagulate, the straws will stop moving; note the time at that point.

If 24 seconds have elapsed, the acidity of the milk is 0.20 percent.

If 21 to 22 seconds have elapsed, it is 0.21 percent.

If 20 seconds have elapsed, it is 0.22 percent.

If 18 seconds have elapsed, it is 0.24 percent.

Normally, hard-pressed cheeses need a milk at about 0.21 to 0.23 percent, and soft cheeses a milk at 0.18 to 0.20 percent.

One degree variation from 84 degrees will make a difference of two seconds in the test; a higher temperature will speed up the action of the rennet that much. So you might want to stir the milk you are testing with a thermometer and read the temperature when you remove it, to be sure you are exact, or have somebody help you by keeping track of the temperature.

If you know the acidity of the milk, you can use this same test to determine the strength of your rennet, as you will agree if you think about it.

Or, if you have two bottles of rennet, you can run this test twice, once for each of the rennets, and compare their strength.

Uses of pH testing have been widely experimented with, and have largely been rejected in England as unsuitable. Some factories in the United States use both acidity and pH tests and have begun using pH machines of a type which gives them a printed record for each batch of cheese, one inch per hour or whatever. They use the readings chiefly to help judge when to cut.

7. Rennet is an almost odorless natural chemical with the color of a brown sherry. Not only does it increase the coagulation process, but it retards and delays the acidifying of milk. The amount used and the temperature at which it is used are critical bits of information in almost every cheese recipe.

Rennet is available in powder, tablets, and liquid. The commercial tablets are equal to about 6 cc. of the liquid. As a general rule, liquid rennet extract is the easiest to use.

As I said earlier, liquid rennet can be kept in the refrigerator and will lose only about 10 percent of its power in a year's time.

Rennet you plan immediately to use should be diluted with tap water, anywhere from six to forty times its own volume. The larger the quantity of milk you are renneting, the more water you will want to add, in order to be able to stir the diluted rennet to all corners of the vat evenly.

8. You ought not to stir the milk once it has begun to coagulate. To do so will cause a severe loss of butterfat. Once the coagulation begins, the pot should not be moved, either.

To tell when coagulation starts, you can, as Mrs. Kirby said, use pieces of a clean toothpick, wooden matchstick, or clean broomstraw. Float them. They will stop moving the instant the milk begins to coagulate. If you notice how long the rennet takes to start the coagulation, you can be pretty sure the coagulum will be in the proper state for cutting after waiting an additional 2 ½ times that long.

Another method of telling when coagulation is under way is by dipping a small glass in the milk, then holding the glass up to the light; uncoagulated milk will flow off the glass evenly, while coagulated milk will try to cling to it, forming wavy patterns. Still another way is to put a drop of water on the milk; if the drop of water disappears, the milk hasn't begun to coagulate, but if it lies on the surface of the milk or makes a slight hole for itself, coagulation is in process. Some cheesemakers float a tin bowl in the milk, and when they lift the bowl they look for the presence or absence of small particles of curd on the bottom of the bowl.

In a 3- to 4-gallon pot, only three minutes for stirring are needed for the rennet to become thoroughly distributed; in a larger pot, another minute or so is needed. After that you might want to stir the surface, that is, ripple the surface, now and again for a few minutes, since it is important in the making of most cheeses for the cream not to rise. Stir gently, trying not to have the milk in motion when coagulation first begins. This is the ideal and, like most ideals, is almost never attained in the real world. Better to stop stirring too soon than too late.

9. The purpose of cutting is to divide the curd into pieces that can easily exude whey, without causing them to exude much butterfat as well. You can use a kitchen knife, or you can purchase curd knives, contraptions which make four to thirty cuts at one time, either ½-inch or 1-inch, or whatever. Most curd knives are 8 inches wide and 16 to 24 inches long; there are vertical and horizontal models. The cutting wires are stainless or tinned steel.

Squeezing the bits of curd will cause them to exude butterfat. Whey naturally is clear and has a greenish hue; however, just after cutting it will probably be white, and the whiter it is, the more butterfat you are losing, and the longer it stays white, the more you are losing and have lost.

Also, the softer the curd, the more butterfat you will lose. When a recipe calls for a soft curd to be cut, it might also suggest that the cutting be done in two or three stages, with rests in between for a few minutes, in order to help hold the loss of butterfat to a minimum.

10. Mrs. Kirby breaks her matted cheese into small pieces with her fingers, and for the home maker this is probably the best way, even though it will become tiring. More fat is lost by the use of a cheese mill. Such mills can be purchased. I bought mine in an antique shop. It looks like a grape crusher and can be used for that, too, but the grape crushers will not do for milling cheeses.

11. Salting will put the brakes on the swift advance of ripening and improve the taste of the cheese. In early spring, more salt is needed, the milk having less flavor then than it will have later in the year.

Interestingly, the more you salt a cheese, the less salty it may taste once it is cured. The reason is that the salt you add slows down the curing process which produces natural salts.

NaCl, common salt, is used universally in cheesemaking. A soft cheese requires fine salt, but most other cheeses prefer a coarse salt, such as ice-cream or kosher salt; the larger grains take longer to dissolve, become more evenly distributed, and suffer less loss in the whey. Iodized salt should not be used in cheeses.

Salt is usually sprinkled on the curd. An alternate way of salting is from the outside, once the cheese has taken on its shape, either with dry salt or by putting the whole cheese in brine.

12. *Vatting* is a term cheesemakers use for the process of putting pieces of curd in molds, in hoops, in tins, in the baskets of presses, or in vats, all of which are words for the same thing. We use the word *molds* as a general rule. Vatting should not be undertaken until the curds have had a chance to cool.

A cheese should not be pressed until it has cooled to about 70 degrees, except in the case of Gruyère. If pressed at a higher temperature it will lose excessive amounts of butterfat.

A hard-pressed cheese has a tough curd and must be pressed early and with comparatively high pressure, or it will not go together as a cheese and will have an open texture, which such a cheese does not want. A cheese with a soft curd does not need to be pressed heavily or under high pressure, and the curd is likely to go together nicely to make a cheese with any little help given it. The open texture is desirable.

13. Some cheeses need a press; others do not. As to presses, one of the marvels of science is this: If you press two or more cheeses vertically, one on top of the other, the full force of the press is delivered to each, and the lower one has in addition the weight of any above; if you press two or more cheeses side by side, horizontally, the force of the press is half as great for each in the case of two cheeses, one-third as great in the case of three cheeses, and so forth.

A wine press or other ratchet or screw press will do very well. Its only fault is that it has no persisting weight; once the curd has exuded enough whey to shrink in the mold, the pressure is relaxed somewhat. That is different, you see, from the pressure of a dead weight that is set on the mold. A dead-weight press, or hydraulic press, is difficult to come by, I find.

A lard press has the same fault but it is what I use. I have three wine presses, too, but prefer the lard press. Lard presses can be found sometimes in junk or antique shops and can be ordered new from hardware stores.

A car jack can be used, but you will need to build a frame, or use a sturdy wooden box or metal footlocker.

I find it helpful in estimating the force of a press to operate it a few times with a bathroom scales receiving its pressure. Only a slight turn of the handle on my presses will exert 40 pounds of pressure, and with one finger I can exert well over 300 pounds. It is important that one get a sense of what his press is doing before he presses cheeses.

You can press more than one cheese in a press, if you contrive a system. For instance, if the molds have collapsible bands that will sink down as the cheese is pressed, you could put boards between the molds in a stack and put a flat board over the top one or a follower inside the top mold, as you choose.

14. A cheese cellar, the type needed by pressed cheeses, such as Cheddar, can be in a cellar or in a closet upstairs or in a box, so long as it is reasonably cool, 65 degrees or less, and reasonably moist. Usually a wine cellar is ideal. Mold- or bacteria-ripened cheeses have special needs which are discussed in the particular chapters and at the close of this section.

The cellar can fluctuate moderately in temperature and humidity. Cheese, like wines, can breathe; both are alive and are natural creatures.

If kept above 65 degrees, the cheese is likely to develop a sharper, more pungent flavor than you will like, and the mellow texture might begin deteriorating too soon. At a low, low temperature cheese will ripen—even at 40 degrees it will ripen, but it takes longer and will not develop as full a flavor. Many cheese factories age their cheese at just such a low temperature, since this does help to avoid bacteria and mold problems and loss of moisture; then they stamp the cheese as having been aged four months, when effectively it has not been aged two.

In a 60- to 65-degree cellar, a pressed cheese such as Cheddar will lose about 12 percent of the water it contained just after pressing; a Cheddar containing 41 percent water after pressing will, when ripened, contain about 35 percent, most of the loss having taken place during the early weeks. For this reason cheeses in a cellar should be turned now and then, every few days when young, less often later on, so that the moisture inside the cheeses will remain evenly distributed and the curing will be uniform.

If the cheese cellar is not moist, the cheeses might shrink unduly, or even crack. Should one crack, put lard or butter in the opening, or paste a piece of muslin over the injury with flour paste.

If the room is too damp, mold might appear on the cheeses and have to be wiped off. Use salty water, if you need to.

If a brown dust appears on your shelves or cheeses, then you might have cheese mites, famous in literature through ages past. Brush the mites off. If they are damaging the cheeses, dip the cheeses in scalding water briefly. Most pressed cheeses develop hides thick enough to protect themselves. To be sure cheese mites are alive, disrupt their orderly patterns; if in a day or so the damage to their patterns has been corrected, you can be sure mites made the correction.

Cheese flies, another pest, are not active in dark rooms, so you can control them by darkening the cellar.

As for cleaning the cellar, a washing with a saline solution usually will do very well. The old people, when pushed to it, disinfected the place, then whitewashed the walls and ceiling. It is best to disinfect or paint one wall at a time, in order not to eradicate the colonies of bacteria.

In a cellar temperature and ventilation influence the molds that appear. The most common mold is *Penicillium glaucum,* which has a greenish-blue color; its range of temperature is 50 to 60 degrees. It is of trifling importance and does little harm unless it manages through a crack or a hole to get inside a cheese. A black mold might appear, and it can cause a poor flavor in the cheese; it should be wiped off; once encountered in a cellar, it is difficult to get rid of entirely. Red and yellow molds are found occasionally in cheese rooms. When seen on pressed cheeses, they usually indicate that the room is too moist. It is desirable in the case of these pressed cheeses to keep the molds fairly well checked, though not necessarily to banish them. You can rub the cheese surface with your hand or a brush, and if necessary you can use boiling water

or salt water, attacking the fresh colonies at sight. It is well
to take the shelves outdoors from time to time to wash them in
soda water and let them sun.

Cheesemakers like to bore plugs from their cheeses to see
how they are getting on, and this can best be done by a tryer,
a 4- to 6-inch cheese borer, in a semidark cellar room when

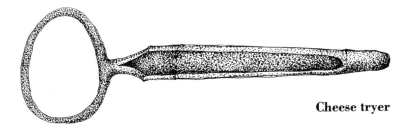

Cheese tryer

one is alone; the guilt of doing it is less oppressive that way.
Metal cheese borers are available. When you take a plug
from a cheese, return the plug's rind quarter to the cheese in
order to close the hole and smear wax or butter or lard over
the injury.

My own efforts to make a cellar for wines and cheeses at
my mountain house led me into considerable involvement,
simply because my ambitions overcame my need. The excava-
tion continued until the hole under the house was 9 feet deep,
floor to ceiling, and 20 by 22 feet wall to wall. That proves
to be large enough for several hundred cheeses and is too
large for practical temperature and humidity controls. The
earth excavated I used to make the dam for a fishpond, and
that I like much better, though, of course, it doesn't serve the
same purposes. Even if some say Blue Vinny was sometimes
cured immersed in cider, we have no authority for curing any
cheese in a trout pond.

The smaller the cellar, the better. The cheeses need to

occupy it. A closet is sometimes ideal, if it can be ventilated when it needs to be, this varying with different cheeses at different stages, and properly cleaned.

As you know, mold- or bacteria-ripened cheeses require high humidity and friendly colonies of organisms. For a small number of cheeses you might consider half filling a bowl or bucket with water; set a wooden or metal grid on top of it, put the cheeses on the grid and cover them with a bowl or box which is about the size of the container holding the water. This will help solve the humidity problem and will also furnish the organisms with a small area for colonization.

15. You perhaps have noticed that the method for making one cheese is similar to that of others which taste unlike it. The maker uses slightly more rennet in one than another, or rennets at a higher temperature, or scalds to a higher temperature, or whatever, but the differences are slight.

The differences in the cheeses are slight, too, if they are analyzed. I will include here two charts which are interesting to speculate about. The information for both comes from *A Textbook of Dairy Chemistry* by Edgar R. Ling (New York: Philosophical Library, 1957: Chapman & Hall, Ltd.).

If your Caerphilly or Cheshire or Wensleydale or other

Cheese	Water (%)	Fat (%)	Protein (%)	Ammonia (%)
Coulommiers (double cream)	57.8	25.0	13.0	0.13
Camembert	53.8	22.0	17.1	0.23
Brie	53.5	22.5	18.0	0.18
Pont l'Evêque	51.0	23.1	17.8	0.13
Gruyère	35.7	28.0	28.9	0.05

Cheese	Water (%)	Fat (%)	Fat in Dry Matter (%)	Protein, Ash and Lactic Acid (%)
Wensleydale	45.03	27.72	50.23	27.25
Caerphilly	44.67	28.43	51.23	26.90
Lancashire	44.28	27.39	49.10	28.33
White Stilton	41.76	32.44	55.37	25.80
Gloucester	41.0	28.8	49.0	30.2
Cheshire	40.53	29.96	50.30	29.51
Derby	39.95	30.59	50.70	29.46
Leicester	39.79	30.21	50.00	30.00
Blue Stilton	37.64	35.71	57.20	26.65
Cheddar	36.69	31.82	50.20	31.49
Cream	24.5	71.6	—	3.9

pressed cheese is too soft or weak or wet for your liking, one or more of the following situations might have occurred.

Too little acidity at renneting and vatting.

Too little temperature at renneting and scalding.

Too little rennet was used.

Cutting too large or too uneven.

Pitching too soon (that is, stopping the stirring too soon).

Allowing the curd to chill.

If the cheese is, on the other hand, too dry or hard, then one or more of the opposite situations might have occurred. Or you might have used too much salt or used a milk with too little butterfat.

I am sometimes asked how to make processed cheese at home. It is often useful to have the recipe, for you can use various bits of cheese that are left over. Use only hard cheeses. Remove the rind. Mince the cheese. Weigh the minced cheese and add 3 percent neutral sodium phosphate and 15 percent water by weight. Mix the three together.

While stirring, at once cook them in a double boiler or double saucepan to 160 degrees F., taking twenty-five to thirty minutes.

When the cheese has the consistency of thick cream, pour it into molds lined with tinfoil or aluminum wrap. Fold the foil over the top and allow the cheese to cool. It is then ready to eat any time.

If you invert the molds onto a flat surface, you will get a smooth top for the cheese.

Before pouring the cheese into molds, or as you pour it, you can add pimentos, olives, caraway seeds, or whatever flavorings you choose, or none at all.

The Switzerland Cheese Association in New York City has recently printed a folder which describes how to make a one-pound Emmenthal cheese. We will review here their suggested method.

Needed is a pot to hold 5 ½ quarts of fresh milk. As a starter they suggest you use a heaping teaspoon of yogurt. Let the mixture stand for twenty-five minutes. Now take out 1 quart of the milk and heat the remaining 4 ½ quarts to 110 degrees, stirring it meanwhile. Add the quart of cooler milk and adjust the temperature of the milk to 88 to 90 degrees.

Crush a rennet tablet and dissolve it in half a cup of water and stir this into the milk. Cover the pot and wait twenty to twenty-five minutes.

Cut the coagulum with a knife, the knife entering from the top straight down to the bottom; cut it into half-inch columns.

Let the curd rest for four or five minutes.

Now break the columns of curd, using an 8-inch-long whisk or a miniature cheese harp. Stir with a figure-eight motion. Let the curd set for three minutes. Repeat the breaking two more times. In all, the breaking should take about fifteen minutes, and the bits of curd should then be about the size of corn kernels.

Stir the curds and whey while slowly reheating them to renneting temperature, about 89 degrees. This should take about five minutes.

Remove the pot from the stove and keep the curds in motion for five or ten minutes longer, using the whisk or the harp.

The mold or hoop recommended to receive the curd is a gallon-size can with about 60 small holes punched in its sides and bottom from inside out. With a ladle or slotted spoon, the bits of curd are transferred to the mold. Fill it evenly and smooth out the surface to make it flat.

No press is used on a cheese this small. The mold is simply left at room temperature, about 72 degrees, for twenty-four hours; however, after six hours the cheese is turned. It is turned again once or twice during this same twenty-four-hour period. It can be removed from the mold during turning, if you like.

At the close of the twenty-four-hour period, remove the cheese from the mold and put it on a wooden or metal grate. Salt it with one teaspoon of salt over the upper surface and the sides. When the salt has dissolved, rub it into the rind with your fingertips. Put the cheese in a cool room or cabinet, one about 58 degrees. Turn the cheese next day and salt the untreated surface and once more salt the sides. (Instead of using the dry-salt method, you can if you prefer put the cheese for three hours in a salt bath made of 1 quart of water and 4 ounces of salt; the cheese should be turned once, so that both surfaces are equally treated.)

You can best cure the cheese at 55 degrees. One way to help sustain the humidity is to fill a salad bowl two-thirds full of water. Place a grate on this bowl. Place the cheese on the grate and cover it with a second bowl. Leave the cheese alone for

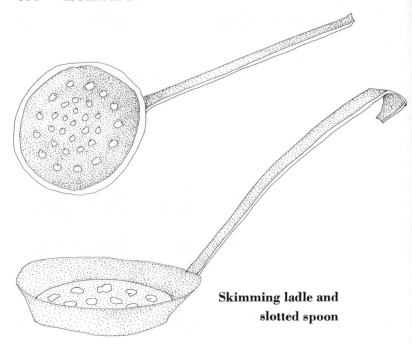

**Skimming ladle and
slotted spoon**

two or three days. After that, turn the cheese once a day for
the curing period, three to five weeks. Each time before you
turn the cheese on the grate, wipe the grate dry, set the cheese
on the dried grate and lightly dampen its top surface with a
cloth wet with salt water, then massage the cheese gently to
spread the moisture evenly, but do not rub or wash an Emmenthal. (Two teaspoons of salt dissolved in half a quart of water
will make a suitable bath for this operation.)

A white and then a pinkish, smeary-looking rind will develop. The cheese is ready once the rind takes on the pink hue,
which will be three weeks in a cellar warmer than the one recommended, about five in a cellar as cool as the one recommended.

If you don't have a whisk long enough, you can make a
cheese harp out of three sticks and some copper or tinned

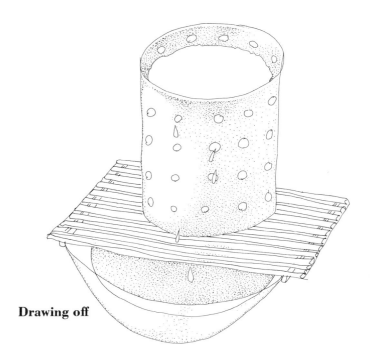

Drawing off

wire. One stick 20 inches long can be the handle and spine of the harp. To one end secure a 6 ½- to 7-inch stick, making a "T." Now measure down the spine 8 inches and at that point secure the other 6 ½- to 7-inch stick, setting it parallel to its small brother, thus making a little telephone pole with two crosspieces. To complete the harp, stretch wire in parallel rows between the two small sticks, so that one wire is about an inch from another or from the spinal stick.

I suspect this particular cheese would be improved if the appropriate bacterial culture were to be introduced, as in the description for Gruyère in Chapter 8.

The old recipe we mentioned in the chapter on Double Gloucester cheese is entered here just as it was printed in 1796.

THE

RURAL ECONOMY

OF

GLOCESTERSHIRE;

INCLUDING ITS

D A I R Y:

TOGETHER WITH THE

DAIRY MANAGEMENT

OF

NORTH WILTSHIRE;

AND THE

MANAGEMENT

OF

ORCHARDS AND FRUIT LIQUOR,

IN

HEREFORDSHIRE.

By Mr. MARSHALL.

SECOND EDITION.

IN TWO VOLUMES.

VOL. I.

LONDON:

PRINTED FOR G. NICOL, BOOKSELLER TO
HIS MAJESTY, PALL-MALL; G. G. AND J. ROBINSON,
PATERNOSTER ROW; AND J. DEBRETT,
PICCADILLY.
1796.

III. CHEESE. The art of making GLOCESTERSHIRE CHEESE was, originally, one of the principal objects which induced me to make choice of Glocestershire, as a STATION. My practice in Norfolk had shown me, that, in the quality of cheese, although much may depend upon SOIL and HERBAGE, much is certainly due to MANAGEMENT.

GLOCESTERSHIRE has long been celebrated for its excellency in this art: and where shall we study an art, with so much propriety, as in the place where it excels? It may be proper to add, that although my own experience had not led me to perfection, it had sufficiently enabled me to make accurate observations, on the practices of others. An ANALYTICAL ARRANGEMENT, of the several departments and stages of the art, was a guard against my suffering any material part to escape my notice; and the THERMOMETER a certain guide, in those difficult passages, in which an accuracy of judgment is, more peculiarly, requisite.

The objects of my attention have been

Soils.	Management of the curd.
Water.	Management of the cheese.
Herbage.	Defects and Excellencies.
Cows.	Markets.
Quality of milk.	Produce.
Coloring.	
Rennets.	
Method of running.	

The managements of the two vales under survey differ in one most material article;—the *quality* of the milk. In the lower vale, the milk is run neat from the cow (or nearly so.) In the upper vale, it has been already said, the prevailing practice is, to set the evening's meal for cream; in the morning to skim it; and then to add it to the new milk of the morning's meal. The cheese made from this mixture is termed "TWO-MEAL CHEESE:" that from the neat milk, "one-meal cheese" or "BEST MAKING."

Besides this difference in produce, or SPECIES OF CHEESE, there are other differences, in the practices of the two vales. It will, therefore, be proper to register them, separately; lest, by mixing them, the perspicuity, which is requisite, in describing the minutiæ of an art so complex, and so difficult, as this under consideration, should be destroyed.

Of the UPPER VALE the *soil*, the *herbage*, and the *cow*, have been already mentioned: the subjects which remain to be noticed, in this place, are

1. The season of making.
2. The quality of the milk.
3. Coloring.
4. Rennets.
5. Running.
6. Management of the curd.
7. Management of the cheese.
8. Markets.

1. THE SEASON OF MAKING. From the beginning of May, to the latter end of October, including seven months, may be considered as the season of cheesemaking, in this district.

2. THE QUALITY OF THE MILK. The mixture for two-meal cheese has been mentioned, in general terms, to be one part skim milk (namely milk which has stood *one* meal for cream) and one part new milk, *neat* from the cow. But *this* is seldom, I apprehend, strictly the case. A little *fraud* is, I am afraid, generally practised. A greater or less proportion of the morning's meal is set for cream, and returned the next morning to the cheese cowl,—*robbed* of its better part. This is a trick played upon the cheese factor: but he being aware of the

practice, little advantage, probably, is gained by it. However, where the soil is superiorly rich, a small proportion may be "kept out," and the cheese, nevertheless, be of a *fair* quality.

3. COLORING. This is another *deception*, which has long been practised by the Glocestershire dairywomen, and which, heretofore, probably, they carried on exclusively. The coloring of cheese, however, is now become a practice in other districts.

The artifice, no doubt, has arisen, from the Glocestershire dairywomen having observed, that, on some soils, and in some seasons, cheese naturally acquires a yellow color; and such cheese having been found to bear a better price, (either from its intrinsic quality, or because it pleased the eye better) than cheese of a paler color, they set about *counterfeiting nature;* and, in the outset, of course, found their end in it.

There is some difficulty, however, in this, as in other cases, to copy nature, exactly. Much depends on the material; and something on the method of using it. If the coloring material be improperly chosen, or injudiciously used, the color appears in streaks, and instead of pleasing the eye, offends it. On the contrary, with a suitable material, properly used, the artifice may be rendered undetectable.

The material which has at length obtained universal esteem, and which, I believe, is now, almost invariably, used, is a preparation of ANNOTTA; a drug, the produce of Spanish America. It is brought to England (for the use of the dyers, principally, I believe) under the appearance of an earthy clay-like substance; but is well known to be a vegetable production.*

---

* ANNOTTA is the produce of *Bixa Orellana* of Linneus. Miller describes the plant and its propagation. It is a tallish shrub, somewhat resembling the lilac. The coloring material is the pulp of the fruit; among which the

It has been tried as a coloring of cheese, in its genuine state; but without success. The PREPARATION, which is here used, is made by druggists, both in London and in the country; and is sold, at the shops in Glocester and other towns of the district, in rolls or knobs of three or four ounces each. In color, and contexture, it is not unlike well burnt red brick. But it varies in appearance and goodness: the hardest and closest is esteemed the best.

The method of using it is this. A piece of the preparation is rubbed against a hard smooth even-faced pebble, or other stone; the pieces being previously dipped in the milk, to forward the levigation, and to collect the particles as they are loosened. For this purpose, a dish of milk is generally placed upon the cheese-ladder; and, as the stone becomes loaded with levigated matter, the pieces are dipped in the milk, from time to time; until the milk in the dish appear (from daily practice) to be sufficiently colored.

The stone and the "coloring" being washed clean in the milk, it is stirred briskly about in the dish; and having stood a few minutes for the unsuspended particles of coloring to settle, is returned into the cheese cowl; pouring it off, gently, so as to leave any sediment, which may have fallen down, in the bottom of the dish. The grounds are then rubbed, with the finger, on the bottom of the dish, and fresh milk added; until all the finer particles be *suspended:* and in this the skill in coloring principally consists. If any fragments have been broken off in the operation, they remain at the bottom of the

seeds are bedded, in a manner somewhat similar to those of the rose, in the pulp of the hep. It is a native of the West Indies, and the warmer parts of America: Annotta Bay in Jamaica takes its name from this shrub. The pigment, it is said, was formerly collected in Jamaica: but has of later years been brought there (in seroons, or bags made of undressed hides) from the Spanish settlements.

dish; hence the superiority of a hard closely textured material, which will not break off or crumble in rubbing.

The price of annotta is about tenpence an ounce; which will color about twenty thin cheeses (10 or 12 pounds each). The coloring, therefore, costs about a halfpenny a cheese.

4. RENNETS. Rennets are here learnedly spoken of,—by those who are superficially acquainted with their use. Experienced dairywomen, however, speak modestly on the subject: what they principally expect from rennet is the *coagulation* of their milk; having little faith in its being able to *correct* any evil quality which the milk may be possessed of.

The universal *basis* is the stomach of a calf; provincially a "vell;" from which an extract is drawn, in various ways; according to the judgment or *belief* of the dairywoman.

1. The *curing of the vell*,—namely, the cleansing and pickling,—is generally done to their hands. Besides the internal supply, London and Ireland furnish this country with great numbers of vells; which are brought in casks, in pickle, and sold by the grocers and other shopkeepers. The price of English vells is about sixpence, a piece,—of Irish, about fourpence; these being comparatively small.*

2. *Preparation of the rennet.* In the dairy which I more particularly attended to, in the upper vale, the rennet underwent no *established* mode of preparation. The *prevailing* method is this: some *whey* being *salted,* until it will bear an egg, is suffered to stand, all night, to purge itself: in the morning it is skimmed, and racked off clear: to this is added an equal quantity of *water-brine,* and into this briny mixture is put some sweet briar, thyme, hyssop, or other "sweet herbs;" also a little black pepper, saltpetre, &c.; tying the herbs in bunches, and letting them remain in the brine, a few

* Some of them, it is apprehended, are "lambs' vells."

days. Into about six quarts of this liquor, four English vells, or a proportionate number of Irish ones, are put; and having lain in it, three or four days, the rennet is fit for use. No part of the preparation is boiled, or even heated: and, frequently, no other preparation whatever is used, than that of steeping the vells in cold salt and water. Indeed, in another dairy, which I had an opportunity of observing, in the upper vale, no other mode of preparation was used; and few, if any, dairies make better cheese: I speak from my own knowledge.

Therefore, from the evidence which I have collected, in the upper vale, it appears, that, provided the *vells* be duly *prepared*—be thoroughly cleansed and cured—no subsequent preparation of *rennet* is necessary. Nevertheless were I to recommend a practice, in this case, it would be that of doing away the natural *faint* flavor of the vells, by some aromatic infusion. But I should prefer *spices* to *herbs* for this purpose.

5. RUNNING. In this, as in every other stage and department of cheesemaking, there are *shades of difference,* in the practices of different dairywomen. No two conduct the business exactly alike; nor is the practice of any individual uniform. There are, at present, no fixed principles to go by. Every thing is left to the decision of the senses; uncertain guides. Nevertheless, *practice,* carried on with attention, and assisted by good natural abilities, will do much; though it cannot, alone, attain that degree of perfection, which, when joined with *science,* it is capable of reaching.

The mistress of the dairy, whose practice I am more particularly registering, has both natural and acquired advantages, which render her dairy, though not of the first magnitude, a proper subject of study. Her father was possessed of the best breed of cows in the vale, and was one of the largest dairy farmers in it. Her mother, the first among its dairywomen;

and herself possessed of that *natural cleverness*, without which no woman, let her *education* be what it may, can conduct, with any degree of superiority, the business of a cheese dairy.

In giving a detail of my own practice, in Norfolk, I mentioned some known principles of coagulation; as well as some received opinions of dairywomen, respecting the nature of this process. The same opinions are held in this district; in which some other received ideas prevail: namely, that the quantity of curd is in proportion to the length of time of coagulation; there being "the least curd when longest in coming."

That setting the milk, hot, inclines the cheese to "heave:" (a defect which will be spoken to hereafter.)

And that lowering the heat of the milk, with cold water, has a similar effect.

To give some idea of the practice of the upper vale, in this most delicate stage of the art, I will detail the observations made, during five successive mornings, in the dairy which has been spoken of.

Tuesday, 2 September, 1783. The quality of the milk, that which has been described. Part of the skim milk added cold,—part warmed, in a kettle, over an open fire, to raise the whole to a due degree of heat. Colored in the manner described. An estimated sufficiency of rennet added. The whole stirred and mixed evenly together. The exact heat of the mixture 85° of Fahrenheit's thermometer. The morning close and warm, with some thunder. The cheese-cowl covered;—but placed near an open door. The curd, nevertheless, came in less than forty minutes: much sooner than expected: owing, probably, to the peculiar state of the air. The retained heat of the curd and whey, when broken up and mixed evenly together, 82°. The curd deemed too tough and hard; though much the tenderest curd I have observed.

Wednesday, 3 September. The morning moderately cool. The heat of the milk when set 83 ½°. The cowl partially covered, and exposed to the outward air, as before. Came in an hour and a quarter. The heat of the curd and whey, mixed evenly together, 80°. But at the top, before mixing, only 77°. The curd extremely delicate, and esteemed of a good quality.

Thursday, 4 September. The morning cool—a slight frost. The milk heated, this morning, to 88°. The cowl more closely covered; and the door shut part of the time. Set at half past six: began to come, at half after seven: but not sufficiently firm, to be broken up, until eight o'clock:—an hour and a half. The whey, when mixt, exactly 80°! The curd exceedingly delicate.

Thus, it would seem, it is not the heat of the milk when it is run, but the heat of the whey, when the curd is sufficiently coagulated, which gives the quality of the curd. My own practice led me to the same idea. And the Glocestershire dairywomen, by their practice, seem fully aware of the fact. As autumn advances, the heat of the milk is increased; and as the given morning happens to be warm or cool, the degree of warmth of the milk is varied.

Friday, 5 September. This morning, though mild, the curd came exactly at 80°! What an accuracy of judgment here appears to be displayed! Let the state of the air be what it will, we find the heat of the whey, when the curd is sufficiently coagulated, exactly 80°; and this, without the assistance of a thermometer, or any other artificial help. But what will not daily practice, natural good sense, and minute attention accomplish.

Saturday, 6 September. This morning, the curd came too quick. The heat of the whey (after the curd had been broken and was settled) full 85°! The curd "much tougher and harder than it should be." Here we have a proof of the inaccuracy of the senses; and of the insufficiency of the natural judgment, in the art under consideration: it may frequently *prove to be right;* but never can be *certain.* Some scientific helps are evidently necessary to UNIFORM SUCCESS.

6. THE MANAGEMENT OF THE CURD. This stage of the process has five distinct operations belonging to it.

1. Breaking.
2. Gathering.
3. Scalding.
4. Vatting.
5. Preserving spare curd.

1. *Breaking.* Here, new ideas arise.—The curd while suspended in the whey, is never touched with the hands.* The curd is broken, or rather cut, with the triple "cheese knife," which has been described. This mode of separating the curd and whey, though not universal, appears to be highly eligible: the intention of it is that of "keeping the fat in the cheese:" a matter which, in the manufacture of two-meal cheese, is of the first consideration. The operation is performed in this manner.

The knife is first drawn, as deep as it will reach, across the cowl, in two or three places; and likewise round by the sides; in order to give the whey an opportunity of escaping, as clear as may be. Having stood five or ten minutes, the knife is more freely used; drawing it briskly in every direction, until the upper part of the curd be cut into small chequers. The bottom is then stirred up with the dish, in the left hand; and, while the lumps are suspended in the whey, they are cut with the knife, in the right: thus continuing to stir up the curd with

* In another dairy, however, whose manager ranks high among dairy-women, the curd is broken with the hands alone . . .

the dish, and separate the lumps with the knife, until not a lump, larger than a bean, is seen to rise to the surface.

2. *Gathering.* The curd having been allowed about half an hour to settle in, the whey is laded off, with the dish; passing it through a hair sieve into some other vessel.

The principal part of the whey being laded off, the curd is drawn to one side of the cowl, and pressed hard with the bottom of the dish: the skirts and edges cut off with a common knife, and the cuttings laid upon the principal mass; which is carried round the tub, among the remaining whey, to gather up the scattered fragments that lie among it. The whole being collected, the whey is all laded or poured off, and the curd left in one mass, at the bottom of the cowl.

3. *Scalding.* It is, I believe, the invariable practice of the dairywomen of Glocestershire, to *scald the curd.* This accounts for their running the milk so comparatively cool. Were the delicate cool-run curd, of this district, to be made into cheese, without being previously scalded, the cheeses made from it would require an inconvenient length of time to fit them for market.

The method of scalding the curd, here, varies from that mentioned in the Minutes, in Norfolk. There, it was scalded in the mass; pouring hot water over the surface, as it lay at the bottom of the cheese tub: but, here, the mass is broken; first by cutting it into square pieces with a common knife; and then reducing it, with the triple knife, into small fragments; mostly as small as peas: none of them is left larger than a walnut: and among these fragments, the "scalding stuff" is thrown; stirring them briskly about; thereby effectually mixing them together; and, of course scalding the whole as effectually, and as evenly, as this method of scalding will admit of.

The *liquid* made use of, here, for scalding curd, varies in different dairies. Some dairywomen scald with *whey;* violently objecting to water; while others use *water;* objecting, with equal obstinacy, to whey: while dairywomen in general, I believe, mix the two together.*

The *quantity* is in proportion to the quantity of curd: enough to float the curd; and make the mixture easy to be stirred about with the dish.

Part of it is heated to near boiling heat; and this is lowered, with cold liquid, TO A HEAT PROPORTIONED TO THE STATE OF THE CURD: soft curd is scalded with hot, hard curd with cooler liquid.

In scalding, therefore, the dairywoman has a remedy, for any misjudgment her sense of feeling may have led her into, in the stage of coagulation: let the curd come too soft or too hard, she can bring it to the desired texture, by the heat of the scalding liquor. And here seems to hinge, principally, the superior skill of the Glocestershire dairywoman: by running the milk cool, she can, in scalding, correct any error which has been committed in running.

Saturday, 6 September. This morning, the curd being too tough, the *whey* was used cooler than it was, yesterday morning, when the curd was sufficiently tender. Yesterday morning, 104°, this morning, 125°.

Tuesday, 9 September. This morning, the curd came at its proper heat 80°, and the heat of the scalding whey was 142°.

The curd being thoroughly mixed and agitated among the whey, and having had a few minutes to subside in,—the dairymaid began immediately to lade off the whey. This, however, is not the universal practice: in some diaries, the curd is suf-

* It seems to be understood, that different grounds require different kinds of scalding liquor.

fered to remain among the scalding liquor, half an hour: thus (as has been observed) there are *shades of difference* in every stage of the process.

Wednesday, 24 Sept. This morning, the curd came too tender; and, the morning being cool, the scalding whey was heated to 161°, and stood upon the curd, near ten minutes: this changed it from a state of jelly, as to softness, to the same tough hard mass it is always left after scalding.

4. *Vatting.* The scalding liquor being mostly laded off, a vat is placed on the cheese ladder, laid across the tub, and the curd crumbled into it, with the hands, scrupulously breaking every lump; squeezing out the whey, as the handfuls are taken up; and again pressing it with the hands in the vat; which is, from time to time, set on-edge, to let the whey run off.

The vat being filled, as full and firmly as the hand alone can fill it, and rounded up high in the middle, a cheese cloth is spread over it, and the curd turned out of the vat into the cloth; the vat washed, or rather dipped in the whey, and the inverted mass of curd, with the cloth under it, returned into the vat. The angles, formed by the bottom of the vat, are pared off, and crumbled upon the top, with which they are incorporated by partially breaking the surface, and rounding up the middle as before; the cloth is then folded over, and tucked in; and the vat, with its contents, placed in the press.*

5. *Spare curd.* Preserving the overflowings of the last vat of today's curd, to be mixed up with that of tomorrow, is a common practice in this country; where cheeses, if they be

---

* It is observable, that only one CHEESEBOARD is used, in the Glocestershire dairies, let the number of vats be what they may. The bottoms of the vats, being made smooth and even, answer the purpose of cheeseboards to each other—the uppermost, only, requiring a board. No "sinking boards" are ever made use of, here, as they are in other districts; the vats being rounded up with curd in such a manner, as, from experience it is known, will just fill them when sufficiently pressed.

intended for the factors, are obliged to be made of some certain size. The vats are all nearly of the same bigness; and cannot be proportioned to the curd, as they may, where vats of various sizes are made use of.

In the neighbourhood of Glocester, when the quantity of spare curd is considerable, as four or five pounds, it is frequently made into a small cheese, for the Glocester market; in which it may be sold, in a recent state, (namely at three weeks to two months old,) for $2d.\frac{1}{2}$ to $3d.\frac{1}{2}$ a pound; according to its age: three pence, a pound, is the ordinary price, for such little two-meal cheeses.

When the quantity of spare curd is small, or where the making of little cheeses is not practised, the whey is pressed out, and drained off, as dry as may be, and the curd preserved in different ways. In the upper vale, I have seen it put into an earthen vessel, and covered with cold water. The next morning, it is rescalded thoroughly, once or twice; broken as fine as possible; and either mixt evenly with the fresh curd; or, less eligibly, put into the middle of a cheese. *This*, however, is, with good reason, objected to by the factors. A harsh, crumbly ill tasted seam is formed in the middle of the cheese; a disagreeable circumstance, which, is too frequently met with. Mixing the stale curd, more evenly, among the fresh, has an effect almost equally disagreeable: the particles of stale curd ripen faster than the rest of the cheese; which is thereby rendered unsightly and ill flavored.

In a small dairy, it is impossible to make cheeses sufficiently *sizeable*, for the Glocestershire factors, and, at the same time, to avoid having, frequently, spare curd. But, in a large dairy, where three or four cheeses are made from one running, it might, by a proper number and assortment of vats, be generally avoided; and the cheeses be at the same time made within size.

7. THE MANAGEMENT OF THE CHEESES. This requires to be subdivided, agreeably to the different stages of management.

1. The management in the press.
2. The management while on the dairy shelves.
3. The operation of cleaning.
4. The management in the cheese chamber.

1. *The management while in the press.* Having stood some two or three hours in the press, the vat is taken out; the cloth pulled off and washed; the cheesling turned into the same cloth and the same vat (the cloth being spread under and folded over as before,) and replaced in the press.

In the evening, at five or six o'clock, it is taken out of the press again, and *salted,* in this manner: the angles being pared off, if wanted, the cheesling is placed on the inverted vat; and a handful of salt rubbed hard round its edge; leaving as much salt hanging to it as will stick. Another handful is strowed on the upper side, and rubbed over it pretty hard; leaving as much upon the top as will hang on in turning. It is now turned into the bare vat, that is, without a cloth; and, a similar quantity of salt being rubbed on the other side, is again put into the press.

Next morning, it is turned in the bare vat; in the evening, the same; and, the succeeding morning, taken finally out of the press, and placed upon the dairy shelf.

Each cheese, therefore, stands fortyeight hours in the press. At the second or third, it is turned in the cloth. At the tenth, the cloth is taken off, and the cheesling salted. At the twenty-fourth, it is turned in the bare vat. At the thirtyfourth, the same. And at the fortyeighth, finally taken out.*

* SAGE CHEESE. The method of making "green cheese," in this district, is the following. For a cheese of 10 or 12lb. weight, about two handfuls of sage, and one of marigold leaves and parsley, are bruised, and steeped one night in milk. Next morning, the greened milk is strained off, and mixed with about one third of the whole quantity to be run. The green

2. *The management on the dairy shelves.* Here, the "young cheeses" are turned every day, or every two or three days, according to the state of the weather, or the fancy or judgment of the manager. If the air be harsh and dry, the window and door are kept shut, as much as may be: if close and moist, as much fresh air as possible is admitted.

3. *Cleaning.* Having remained, about ten days, in the dairy (more or less according to the space of time between the "washings") they are cleaned; that is washed and scraped; in this manner: a large tub of cold whey being placed on the dairy floor, the cheeses are taken from the shelves, and immerged in it; letting them lie, perhaps an hour or longer, until the rind become sufficiently supple. They are then taken out, one by one, and scraped with a common case-knife, somewhat blunt; guiding it, judiciously, with the thumb placed hard against its side, to prevent its injuring the yet tender rind: continuing to use it, on every side, until the cloth marks and every other roughness be done away; the edges, more particularly, being left with a polished neatness. Having been rinced in the whey, and wiped with a cloth, they are formed into an open pile (in the manner raw bricks are usually piled) in the dairy window, or other airy place, to dry: and from thence are removed into the cheese chamber.

4. *The management in the cheese chamber.* The FLOOR is generally PREPARED, by rubbing it with bean tops, potatoe

---

and the white milks are run separately; keeping the two curds apart, until they be ready for vatting. The method of mixing them depends on the fancy of the maker. Some crumble the two together, mixing them, evenly, and intimately. Others break the green curd into irregular fragments, or cut it out in regular figures, with tins for this purpose. In vatting it, the fragments, or figures, are placed on the outside. The bottom of the vat is first set with them crumbling the white, or yellowed, curd among them. As the vat fills, others are placed at the edges; and the remainder buried flush with the top. The after-treatment is the same as that of "plain cheeses."

halm, or other green succulent herbage, until it appear of a black wet color. If any dirt or roughness appear upon the boards, it is scraped off; and the floor swept clean. The cheeses are then placed upon it, regularly, in rows; and kept turned, twice a week; their edges wiped hard with a cloth, once a week; and the floor cleaned, and rubbed with fresh herbs, once a fortnight.

The preparation of the floor is done, with the intention of encouraging the blue coat to rise. To the same intent, the cheeses are not turned too frequently; for the longer they lie on one side, the sooner the blue coat will rise. If, however, they be suffered to lie too long, without turning, they are liable to stick to the floor, and thereby receive injury. If, by accident, or otherwise, the coat come partially, it is scraped off. This, however, seldom happens, in a rich-soiled country, and all the care and labor requisite, in this stage, as has been said, is to turn them, twice a week; wipe their edges, once a week; and to prepare the floor, afresh, once a fortnight. If the cheese chamber be too small, to admit of the whole being placed, singly, the oldest are "doubled:" sometimes put "three or four double."

It is striking to see how the cheeses of this district will bear to be handled, at an early age: even at the time of washing, the dairymaid will frequently set the cheese, which she is scraping, on-edge upon another, and this without injury. At a month old, they may be thrown about as old cheeses. Their rinds appear tough almost as leather. This must be owing to the scalding. It cannot be owing to their poverty. They are evidently richer "fatter" than the new milk cheeses of many districts.

8. MARKETS for CHEESE, in the upper vale. In large dairies, cheese is here sold and delivered, three times a year; namely,

in July, again at Michaelmas, and finally in the spring. In small dairies, only twice; about the latter end of September, and again in the spring.

It is bought, principally, by cheese factors, who live in or near the district. The same factor, generally, has the same dairy, year after year; frequently without seeing it, and, perhaps, without any bargain having been made, previously to its being sent in. There is, indeed, a degree of confidence, on the parts of the buyer and seller, which we seldom meet with, among country dealers. Millers and maltsters buy, by sample, and generally take care to make a close bargain, before the corn be sent in.

In summer and early autumn, the factors will take them down to six weeks old; provided they be found firm marketable cheeses; that is neither broken nor "hove;"—a defect, which even the best dairywomen cannot always prevent. During winter, provided their coats be perforated, to give the internal air an opportunity of escaping, the swoln cheeses are generally found to go down, and in the spring, to become marketable.

The *consumption* of two-meal cheese is chiefly, I believe, in the manufacturing districts of this, and other counties. Some of it goes to the London market; where, probably, it is sold under the denomination of Warwickshire cheese: and some is said to go to foreign markets. The *size* mostly "tens" —that is, ten to the hundredweight; or 11 to 12lb. each.

The *price* of two-meal cheese varies with that of newmilk cheese. At Barton fair, in 1783,* the "best making" sold

* BARTON FAIR. A fair held, annually, on the 28th of September, in Barton street, Glocester. It has long been the principal cheese fair of the district. Formerly, a principal part of the cheese, made in the two vales, was brought to this fair. At present, it is mostly brought up by factors, previously to the fair. In 1783, there were about twenty waggon loads

from 34s. (to the factors by the waggon load together) to 36s.
(to families who bought by the hundredweight). "Two-meal,"
from 28s. to 29s. 6d. by the cwt. of 112lb. In 1788, "best
making" 30s. down to 27s. "Two-meal" 25s. down to a guinea.
Prices, which have not been heard of, for many years past.

(besides a number of horse loads) exposed for sale, in the fair. Some
bought by factors but principally, I believe, by the housekeepers, and the
retail dealers of the neighbourhood. In 1788, the quantity in the market
was much greater about forty loads; cheese being then a drug.

Appendix 2

Winemakers' Notes

The following suggestions might be of use to you in connection with winemaking, particularly from fruit, which permit the higher attainments of winemaking and justify particular care.

Concerning the Grapes

Just as obtaining the best milk presents a problem for most city cheesemakers, obtaining the best grapes for making wines is a problem for every vintner in England and the United States, and one more difficult to solve.

In the United States, along the west coast, the European,

the vinifera grapes, grow well, for which all of us in North America should be grateful. For the red wines the best ones are the Cabernet Sauvignon from Bordeaux. If grown in Napa or Sonoma County, in the high country above San Francisco, these give a quality red wine, which improves if aged ten to fifteen years. Rarely will a factory age a wine more than one or two, so you must age your own. The Pinot noir has not proved as satisfactory but is in the upper band of quality. Zinfandel from the mountains produces a delicious wine when aged five to eight years, and it also serves well in blends; it is a European grape, though no one is sure from where. The Gamay, which does well in Beaujolais and poorly in the rest of Burgundy, does well in California. Barbera makes a heavy wine which responds to aging. Ruby Cabernet, a hybrid, is quite respectable. Grapes from California can be obtained by refrigerated truck through your local fruit distributors, though usually the best grapes from the best parts of the West are not available to them—they prefer to sell Bouschet and Carignane from Lodi or another hot valley town, which are not as good, or valley-grown Zinfandels, which are not as good as mountain ones, but are good enough to use if you have no other, or so I have found. Excellent wine grapes (Cabernet Sauvignon and Zinfandels, among others) from Napa and Sonoma, picked when ripe, can be obtained by air freight, properly refrigerated, from at least one California supplier.

Until recently, eastern America has had few of its own grapes to choose from for dry red wines. The native muscadines, scuppernong, fox, and possum grapes make wild-tasting, chemically beset wine unless they are sweet—usually quite sweet. Early in American history, attempts were made to bring European grapes to this country. Thomas Jefferson was one person who tried to do so. Almost all such efforts have proved disappointing, but in the last ten years there has been immense progress and experimentation continues. Of course, a few native grapes have been developed, among them the hardy, productive Concord, but it and most of the others need to be used for a sweet wine, not a dry. Norton and Fredonia make neutral wines. Lenoir and Buffalo are pleasant enough, though without distinction. We also have the Ives, a tough customer but durable, and I prefer it to the others. To join these varieties, the East now has the French-American hybrids, sometimes called "direct producers," hardy vines developed during the past several decades in France and Germany, using European and American stock, and nurtured in our own country by Phillip Wagner at his Boordy Vineyard near Baltimore, by the New York State Experiment Station, by Everett Crosby at High Tor Vineyard in New York, and by others. These grapes have begun to make a place for themselves and have taken special names, at least in this country. A wine made principally of Baco #1 is called Baco Noir; Seibel 10878 makes a wine called Chelois; Landot 244 is called Landal; Johannes-Seyve 26-205 is called Chambourcin; Foch, one of the best of them, is called Foch; and Millot, another of the best, is called Millot, as far as I know. There are many others, most of them appearing as blends, rather than each on its own. They can be grown in most parts of America. In good years they develop balanced acid and sugar content, are healthy and durable, and, if you don't want to grow them for yourself, can be shipped to you from eastern vineyards in September or October. The cost is by the pound. A lug of grapes weighs 36 pounds and one lug will make approximately fifteen bottles of wine.

Many of these hybrids are grown in France, are recommended for planting there, but as yet are not permitted for wines carrying an *Appellation Contrôlée* classification. Among the red "direct producers" recommended for growing in France are the following: in Burgundy, Foch and Landot 244; in Bordeaux, Ravat 6; in the Rhône, Ravat 6, Landot 244, Seyve-Villard 5276; and in Beaujolais, Foch, Ravat 6, and Landot 244. These vines are available in the United States.

We also have red-grape juice concentrates available for winemaking, sold in most winemaking shops. The grapes used are not usually identified by name, which is a pity and should be corrected. At the moment these concentrates make serviceable *vins ordinaires* at moderate cost.

Among the white-wine grapes are the following:

The best in California are the Chardonnay, the Semillon, the Pinot blanc, and the Sauvignon blanc, the latter being better for sweet wines than dry. Of above average quality is the Folle Blanche, used in California Chablis and Champagnes.

Less desirable are the Ugno blanc, called Trebbiano in some places, the Palomino, the Sauvignon vert, which has too little acid, and the Thompson seedless, which is a California table grape included here simply because it is extensively used for common wines, when it really doesn't want to be. German grapes available in California are the white Riesling (excellent) and the gray Riesling (not so good). The Italian grape, the Peverella, does very well.

In the eastern United States, over the years a number of varieties have been developed. The Delaware and Catawba are perhaps the best known of them, and are often blended. The Niagara is a poor dry-wine grape. The Dutchess, the Diamond, the Diana, and the Noah are all serviceable but undistinguished.

However, the French-American hybrids make good white wines. The Seyve-Villard 5276 makes a white wine named Seyval-Blanc which has pleasant taste and bouquet. Seibel 5279 makes a pleasing wine called Aurora. Roucaneuf is actually Seyve-Villard 12-309 in disguise, and is above average. Ravat Blanc is Ravat 6 in disguise; it is sometimes the best of them all. Vidal 256 is quite delicate and acceptable. Ravat 51 is light and healthy. Blends of these and their kin present us with excellent prospects for experimenting. On the whole the white hybrids are even more successful than the red.

Sugar Testing

Whatever fruit juice you find to use, a hydrometer, also called a saccharometer, will quickly tell you what sugar content the juice has. Then you can add sugar if necessary to bring the wine up to 10 or 11 percent, where it is quite stable, or soft water to reduce the alcohol potential to 12 percent, which is a practical maximum, considering the need for your wine to have a balanced taste.

As we said earlier, you simply need to float your hydrometer in a jar of the juice and read the amount of sugar. Some hydrometers have readings which must be translated; for instance, a gravity reading of 1.059 indicates a sugar content by weight of 15 percent, which will yield 7.8 percent alcohol if all the sugar is converted by the yeasts. Some hydrometers show the percentage of sugar; others show the alcohol potential itself.

Read the hydrometer at eye level. You will see that the top surface, if you use a hydrometer jar, forms a shallow U, simply because the liquid clings to the sides of the jar; the correct reading is the bottom of the U, not the top.

A hydrometer is calibrated to a certain temperature, usually 60°. If the must or wine you're testing is cooler than the calibrated temperature, subtract 1/10th of 1 percent from the potential-alcohol (DuJardin) scale for every 6 degrees difference. If the must is warmer, add the same tiny amount for each 6 degrees.

The accompanying chart tells how much sugar you must add to change the alcohol potential of a juice you are using. Hydrometers use different scales, so I have listed the most common three in use by home winemakers: the specific gravity, the crude Balling, and the potential alcohol.

HYDROMETER READING			TO MAKE A 10% WINE BY VOLUME ADD SUGAR:		TO MAKE A 12% WINE BY VOLUME ADD SUGAR:	
SPECIFIC GRAVITY	BALLING SCALE	POTENTIAL ALCOHOL				
At 60°		Percent	In pounds per 10 gal.	In ounces per gal.	In pounds per 10 gal.	In ounces per gal.
1.039	10	4.5	7.431	11.80	10.12	16.19
1.043	11	5.1	6.440	10.13	9.23	14.77
1.047	12	5.7	5.54	8.86	8.34	13.33
1.051	13	6.2	4.63	7.41	7.43	11.90
1.055	14	7.2	3.72	5.94	6.52	10.43
1.059	15	7.8	2.90	4.64	5.60	8.92
1.064	16	8.4	1.88	3.00	4.67	7.47
1.068	17	9.2	0.942	1.50	3.74	5.98
1.072	18	9.8			2.80	4.31
1.076	19	10.5			1.85	2.95
1.081	20	11.2			0.89	1.42
1.085	21	11.9				
1.090	22	12.6				
1.094	23	13.4				
1.099	24	14.1				
1.104	25	14.9				
1.108	26	15.5				

Acidity Testing

Most home winemakers do not make any other test than for sugar, but one other is important, even though not as important, and is easy to make. It has to do with acidity.

French grapes are adequately endowed with acids, eastern American grapes usually have a surplus, and California grapes tend to be lacking.

Home winemakers, if they bother with this factor at all, make a simple test to determine the acidity in their must. You can use a burette if you want to, as cheesemakers must (see Appendix 1), but winemaking need not be as exact as they. I find this method works well enough, and all you need in the way of equipment is a 10-ml. graduated measure and a coffee cup.

Also you must obtain an N/5 NaOH solution or use an N/10 solution and cut the findings in half.

Measure out 15 ml. of the grape juice and pour it into a cup. Add 3 ml. of the N/5 solution, stir, and with a spoon or rod put a drop of the mixture on a blue and red piece of litmus paper. It will turn the blue paper red and will not change the red one. Now add some more of the NaOH solution and test again. When the blue litmus no longer turns red, and when the red litmus turns barely blue, the liquid is approximately neutral.

The acidity of the juice is the number of milliliters you used to neutralize this sample—let's say 5 ml. in the case of a California Ruby Cabernet, 10 ½ ml. in the case of a Baco grown in the East, or 8 ml. in the case of a French-grown Gamay in Beaujolais. If the juice is 0.8 percent acid, you used 8 ml. of N/5 NaOH. Any point between 0.8 percent and 1.2 percent is tolerable. If your juice registers over 1.2 percent, you can add water—up to 15 percent I find acceptable in home production myself. (Remember to dissolve ½ pound sugar in every quart of water added.) If you have too little acid, you can add acid to the wine. Some vintners use tartaric acid. Others will use a mixture of 50 percent tartaric, 30 percent malic, and 20 percent succinic acids, this being a newer method, especially recommended for wines to be kept for as long as two years because of a special aroma and flavor these acids develop, given time. To increase 1 gallon of wine 0.1 percent in acidity, you will need to add 3.8 grams of tartaric acid (or of the acid mixture). Use U.S.P. dry tartaric acid, dissolve it in a bit of warm water, and stir it in. Citric acid can serve as a partial substitute but not until fermentation is over and the wine is still. It isn't as satisfactory. English makers also now recommend the addition after fermentation of 1 teaspoonful of 50 percent lactic acid for each gallon, also only for wines that are to be kept for two years.

The pH of a must is a measurement of acidity as well as other qualities. It is rarely encountered in England or France, but is sometimes used in California, where factories look for a pH of not more than 3.8 in the must of a dry wine and 3.6 in the must of a prospectively sweet wine. They say that other musts, even slightly out of range, make less healthy, inferior products. Papers that test for a pH of 3.0 to 4.0 are of general use; a pH meter is better.

Crushing

In making red wine, the crushing is more important than the pressing. If you can afford only a press *or* a crusher, buy the crusher. If you can afford neither, you can crush grapes with your feet, or your children's feet, or you can put the grapes in a plastic pan and crush them with the bottom of a quart bottle or a piece of two-by-four until your hands tire, which they will. Or you can put on clean golashes and walk about in them. Or your child can.

Put the crushed grapes in a vat—it can be a crock or a plastic garbage can provided it is polyethylene or has a polyethylene liner—and twice a day push the skins that rise to the top down into the juice to moisten them, so they will not sour. Cover the container with a pillowcase and, if you like, a loose-fitting top.

The pressing of a red wine comes in three to five days, when the alcohol fermentation is two-thirds to three-quarters complete. The earlier the pressing, the softer the wine; to make a big-bodied, durable wine you can leave the wine on the skins for a week, or even two weeks for a Chianti.

After three days the skins have been softened and the pressing amounts to little; actually, it can be done with moderate effectiveness with a clean flour sack or a pillowcase, if you put the must in and tighten the sack around it. A press is more satisfactory, and a press is an object of pride, too. Home winemakers have been known in their dreams to imagine their house is on fire and to wrestle with the worry of whether they can save their family as well as their press.

Sulfiting and Yeasts

Sulfiting is discussed briefly in the introduction to the wine section of this book. In most cases I do not sulfite at all, or if the fruit is overripe or has been stored somewhere, I sulfite fifty parts per million initially (one Campden tablet for each gallon), which will not kill the wild yeasts and will allow these wild yeasts to ferment the wine. If using wild yeasts makes you uneasy, remember that all yeasts are wild. If you are still nervous, you can simply add to the juice a purchased yeast and let it work with the wild yeast already there. They will be companionable.

But if you are uneasy about this, too, or are using grapes low in acid and therefore vulnerable to bacterial attacks, you might reasonably decide to sulfite the wild yeasts and use your own. To do so, sulfite the juice one hundred parts per million, using this scale:

> One Campden tablet for one gallon equals 50 PPM, as we said.
> Two grams (½ level teaspoon) of potassium metabisulfite equals 60 PPM in 5 gallons.

Dissolve the meta dose in a glass of water. Stir it into the wine. Wait two hours. Stir the liquid vigorously. Then add whatever wine yeast you want to. Use only wine yeast; baker's or brewer's yeasts give an off-flavor to all dry and many sweet wines. An excellent yeast is Montrachet, available in dry form in vacuum-packed packets. Unopened, they will keep for years. Vierka yeasts are also excellent. Madeira is my favorite among them, simply because it gives a more dramatic cap than does any other I have used. A poor reason, actually. Champagne and Bordeaux are popular favorites. To make the most of any liquid yeast, mix it a day or so early with a pint of sweet fruit juice you have boiled briefly, then cooled to 70 to 80 degrees. Put this fruit juice starter in a dark place and cover it with a cloth or lightweight lid. The yeast will begin multiplying and will be all the more effective when you pour the starter culture into the grape juice.

The dry wine yeast can be stirred into the grape juice when you need it, one packet for up to 10 gallons.

The English winemakers have experimented with various yeasts for their country wines, and I pass along the recommendation of one of them.

For apple: Sauternes for sweet and Champagne for dry wine

Blackberry: Burgundy for sweet, Bordeaux for dry

Black currant: Port and Bordeaux, respectively

Cherry: Bordeaux and Burgundy

Dandelion: Champagne and Champagne

Elderberry: Port and Burgundy

Gooseberry: Sauternes and Hock

Orange: Sherry and Hock

Peach: Tokay and Hock

Plum: Port and Burgundy

Raisin: Tokay and Sherry

Raspberry: Bordeaux and Hock

Red currant: Bordeaux and Champagne

Rhubarb stalks: Sauternes and Bordeaux

Rose hip: Madeira and Tokay

You can use yeast left in the bottom of a fermenting vat, incidentally, or if you have a vat of wine actively fermenting you can transfer a pint of this wine into a few gallons of juice and the yeasts in the fermenting wine will take charge.

Fermentation

Scientists say that in general the best fermenting temperatures for red wines are the 70s. Pinot Noir, even in California, prefers 80 degrees or higher, and in Burgundy much higher. A California Cabernet Sauvignon prefers the low 70s in California, the 80s in Bordeaux. The Cabernet Sauvignon and the Pinot Noir are better when fermented at these warm temperatures than when given a cold fermentation in the 50s.

For white wines Burgundy makers ferment in the 80s and 90s; California makers ferment in the 70s and low 80s.

Should fermentation cease for any reason—that is, should the bubbles stop rising, or your hydrometer show no drop in sugar content over a day's time—you can try several different measures:

Stirring is one, and the easiest.

Increasing the temperature in the fermenting room is one, should cold temperature possibly be a reason.

If the must has got too hot, you can cool it 10 degrees or so.

Adding more wine yeast is a possibility.

If none of these correctives work, you can heat a small portion of the juice to 140 degrees and mix it with the whole lot, as is often done in such cases in Burgundy.

If the must still won't resume its fermentation, take out about 10 percent of the lot of stuck wine and to it add 20 percent soft water, which will lower its acidity and might start the fermentation in that portion; then over a two-day period add the other stuck wine to it.

Or use fresh juice to start a new, small batch in another vat, and when it is fermenting well, add the stuck wine to it over a two- to six-day period.

When a red wine has fermented actively for three days in its vat, you can rack it off its skins and pips. Or, if you prefer, you can let the wine ferment on the skins another two or three days. This delay will make it heavier, will cause it to take longer to mature, and will result in a fuller, probably a better wine and one with longer life expectancy. If you like Italian Chianti, you can do as the Italians do and leave the wine on the skins for up to two weeks.

White wine, which is not fermented on its skins, permits more leeway as to the time of this first racking.

Usually the initial fermentation takes place in a vat. For one reason, a vat is easier to clean than a cask or carboy. Plastic, wood, stainless steel, enameled or ceramic containers are equally serviceable, but lead-glazed ceramic or galvanized metal ones ought not to be used, of course. The manufacturers of plastic containers sometimes do use poisons in their dye-stuffs and lubricants, and it is not safe simply to go down to the local hardware store and buy a plastic container to ferment wine or beer in. Polyvinylchloride vessels are not usually suitable, and the colored vessels of any plastic family ought to be avoided, simply to be safe. Polyethylene is thought to be safe if undyed, but one biochemist I know has replaced all his beer and winemaking equipment with glass since learning that polyethylene has been found in some tests to contaminate blood plasma stored in it.

Casks and Jugs and Siphoning

After its initial fermentation in vats, the wine is racked off into casks or jugs or carboys, which should be filled with the wine.

A quality wine, such as you might hope to make from a Napa Valley Cabernet Sauvignon or Chardonnay, deserves an oak cask to grow in. This permits the wine to breathe through the staves as well as the bung, and a wine will extract some of the tannin from the oak itself. However, casks are expensive—though they can be used for years to advantage—and coopers are scarce, and you need not get many casks without worrying about the availability of a cooper to repair them.

Casks of under 10-gallon size permit the wine to breathe too much oxygen and are not recommended.

Used whiskey barrels are available from distillers inexpensively (including Jack Daniel Distillery in Lynchburg, Tennessee, whom I judge the best maker in our country), but they are charred inside and are not, therefore, suitable. Paraffined casks are not recommended either.

For most wines, jugs and carboys do well enough. Gallon jugs or 5-gallon carboys are most often encountered. They can be either of glass or of plastic, but the same advice given on page 389 about plastics applies. The wine can breathe through plastic but not through glass, so you should rack glass-contained wine more often.

The cask or jug should be filled, as I mentioned, and a wad of cotton stuck in its mouth; either that or a waterlock. Waterlocks are small glass or plastic devices which permit the carbon dioxide to leave the cask through a water bath; this bath in turn prohibits alien bacteria or yeasts from reaching the wine. They are inexpensive, and you can make them, if you prefer. Use a rubber stopper with a hole through it, fit a plastic or rubber hose through the stopper, and put the free end of the hose in a pint of water. Carbon dioxide as it forms will go through the stopper, through the hose, and force its way in little exploding bubbles up through the water, but bacteria and insects cannot travel the other way. A purchased waterlock is a glass or plastic unit which permits the carbon dioxide to escape through water contained in the waterlock itself.

A friend of mine makes wine with a balloon attached to the glass jug he ferments it in. The balloon acts as a fermentation trap. This system has no advantage over a waterlock, which is more dependable and is reusable, except that my friend's balloons happen to have happy birthday printed on them and give a corner of his cellar a festive appearance.

The wine will continue to cast to the bottom unneeded yeast and other sediments. When it is a month old it should be siphoned off again into a clean cask or jug, one it fills, leaving as many of the lees behind as is practicable. A wine in a glass jug with a waterlock will need racking every two or three months thereafter; otherwise, in the complete absence of oxygen, it will mature quite slowly. A wine in a small cask needs racking every six months; in a large cask or plastic container, every four or five.

A rubber or plastic hose makes a suitable siphon. A hose ¼ inch in diameter, interior measurement, performs too slowly for anything except gallon lots; a ⅜- or even ½-inch hose is better. The rubber or plastic should be soft. One end is put into the wine and the other into the receiving container, which must be positioned lower. To start the flow, simply suck on the lower end of the hose until the flow starts. Let the wine run without splashing into the jug or cask. Soon the wine will cover the end of the hose, and the wine will not be unnecessarily aerated during the process, which it ought not to be, except on the first racking of a red grape wine and except in the very rare instances when a rotten-egg odor has developed—this does sometimes happen—and aerating the wine will usually cure that. Aerating it again in a week or two might be necessary if the offense still lingers. To aerate the wine, simply let the wine flow down the inside walls of the receiving jug or cask.

You will need each time to fill the receiving jug or cask full, and since each time you rack the wine you will leave behind a small quantity with the lees, different-sized jugs or casks will be required, or you will have to consolidate in fewer jugs as you go along. A winemaker who starts with a 5-gallon carboy might end up with four 1-gallon jugs, a half-gallon jug, and a Coca-Cola bottle full of wine. Better to start with a 5-gallon carboy and a half-gallon jug, and end up with 5 gallons of wine in the single container.

The racking a month after making is the most important. The number of additional rackings you should put yourself and your wine through depends on the quality you wish to try to attain. One or two more rackings are enough for a light, fruity wine, three or four more for a hefty wine. The taste of the wine at the first or second racking is likely to be yeasty and flagrant, so be prepared for disappointment.

The first, main fermentation is the conversion of sugar to alcohol, but there are other changes occurring and their nature is still largely unknown. We know that a secondary fermentation takes place involving the acids. Malic becomes lactic acid and carbon dioxide, for instance. This acidic fermentation is of great importance in a wine that has much acid in it—wines of Germany, Burgundy, and eastern America, for instance; in the low-acid wines made in Italy, Spain, southern France, or California it is not as desirable and often is discouraged by sulfiting, pasteurization, or other means.

If you want to permit the secondary fermentation, keep the wine during the autumn and early winter at 65 to 70 degrees. Since this is a bacteria-caused fermentation, you should not have a high percentage of sulfite in the wine—a small dose when you crush the grapes will not now hinder. Should the wine not undergo its secondary fermentation during the fall or winter, perhaps because of low temperature, it will try to do so when warm weather returns in the spring. In the old days vintners were astonished each spring to find their wine returning to life again, and they contended this was an inherent response to the new season. It has a more ordinary explanation, unfortunately. During this fermentation, the gases will need to be allowed to escape from the cask or jug, through a loose bung or a waterlock, and you will need to keep topping up the wine so that it fills the cask or jug.

If you want to discourage the secondary fermentation, you can add potassium metabisulfite, sixty parts per million, at the first month's racking. That is ½ level teaspoon for 5 gallons of wine. Also, at each subsequent racking, every two or three months, you must use the same amount. This will keep bacteria from fermenting the acid.

Fining and Filtering

Most wines clear brilliantly, given six months' time. Occasionally a grape wine will take longer; white wines are more obstinate than red. If you cannot wait, or if the wine is not brilliant enough to suit you, you can introduce a fining agent, gelatine or casein or a mineral such as bentonite, which is a clay (the best of it comes from Wyoming), or you can beat the white of an egg in a few ounces of water and pour it into the wine; one egg white is enough for 10 to 20 gallons of wine and should not be used to excess. Bentonite is better. It infringes somewhat less on the taste and aroma of the wine, though it does rob both slightly and it does tend to decrease color, especially in a young wine. It reduces vitamin content, too. However, any fining agent has disadvantages, and if you decide to use bentonite, mix ⅓ ounce of it in 6 ounces of wine and use that mixture on 6 gallons of wine. Pour it into the cask or jug, then in three or four days rack the wine into a clean container or into the bottles, being careful not to rack any of the clay and other sediment with it. Another fining agent is unflavored household gelatine, 1 gram for 4 gallons. A gram of gelatine is ⅓ level teaspoon. It will remove some of the color, particularly in old wine, and some of the tannin, which can conceivably be an advantage; Bordeaux makers sometimes fine their red wine in its first year not only to help clarify it but to remove some of the tannin from it, if they feel there is an excess of tannin.

White winemakers can add tannin before fining, to protect the wine from loss it can ill afford. To do this dissolve one gram of grape tannin or tannic acid in 3 ½ ounces of boiled water; add one percent of this solution to your wine, each gallon receiving about 1 ¼ ounces, or mix it with the gelatine.

Before bottling, a wine can be filtered through filter papers, which are readily available, or through cloth. This does unfortunately aerate and to an extent rob the wine. The bottled wine will develop fewer lees but less subtlety as well. In the old days filtering was not permitted in France, but today it is and is often done; however, the equipment and methods used do not permit over-oxidation.

A home winemaker need not fine or filter his wine, as a general rule. If you must clear a wine, it is better to fine than to filter. You can easily ruin a wine, particularly a white wine, by an amateur filtration.

The only home-filtering method I respect is this complicated one: Attach a hose to a jug of swiftly fermenting fruit juice and put the other end of it into a carboy. In an hour or so, carbon dioxide gas will have filled the carboy, displacing the lighter oxygen. Filter wine into this carboy, using a closed, airtight filter, such as are now available to amateurs. The filtered wine will displace the carbon dioxide without being oxidized.

Two odd little facts: A wine in a small vessel will clear

quicker than the same wine in a large vessel. A wine in a rough-textured vessel will clear faster than one in a vessel with a smooth interior.

Blending

Often wines can be improved by blending two or more wines together, or by blending two or more grape juices at the start of fermentation and allowing them to work off together. A wine of too little acidity can be put with one high in acidity, or a wine with an excellent bouquet can be put with one of but little. A Cabernet Sauvignon from California should not, in most people's opinion, be blended; a Cabernet Sauvignon from Bordeaux is always blended and profits from it. It is difficult to say yes or no, as you see, even for a single species of wine. The French hybrids benefit from blending—Foch with Baco, for instance. Taste is the determiner.

Remember that further aging in the bottle will rub off most sharp edges as it modifies and enriches the wine. To blend wines, use small samples of wine, at 60 to 65 degrees temperature, to determine the proportions you want.

Sweet and dry wines are not usually blended.

Red and white wines are not usually blended, except as one way of making *rosé* wines.

A native American red wine, such as Concord, ought not to be blended with a vinifera grape or a French-American hybrid.

Aging and Bottling

If left too long in a wooden cask or most types of plastic containers, a wine will become exhausted by the growing process. It breathes in these vessels, and it breathes during the seasonal rackings. In a glass jug, particularly one with a waterlock, maturing is slow even with two-month or three-month rackings, and the time for bottling is not as critical.

The more a wine is racked, the faster it matures. The smaller the cask, the faster it matures. The warmer the wine, the faster it matures.

There is no way to say here when a wine is ready to be bottled and corked, after which it will age very slowly. To make a guess, six months for fruity wines, one year for most wines, two years for Cabernet Sauvignon and other such long-lived wines. You don't want to bottle it too soon. Properly made wines, "bottle ripe" when bottled, will in the bottle improve with age for one to fifteen years, depending on the juice used.

Before bottling a dry red wine it is well to check to be sure the sugar has fermented out of it completely. A hydrometer in a dry wine will read under 1.000 since alcohol has less weight than water. Another way to judge is to supply yourself with the testing tape used by diabetics to see whether sugar is present in a liquid. Test the wine with that. If the wine still has sugar in it, you should before bottling ferment it out or kill the yeast with a one-hundred-parts-per-million dose of potassium metabisulfite.

Some vintners sulfite their wine just before bottling it, to kill bacteria and thus help stabilize the wine's health and color for its years of rest. Thirty parts per million will kill bacteria. Some use twice as much, reckoning that much of the dose will dissipate before the bottling is done, leaving only thirty parts per million in the wine to stabilize it.

Only in a corked bottle can most wines reach maturity graciously. The wine will need to be in the bottle six months to a year as a minimum, except that wines made from concentrates and fruity wines need about half as long; they can even be capped in quart bottles if you plan to use them quite soon.

Bottles can be of almost any sort that will take a cork or a cap. Only a bottle with a straight, untapered neck will allow a wine cork to fit it. A whiskey bottle won't do; also, it is against the United States laws to reuse whiskey bottles. The best bottles are wine bottles, and the heavier ones are preferred; they are less likely to break when being corked or moved about. European wine bottles are heavier than ours in America and are less likely to break during corking and handling. Bottles are thrown away every day by restaurants which serve wines, and new ones can be purchased from winemakers' stores.

Brownish bottles are best for red wine; greenish bottles will do.

Wine corks have untapered sides. Number 9 corks fit most wine bottles. Champagne bottles are likely to require number 10 corks. The corks should be first-quality Spanish or Portuguese and should be at least 1 ½ inches long; 1 ¾ inches is preferable for wines which are to be kept for several years. A cork permits passage of 0.01 ml. of oxygen per month. The corks are available from winemakers' supply houses, as are inexpensive corking devices. Only new corks should be used. If you must, you can use old ones for your less-than-valuable wines if you sterilize them and if they have not been punctured. A French cork remover, called Sanbri, which does not puncture corks, is now available.

Bottles can be sterilized in hot water. My own experience, which involves much luck—I have never lost a bottle of wine —indicates that hot water from the hot water tap is quite adequate. I have kept even white wine as long as eight years before drinking the last bottle. Do not use detergents, in any event; their taste will often linger in the bottles. For quite dirty bottles use baking soda and water, or sterilize the bottles with a solution of potassium metabisulfite and water, about two hundred parts per million, or even stronger, pouring the same solution from one bottle to another. Bottles should not be baked to sterilize them; baking weakens them. The caps or corks should be sterilized with hot water or a mild meta solution. If once you finish a bottle of wine you rinse out the bottle, you will not need to exhaust yourself later on cleaning it. The brown stain which sometimes clings to the inside of a wine bottle is not harmful, incidentally, and need not be removed.

The corks should be soaked in water for at least thirty minutes before insertion, to soften them, and it is wise to dip them in wine just before use to keep them from sticking to the glass.

Leave as little air space in the bottle as practicable—say, half an inch or so.

A wine suffers bottle sickness the first few days after bottling. It has absorbed much oxygen in the process and must assimilate it and settle down, must meld again. If you taste it during the first week after bottling you will be dealing unfairly with it.

After you bottle it, leave the bottles sitting cork up for twelve hours or so, until the corks have set. Then lay the bottles on their sides in your wine cellar.

Foil need not be put around the cork and neck of the bottle. An unfoiled bottle will in time develop a mold on the cork, but this mold is of no danger. If you decide to use a foil, avoid lead foil; French scientists' tests show that some of the lead does pass through the cork and into the wine over a period of years—it's hard to believe, I admit. Aluminum foil and a small applicator are available.

If a residue does develop in a bottle of wine, the wine can be poured carefully or can be decanted before using. The residue is harmless. In olden days a residue was a mark of distinction, but it can be a nuisance even so.

Wine Cellar

Your wine cellar should be within easy access of your table and should not have steps too steep or dangerous for an intoxicated man to use. An earthen floor is traditional. It has obvious disadvantages but does serve to cool the cellar and help stabilize the temperature. Also, earthen floors develop an aroma, most delicious, and, as I said earlier, I think that might contribute to the fermenting wine, as well as please the vintner. The ideal average temperature is 55 degrees. It can fluctuate as high as 70 degrees, where the maturing will be much sooner attained, and some authorities say it can spurt as high as 80 degrees briefly and infrequently. The minimum temperature ought to be 40 degrees. Slow, gentle fluctuations do not trouble the wine. Abrupt and frequent changes probably do.

If labeled, the bottles ought not to be put on the floor; even when on shelves the paper labels in a moist cellar soon deteriorate. Burgundy winemakers do not label their bottles until they are sold and are leaving the cellar.

A cellar should be dark, or nearly so.

You will find it necessary to lock your wine cellar, and it is not without reason that some home winemakers have decided to have two cellars, only one of which they show visitors.

I once caught a friend of mine, incidentally, preparing his showroom cellar by shaking a bag of dust over the bottles. The reason for secrecy is not only the possibility of theft but the trouble of making an inventory. If wine is stored in all sorts of different bottles and jugs, there is no way to know whether you are losing wine or not, day by day. Once every year I try to make an inventory but always find that more wine has been used than my records account for, which is merely a comment on my enthusiasm for wine.

Memory is a sorry recorder—mine is anyway—and notes should be taken. Everything pertaining to a given wine would, in a perfect world, be recorded on a card and set aside for that wine. The record would note the juice, the hydrometer reading, the acidity, any sulfiting, the yeast, the fermenting period, any sugar added, any water added, the rackings until bottling, and the aroma and taste at various times, including when the wine is finally served. Such a record can be coded with a number—G173 might be grape wine number 1 in 1973, for instance. This number should be put on the bottle with a grease pencil or by means of a strip of plastic tape, perhaps green for grape wines, purple for mead, etc.

The rooms in which wine is made and stored in Burgundy all seem to have a somber, old-age, relaxing atmosphere. They yield themselves to being washed down from time to time but they are not marred by brightness. Sometimes I enter the winemaking rooms of friends and feel that good wine cannot be made there. It is not the sterility of the room which is basically at fault but the personality of the friend, for anybody who would create such a room for winemaking cannot at heart be a vintner.

Serving and Drinking Red Wines

A great wine should be inhaled and sipped. A fruity wine can, if you prefer, be guzzled. A wine should have a complexity of aroma, of bouquet and flavor. It should have in aroma and flavor a mild reminder of the fruit from which it is made. Beyond that it should have elegance. The flavor should be balanced, with the acids, tannin, and alcohol all contributing, none out of place. The wine should be crystal clear and should be handsome when poured into a clear wineglass.

A 6- to 8-ounce wineglass one-third filled is a nice sight to see. A wineglass should be that large, of clear glass, and should never be filled more than half full. This permits the bouquet to accumulate in the glass and lets you swirl the wine gently, to awaken it, if you need to.

The best temperature for serving red wines is not room temperature, as so often is stated. It is about 65 degrees, which is room temperature in Europe (or often is), but rarely in the United States. A red wine should never be heated. If you bring a bottle from your cellar an hour before serving, it will become warm enough. However, since the moving will have irritated it slightly, it is advisable to bring it to the dining room earlier, even the day before its use. Leave it sitting cork up, proudly we trust, until you open it thirty to sixty minutes before serving, to allow it to breathe and to let oxygen awaken it.

Appendix 3

Markets

Cheesemaking

So far as I can determine, there is only one shop in the country specializing in supplying equipment, cultures and other items needed by home cheesemakers and it is only now opening. You can write its director for a free catalogue: Homecrafts, 111 Stratford Center, Winston-Salem, North Carolina 27104.

The stock includes various cheese presses, molds (including wooden molds like the Mossholders use), curd knives, insulated vats, shielded thermometers, rennet, cheese coloring, starter cultures, bacterial cultures and molds for Camembert, Brie and Gruyère (and they hope to get *B. linens* for Port Salut), acid testing kits, books and pamphlets on cheesemaking, bandages, press cloths, cheesemaking kits, and other items.

Should they not have what you want, you can order rennet and cultures from major manufacturers and distributors; however, the packaged amounts are sometimes large for home use. Among the big suppliers are Marschall Division, Miles Laboratories, Inc., P.O. Box 592, Madison, Wisconsin 53701, and Chr. Hansen's Laboratory, Inc., 9015 W. Maple Street, Milwaukee, Wisconsin 53214. Pure bacterial cultures can also be obtained from the American Type Culture Collection, 12301 Parklawn Drive, Rockville, Maryland 20852; their prices are high—$35 to businesses or individuals, $6.50 to schools. They do have *B. linens*.

Excellent cheese shops are opening in many cities. Most of them will ship cheeses to you. My favorite shops are Cheese Unlimited, Inc., 1263 Lexington Avenue at 85th Street, New York City; Cheeses of All Nations, Inc., 153 Chambers Street, New York City; Ference Cheese Shoppe, 91 Broadway, Asheville, North Carolina; and the shop Mr. Ference's son operates at 554 Main Street, Bethlehem, Pennsylvania.

Winemaking

Winemakers' shops are now located in most major cities. Some cities have two or three. Look under "winemaking" in the yellow pages of the phone book. In addition, there are a number of well-stocked mail order shops which handle orders expeditiously and reasonably. They carry a wide selection—everything you will need and many things you don't need but they would like for you to have. They stock wine and beer yeasts, grape juice concentrates from this and other countries, fruit juice concentrates, malted barley, malt extracts, waterlocks, jugs, bottles, plastic vats, wooden kegs, glass and plastic carboys, chemicals, corks and corkers, filters, finings, siphons, acidity testing kits, hydrometers, crushers, presses, and so forth. One shop, Homecrafts, has promised me to try to stock crushers which can be used as cheese mills and presses that can be used for cheeses as well as fruit. All the shops have free catalogues. Among them are:

In the West:

Wine Art of America, Inc., 4324 Geary Boulevard, San Francisco, California 94118. They are a major franchiser of shops.

The Compleat Winemaker, 614 San Pablo Avenue, Albany, California 94706

Oregon Specialty Co., 615 N. E. Sixty-eighth Avenue, Portland, Oregon 97213

Aetna Bottle Company, Inc., 708 Rainier Avenue, South, Seattle, Washington 98144

In the Midwest:

Semplex of U.S.A., Box 12276, 4301 James Avenue, North, Minneapolis, Minnesota 55421

The Vintner, 5740 Nicollet Avenue, Minneapolis, Minnesota 55419

In the East:

Presque Isle Wine Cellars, 5422 Glenwood Park Avenue, Erie, Pennsylvania 16509

Homecrafts, 111 Stratford Center, Winston-Salem, North Carolina 27104

The Winemakers Shop, Bully Hill Road, Hammondsport, New York 14840

Wine Grape Vines

Boordy Vineyard, Riderwood, Maryland 21139

New York Fruit Testing Association, Geneva, New York 14456

Sauratown Mountain Vineyard, Post Office Box 66, Rural Hall, North Carolina 27045.

Stribling's Nurseries, Merced, California 95340

Johnston Vineyards, 4320 North Barnes, Oklahoma City, Oklahoma 73112

Grapes and Apples

Ripe grapes can be got in season by writing Presque Isle, 9440 Buffalo Road, North East, Pennsylvania 16428. Their catalogue lists such French-American hybrids as Foch and Vidal, such American types as Delaware and Catawba, and two vinifera grapes, Riesling and Chardonnay.

The Compleat Winemaker, P.O. Box 2470, Yountville, California 94599, has Napa Valley Zinfandel, Cabernet Sauvignon and other excellent grapes, which he ships by refrigerator truck or air express during harvest season.

U.S. Government Registration Forms

Article 240.540 of the U.S. Federal Wine Regulations says "A duly registered head of any family may produce annually for family use, and not for sale, not in excess of 200 gallons of wine without payment of tax."

The head of the family is supposed to fill out two copies of Form 1541 and mail both to his regional office.

If you live in California, Idaho, Montana, Arizona, Oregon, Washington, Nevada, Utah, Alaska or Hawaii, your regional office is at 870 Market Street, San Francisco, California 94104.

If you live in Nebraska, the Dakotas, Wyoming, Colorado, Iowa, Missouri, Minnesota or Kansas, your regional office is at 2124 Post Office Building, Omaha, Nebraska 68102.

If you live in Ohio, Indiana, Kentucky, Virginia, or West Virginia, your regional office is at 222 E. Central Parkway, Cincinnati, Ohio 45202.

If you live in Texas, New Mexico, Arkansas, Louisiana, or Oklahoma, your regional office is at 1114 Commerce Street, Dallas, Texas 75202.

If you live in Georgia, Alabama, the Carolinas, Mississippi, Florida or Tennessee, your regional office is at 275 Peachtree Street N.E., Atlanta, Georgia 30303.

If you live in New England, your regional office is at 55 Tremont Street, Boston, Massachusetts 02148.

If you live in Pennsylvania, Maryland, New Jersey, Delaware or Washington, D.C., your regional office is at 2 Penn Center Plaza, Philadelphia, Pennsylvania 19102.

If you live in Illinois, Michigan or Wisconsin, your regional office is at 17 North Dearborn Street, Chicago, Illinois 60602.

If you live in New York State, your regional office is at 90 Church Street, New York, New York 10013.

If you live in Puerto Rico, you are supposed to use the New York City office, given just above.

Index

407

412   INDEX

French-American hybrid grapes, 286, 378, 379, 381, 395
French Camembert, 179-180
French cooking, 154, 335-336
French double-cream cheese, 36, 352
French Longtail apples, 207
Frequin Audième, Frequin Rouge apples, 215
Frisian-Holstein milk, 159, 337

Gamay grapes, 256, 266, 378
Gautrias cheese, 84
Gavot cheese, 92-93
Gelatine, for fining, 393, 394
Géromé cheese, 83
Gervais cheese, 34
Gex, Gex Bressons cheese, 93, 123-124
Ginger wine (beer, ale), 248-249
Glass jugs, 390, 396
Gloucester cheese, 56-62, 353, 359-376
Goat's milk cheese, 92-93
Golden Ball apples, 207
Golden Guinea (wine), 308
Gooseberries, gooseberry wine, 237, 240-241, 387
Gournay cheese, 37-38
Goût Américain, 306
Grape juice, for mead, 228
Grapes, 237, 238, 377-381
  for Champagne, 303, 308
  hybrid, 286, 378, 379, 381, 395
  for red wine, 255-256, 266
  for *rosé*, 280
  where to buy, 405

white-wine, 268, 271, 274, 276, 279, 380, 381
Gravenstein apples, 208, 211
Gray mold, 90-91
Greasing of cheese, 140, 176
Green cheese, 372 n.
Green mold, 43, 184, 350
Grenache grapes, 280
Grey Owl yeast, 299
Grinding of cheese. *See* Milling
Gruyère cheese, 144-153, 352
Guernsey milk, 12, 22, 28, 31, 337, 338
Guinness, 300

Hangdown apples, 207, 208
Hanging of cheeses, 18, 33, 43, 69, 113, 118
Hard cheeses, 53-80, 144-157, 347
Harel, Marie, 179
Harp, Swiss, 85, 107, 147, 356-357; *see also* Curd knives
Hermitage wine, 267
Holstein milk, 12, 27, 31-32, 48, 159, 337
Homer, 31
Honey, for mead, 223-232
Hoops, cheese, 100, 131, 139, 148, 149, 150, 156, 162, 172, 180, 182, 185, 186, 355; *see also* Molds
Hops, in beer, 295, 296
  "finishing," 297
  to flavor whiskey, 316
  for mead, 226
  for root beer, 251
Humidity, for bread nurturing *P. roquefortii*, 111
  in cave, 184
  of curing room, 82, 87,

94, 102, 109, 122, 141, 151, 173, 176, 187, 194, 355
Hybrid grapes, 286, 378, 379, 381, 395
Hydraulic press, 132, 303, 333, 348
Hydrometer, 259, 381-382
  beermaker's, 298
Hydrometer readings, 215, 217, 221, 222, 225, 231, 297, 298, 300, 301, 309, 310, 396
Hypocras (Hippocras), 294

Importing of wine, 288-290, 291
Improved Foxwhelp apples, 207, 208
Ina, king of Wessex, 293
Inventory, wine cellar, 400
Invert sugar, 300
Iodized salt, 347
Irish Archer barley, 310
Irish whiskey, 313-327
Ives grapes, 379

Jack Daniel Distillery, 390
James grapes, 286
Jameson, J., and Son; Jameson, Wm., and Company, 325
Janzen, J. J., xii
Jefferson, Thomas, 378
Jersey Chisel apples, 207
Jersey milk, 22, 23, 31, 337, 338
Johannes-Seyve grapes, 379
Johnson, Samuel, 293
Jonathan apples, 208
Jugs, glass, 390, 396

Kasper, Lester, 26, 176
Keeving, 216
Kindred barley, 311
Kingston Bitter apples, 208
Kingston Black apples, 207, 208

72 73 10 9 8 7 6 5 4 3 2 1